37.95

D0706627

THE NEW BATTLEFIELD

Recent Titles in Contributions
in Military Studies

The Tainted War: Culture and Identity in Vietnam War Narratives
Lloyd B. Lewis

Shaping a Maritime Empire: The Commercial and
Diplomatic Role of the American Navy, 1829-1861
John H. Schroeder

The American Occupation of Austria: Planning and Early Years
Donald R. Whitnah and Edgar L. Erickson

Crusade in Nuremberg: Military Occupation, 1945-1949
Boyd L. Dastrup

The Dogma of the Battle of Annihilation: The Theories of
Clausewitz and Schlieffen and Their Impact on the
German Conduct of Two World Wars
Jehuda L. Wallach

Jailed for Peace: The History of American Draft Law
Violators, 1658-1985
Stephen M. Kohn

Against All Enemies: Interpretations of American Military
History from Colonial Times to the Present
Kenneth J. Hagan and William R. Roberts

Citizen Sailors in a Changing Society: Policy Issues for
Manning the United States Naval Reserve
Louis A. Zurcher, Milton L. Boykin, and Hardy L. Merritt, editors

Strategic Nuclear War: What the Superpowers Target and Why
William C. Martel and Paul L. Savage

Soviet Military Psychiatry: The Theory and Practice of
Coping with Battle Stress
Richard A. Gabriel

A Portrait of the Israeli Soldier
Reuven Gal

The Other Price of Hitler's War: German Military and
Civilian Losses Resulting from World War II
Martin K. Sorge

THE NEW BATTLEFIELD

The United States and Unconventional Conflicts

Sam C. Sarkesian

Contributions in Military Studies, Number 54

GREENWOOD PRESS
New York • Westport, Connecticut • London

Library of Congress Cataloging-in-Publication Data

Sarkesian, Sam Charles.
   The new battlefield.

   (Contributions in military studies, ISSN 0883-6884 ;
no. 54)
   Bibliography: p.
   Includes index.
   1. Low-intensity conflicts. 2. United States—
Military policy. 3. United States—Foreign relations—
1981-   . I. Title. II. Series.
U104.S27   1986   355'.0218   86-3087
ISBN 0-313-24890-7 (lib. bdg. : alk. paper)

Library of Congress Catalog Card Number: 86-3087
ISBN: 0-313-24890-7
ISSN: 0883-6884

First published in 1986

Greenwood Press, Inc.
88 Post Road West, Westport, Connecticut 06881

Printed in the United States of America

∞

The paper used in this book complies with the
Permanent Paper Standard issued by the National
Information Standards Organization (Z39.48-1984).

10 9   8   7   6   5   4   3   2   1

Copyright Acknowledgment

We gratefully acknowledge Crane, Russak & Company, Inc.
for granting permission to use portions of
material which previously appeared in
Conflict, Volume 5, No. 2.

To the officers and men of the 10th Special Forces
Group who tried to show the way in 1952 and 1953

Contents

Figures and Tables

FIGURES

TABLES

Preface

In June 1985, Trans World Airlines flight 847 en route from Athens to Rome with 153 persons on board, mostly Americans, was hijacked by Shiite Moslem terrorists. The flight was forced to fly to Algiers and, after two trips back and forth from Algiers to Beirut, came to rest at the Beirut airport under the control of Amal, the Shiite militia, and the more extreme Shiite Hizbollah, the Party of God. Although the hostages were released after 17 days, the vulnerability of the United States (and, indeed, all other open societies in general) to terrorism was again dramatically demonstrated. Several years earlier, 241 US Marines had been killed by a terrorist attack in Beirut, and before then, the US embassy had been bombed, with scores of casualties. Most of these attacks were attributed to the Islamic Jihad, a fundamentalist Islamic movement intent on terrorizing the United States in order to reduce or eliminate US presence in the Middle East.

Although terrorist acts had increased over the past decade, the ordeal of TWA flight 847 seemed to demonstrate dramatically the challenges and dangers posed by terrorism to the United States. It was clear that the United States was faced with complex problems and serious dilemmas in developing effective counterterror policies and strategies.

Response to terrorism was but a small, albeit dramatic, part of a much deeper and more serious issue, however: unconventional conflicts, which include not only terrorism but also revolution and counterrevolution. The conditions and motivations that precipitate contemporary revolutions and counterrevolutions are essentially those from which terrorism also evolves. They have to do primarily with the problems of the Third World and are directly linked to the internal instability and weakness of many Third World states, the conflicts these generate, and the external forces they attract. These conditions make the problems of the Third World and their conflicts important issues for US security interests.

Following the withdrawal of the United States from Vietnam and the subsequent collapse of South Vietnam, the US military, according to most accounts, began to deteriorate. Certainly its ability to engage in unconventional conflicts was at an all-time low. Because of this, America's ability to influence the Third World also reached its lowest point. Exacerbating matters was the perception that the US military, including its strategic and general purpose forces, was incapable of carrying out US policy. American national will and staying power suffered accordingly. Indeed, it was in the last half of the 1970s that Marxist-Leninist systems were established in Angola, Ethiopia, Mozambique, and Central America. The Third World and its Marxist-Leninist revolutionary forces seemed to be immune from effective US influence. The Soviet invasion of Afghanistan and the Iranian revolution were events that seemed to confirm US impotence.

The 1980s began with a great deal of attention to strengthening America's military capability. The new Reagan administration not only increased defense expenditures for strategic forces and nuclear weaponry but attempted to increase the effectiveness of conventional military forces.

The military services, taking their cue from the administration, expanded their strategic and tactical view to include a wide range of contingencies from nuclear war to limited war. One result was that national capability in unconventional conflicts, which had been seriously neglected since 1970, began to attract the attention of many civilian and military experts. This was sparked not only by the administration's apparent tough policy toward conflicts in general but also by the conflicts in Central America, the Soviet invasion of Afghanistan, and the increasing incidence of terrorism against the United States.

By the middle of the 1980s, it appeared that the United States and the West, in general, were in ascendancy throughout the world. Not only did the United States reassert itself in world affairs, but its economic system and technological capacity grew and improved. The Soviet view in the 1970s that the correlation of forces favored them was replaced by the 1980s' realization that the Soviet system was falling behind the industrialized West; the correlation of forces had shifted to the United States and the West. The new Soviet leadership is faced with troubling internal problems as well. As of this writing, it is not clear what the long range impact these new conditions will impose on US-USSR relationships. It appears that the political and economic turmoil in the Third World and the unconventional conflicts these generate combined with the continuing issues of nuclear warfare provide new opportunities for the Soviet Union.

At the same time, these new challenges pose serious political, military and intellectual problems for US policy makers and for the American people. Moreover, the issues of war and peace have become so complex, ambiguous, and multidimensional that they generate a confusing array of views, interpretations, and policy alternatives. As a result, Americans, seeking clear answers to confusing situations, accept the simplest explanations, which they believe will lead to clear-cut policies and solutions. Unfortunately, the kinds of conflicts that are characteristic of the present decade defy simplistic solutions and virtually preclude any one set of policies or answers.

Nuclear war and nuclear strategy have been the subjects of a great deal of analysis. Most people understand such conflicts because they are related to experiences in World War II and can generally be judged with quantitative data. The number of warheads, aircraft, and personnel in the armed forces are factors that can be measured and translated into assessments of military strength. Although there may be serious disagreements about effective nuclear strategy, the groundwork for debates and the frameworks for critical analysis have been widely argued, discussed, and publicized.

The concern about nuclear weapons and strategic forces dominates strategic thought and defense expenditures. Yet, ironically, the most likely conflicts in the contemporary period and the coming decade are in or emanate from the Third World. The character of such conflicts is far removed from those of nuclear wars, major conventional conflicts, limited conflicts of the Korean War variety, or even those of the Israeli-Arab wars of the past two decades.

Given the nature of the US political system and prevailing mind-sets, civilian and military policy makers are likely to adopt conventional postures and Western-based perceptions in establishing policy and strategy in response to Third World conflicts. But the lack of understanding of unconventional conflicts—particularly revolution and counterrevolution—can easily lead to policy misjudgments and misguided political partisanship, thereby exposing the US military to conflicts and contingencies that are difficult, if not impossible, for it to undertake effectively.

Although increasing concern about unconventional conflict was evident by 1985, it remained rooted in conventional attitudes and misunderstanding about the nature and character of such conflicts. In light of the complex and long-range threat of revolution, counterrevolution, and various forms of terrorism, this posed a particularly serious problem. Although the United States created the First Special Operations Command in 1982 as a direct response to problems of unconventional conflict, much remained to be done in developing an effective political-military capability.

The purpose of this book is to study and analyze the US political-military posture and effectiveness in responding to unconventional conflicts. It includes an examination of the evolution of US policy, the nature and character of unconventional conflicts, and US security interests in Third World areas. The main focus of this book is on revolution and counterrevolution in the belief that these are the most encompassing and long-range unconventional challenges. The study of terrorism is included only as it is directly related to revolution and counter-revolution.

The theme of this book is that the US political-military posture and capability to deal with unconventional conflicts are inadequate and, in the main, ineffective. Many of these challenges cannot be met solely by nego-tiation, economic aid, or a variety of traditional means, contrary to the view held by some in the United States. For many revolutionaries within the Third World, armed struggle is an essential component in the creation of the revolutionary state and in establishing the legitimacy of the revolution. For revolutionaries, therefore, the ulti-mate goal is overthrow of the existing system using any means possible, from assassination, hijacking of aircraft, and taking of hostages to full-scale revolutionary conflict. And for an increasing number of revolutionaries, the United States has become the prime target as the leader of the developed democratic world. In the 1980s a number of anti-Marxist revolutions are in progress. These could prove favorable to US interests, yet they also pose complex and challenging problems. Should the US support such revolutions? If so, what kind of support and how much should be provided? These are the ingredients that make up the new battlefield, the most serious challenge facing the United States in this and the coming decade.

Underlying this theme is the view that this challenge is endemic to the Third World, and unless the United States makes a determined effort to develop a political-military posture and capability to respond effectively to unconventional conflicts, it is likely to find itself undermined in many areas in the world and faced with potentially serious security threats to its own survival. Many extremist Third World states understand this far better than most Americans, and these states have been able to fashion their own political-military policies to exploit America's apparent weaknesses. Moreover, the Soviet Union and its surrogates have found in the Third World and unconventional conflicts a fertile field in which to expand their own power and exploit the weaknesses of the United States and its allies.

This book has three parts. Part I presents a discussion of the nature of unconventional conflicts and the challenges these pose to the United States. This includes an analysis of the changed international political system and the relationships among the Third World, the United States, and the Soviet Union. An important part of this study is on the nature of Third World politics and internal conflicts and their relationships to unconventional conflicts. But the main focus is on the concepts and characteristics of unconventional conflicts, particularly revolution and counterrevolution.

Part II is a study of the US response to unconventional warfare. It begins by surveying the events that led up to the Vietnam War, particularly the issue of US capability in unconventional warfare. This is followed by a study of US involvement in Vietnam and its consequences for the US political-military posture. Next is a discussion of the dilemmas faced by the US political system in developing an effective response to unconventional challenges. A discussion of the various categories of conflicts that are part of the unconventional conflict spectrum, with particular attention to low-intensity conflict (revolution and counterrevolution) and special operations (counter-terror operations), is included. Part II concludes with an examination of the essential elements for developing an effective US political-military posture for unconventional conflict. In addition to the problem of US civic illiteracy, several other components of effective policy are examined: the role of the media, the nature of open societies, the dynamics of the US political system, and how these affect the ability to respond to unconventional conflicts. Following this, a study is made of policy, strategy, and doctrine as the basis of an effective US unconventional capability.

Part III, the conclusion, discusses the philosophical and moral basis of democracy and how these relate to unconventional conflict. The democratic dilemma is examined, and observations are made on how these should be conceived and interpreted to place the United States in a posture to respond more effectively to unconventional conflicts.

The Appendix includes a number of charts showing levels of US and USSR military assistance to various states of the Third World, the number of USSR military advisors in various countries, and the number of Soviet bloc troops outside their home areas. The study in the various chapters addressing Soviet power projections and US-USSR foreign involvement is partly based on the data in the Appendix.

This book is directed at serious students of US political-military policy: those in policy-making circles, military professionals, and the faculty and staff at senior service schools. I hope that such an audience will be concerned about US capability in what I label the new battlefield. I have not attempted to present basic information about policy and the workings of the US system on the assumption that most of this is common knowledge for the audience of this book.

A number of books are available examining various aspects of unconventional conflicts: terrorism, Vietnam, and certain wars of the past. Many are excellent and need to be read to develop a serious and in-depth analysis of the United States and unconventional conflict. However, few single-author books analyze the broad range of unconventional conflicts from a US policy perspective linking these to US capabilities and effectiveness. Nor does any book examine the conceptual and organizational confusion within the US military and policy-making circles regarding unconventional conflicts. Finally, there are few books that link past experience with the problems facing contemporary policy makers. This book attempts to fill these gaps in the literature.

The motivation for this book came from my book, *America's Forgotten Wars: The Counterrevolutionary Past and Lessons for the Future.* It is a selected comparative analysis of four of America's forgotten unconventional wars, drawing from these broad guidelines for the future.   This book begins where *America's Forgotten Wars* left off. Although this book might be considered a sequel, it is much more.   It focuses specifically on the contemporary period and analyzes in detail both policy and strategy by which to deal with unconventional conflicts and the problems and dilemmas these generate. Particular attention is given to the nature and character of open systems, their moral principles and ethical norms, and how these affect the system's ability to engage in unconventional conflicts.

This book is not likely to be comforting to government officials or their critics, to the US military services, to civil libertarians, or to members of the mass media.   Finally, those who do not believe in the utility of military force and just war theorists will find much to criticize here.   In brief, the book is likely to challenge conventional wisdom about the US political system and its responses to unconventional conflicts.

This is not a how-to book.   It is not designed to examine the details of the tactical and operational dimensions of covert operations.   Nor is it designed to explore all of the moral and ethical issues raised in open systems trying to deal with unconventional conflicts.   This book is presented as a landscape to the new battlefield with a map pointing out the directions and identifying critical landmarks.

A number of people have contributed to this book by their interest in the subject and willingness to discuss and debate the issues raised here. I thank them for their role in motivating the writing of this book and for their contributions. The person most directly responsible for assisting me in developing the final manuscript is Jay Walusek of Loyola University of Chicago. His editorial assistance and commentary on the manuscript were invaluable.

PART I

The Nature of Unconventional Conflicts: The Challenge

1

Third World Conflicts and US Interests

The Third World contains three-fourths of the world's population, two-thirds of the world's land mass, most of the world's poverty, and many of the world's most serious political and economic problems. In this turmoil, few Third World governments have been able to protect themselves from internal conflict or isolate themselves from external forces.

The most prudent course for the United States would appear to be arm's-length relationships and nonintervention in the Third World. Unfortunately, too often a state does not have the luxury of choosing between what it desires and what it can do. Thus the United States finds itself drawn into the Third World by a variety of purposes and forces, many over which it has no control. The danger is that in the effort to achieve legitimate policy goals, the United States may become embroiled in Third World conflicts such as Nicaragua and El Salvador, as it did earlier in Vietnam and Korea. What is particularly dangerous is that the United States is likely to find itself in a situation where it is least prepared to win. Compounding the danger is that the Soviet Union has demonstrated a capability to exploit such situations to its own advantage. The Third World has become the new battlefield. But this battlefield is one that cannot be understood by seeing

Figure 1-1
The Third World
(Developing Countries—Least developed shown in boldface)

Developing countries often are divided into subcategories based on income level or stage of industrial development. In 1971 the United Nations established the category of the least developed—a group characterized by the exceptionally small size of gross national product and manufacturing sector as well as a low literacy rate. These are mostly land-locked states or isolated islands, and many have limited physical resources and a declining population due to emigration. In 1980 the least developed countries together received an average of $24 per inhabitant of bilateral and multilateral official development assistance. The average for other developing countries was about $9.

Afghanistan
Algeria
Angola
Antigua and Barbuda
Argentina
The Bahamas
Bahrain
Bangladesh
Barbados
Belize
Benin
Bhutan
Bolivia
Botswana
Brazil
Burma
Burundi
Cameroon
Cape Verde
Central African Republic
Chad
Chile

China
Colombia
Comoros
Congo
Costa Rica
Cuba
Cyprus
Djibouti
Dominica
Dominican Republic
Ecuador
Egypt
Equatorial Guinea
El Salvador
Ethiopia
Fiji
Gabon
The Gambia
Ghana
Grenada
Guatemala
Guinea

Guinea-Bissau
Guyana
Haiti
Honduras
Hong Kong
India
Indonesia
Iran
Iraq
Ivory Coast
Jamaica
Jordan
Kampuchea
Kenya
Kiribati
North Korea
South Korea
Kuwait
Laos
Lebanon
Lesotho
Liberia

Libya
Madagascar
Malawi
Malaysia
Maldives
Mali
Malta
Mauritania
Mauritius
Mexico
Morocco
Mozambique
Nauru
Nepal
Nicaragua
Niger
Nigeria
Oman
Pakistan
Panama
Papua New Guinea
Paraguay

Peru
Philippines
Qatar
Rwanda
St. Lucia
St. Vincent and the Grenadines
Sao Tome and Principe
Saudi Arabia
Senegal
Seychelles
Sierra Leone
Singapore
Solomon Islands
Somalia
Sri Lanka
Sudan
Suriname
Swaziland
Syria
Tanzania
Thailand

Togo
Tonga
Trinidad and Tobago
Tunisia
Tuvalu
Uganda
United Arab Emirates
Upper Volta
Uruguay
Vanuatu
Venezuela
Vietnam
Western Samoa
Yemen (Aden)
Yemen (Sanaa)
Zaire
Zambia
Zimbabwe

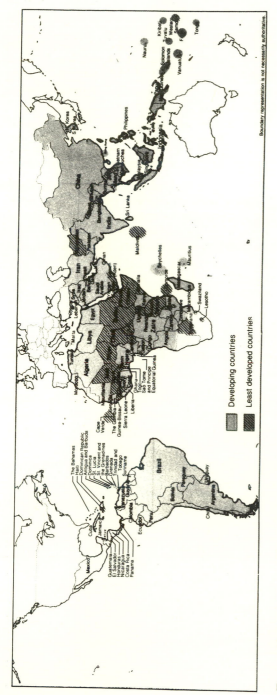

From: United States Department of State, *Atlas of United States Foreign Relations* (Washington, D.C.: U.S. Government Printing Office, June 1983), p. 69.

it through conventional lenses or by applying prevailing democratic norms. And if history is any guide, the United States will have difficulty developing the understanding and political-military capacity to respond effectively to challenges posed by the Third World.

Why is this so? How can the United States with its economic power and military strength be accused of inadequacy in facing the Third World? At first, the reasons may seem varied, but there is one overriding reason: the nature and character of US democracy. Democracy demands a kind of morality and ethics and a value system that are not suitable to successful engagement in Third World conflicts.

In this respect, if the US experience in Vietnam did anything, it did bring (or should have brought) Americans face to face with the realities of the Third World, realities that were beyond the comprehension of many. The same realities exist today and are still incomprehensible to most Americans. The fact is that little in the nature of American society or its political experience and value system can provide the basis for understanding the Vietnam War or, in the broader context, the Third World.

Here is how one observer described the American in Vietnam:

> The American in Vietnam. Caught in a war without fixed battle lines, without stirring slogans or Hitler-type villains, without real estate objectives, without conventional tactics or even conventional weapons, he must share the daily fighting with a smiling ally who at times is as difficult to understand as the enemy, for he too is an oriental cut from the same enigmatic mold. There is an Old West quality about the war in ingenuity and daring. But there is an Old East quality about it too, that is exasperating and wears down even the most dedicated.[1]

More pointedly, a Vietnamese counterpart told a US officer, "You can't help it if you're an American, but you should always remember that very few of our people are capable of genuine positive feelings towards you. You must assume that you are not wholly liked and trusted, and not be deceived by the Asian smile."[2]

Such observations are not necessarily limited to Americans in Vietnam. Tom Mboya, a leader in Kenya, East Africa, who was assassinated early in the independence period, had this to say about non-Africans in general:

> We find that both Westerners and Russians look at Africans through the same pair of glasses: the one lens is marked pro-West; the other pro-Communist. It is not surprising that, looking at Africans in this way, most foreigners fail to understand one great reality about our continent—that Africans are neither pro-West nor pro-Russian; they are pro-African.[3]

Throughout its history, the United States has attempted to keep its relationship with foreign states at a distance. Until recently this was true even with respect to Europe. Although the Southern Hemisphere was an exception, U.S. involvement there did not occur until early in the twentieth century and then primarily as a political-business venture in America's own backyard.

A legacy of this isolation is reflected today in the prevailing view of Americans regarding the Third World. Many Americans see the Third World as backward, poverty stricken, run by military men and oppressive rulers, awash in terror and internal power struggles, with major violations of human rights. Yet it is the same Third World that includes oil-rich sheikhdoms, swimming pools, mansions, luxury autos, massive amounts of US dollars, and even individuals and groups searching for democracy. These disparities are only surface indicators of the deeply rooted, complex forces in the Third World. The Third World includes all kinds of peoples, religions, political systems, weather, climate, geographic factors, and resources. One finds the widest gaps between rich and poor, rural and urban dwellers, the educated and uneducated.

Most Americans have difficulty understanding or relating to the many complexities, ambiguities, and cultural diversities in Third World societies. Yet the Third World has become increasingly important to the United States, not only because of the strategic location of a number of states but also because of mineral resources, energy sources, and cultural linkages to groups within the United States. As its importance to the United States has grown, so too has the Third World's instability and disarray, making it extremely vulnerable to a variety of internal and external forces. As a result, there has developed a high potential for internal conflict that threatens US interests and challenges the US position.

US interest in the Third World is relatively recent. During much of the 1950s and 1960s, not only were Americans mostly concerned about their own domestic politics, but any concern about international politics was focused on Europe, the Cold War, the Soviet threat in Europe, and nuclear warfare. Although major events were taking place in black Africa and Southeast Asia, many Americans regarded these as incidental to the main thrust of domestic life and US-Soviet relationships.

Thus, while the Third World was trying to modernize, struggling against divisive forces within, American concern was primarily turned toward the increasing prominence of the Soviet Union and the dramatic events taking place in China. Only much later did it become clear that these changes in the international system would have an impact on the role of the United States in the Third World.

Almost overnight, so it seemed, a number of Marxist-Leninist states had emerged in areas previously under Western influence. Even more ominous, the network of states that evolved is politically and ideologically diametrically opposed to open societies as represented by the United States. This was reinforced by the linkage between Marxist-Leninist Third World states such as Nicaragua, Cuba, Ethiopia, Vietnam, and the Soviet Union.

The United States belatedly recognized that the location of these states and their relationships to other Third World systems posed potential threats to the security interests of the United States. To understand why this is so, we need to examine the US political-military posture and how the United States got where it is today in the Third World.

US POLITICAL-MILITARY POLICY AND STRATEGY

The international system that emerged in the aftermath of World War II proved to be quite different from and more dangerous than what came out of World War I. Europe was prostrate, millions of people had been killed, new weapons of war had permanently changed warfare, and there occurred a major shift in the power structure of the international system.

Evolution of the International System: The European Connection

The United States and the Soviet Union emerged from World War II as superpowers. Not only did they have the largest military forces, but they were in commanding positions in the heart of Europe as the war came to an end. Although the United States demobilized quickly after World War II, the Soviet Union maintained its military strength and used it to pursue political goals in Eastern Europe and on the periphery of the Soviet land mass. To be sure, the United States developed an atomic arsenal and was already in the process of changing its strategy accordingly, but it seemed primarily disposed to return to peaceful pursuits reminiscent of the prewar period.

Events in Eastern Europe and the ruined political and economic systems of Europe created a vacuum that allowed Soviet military forces to establish Marxist-Leninist systems along the western borders of the Soviet Union.

Virtually all of Eastern Europe came under the control of Soviet-backed elites claiming legitimacy under Marxist-Leninist ideology.

The US response—the Marshall Plan and the Truman Doctrine—placed the United States squarely against the Soviet Union. These initial developments became the basis for the bipolar structure that still determines the basic patterns of the international system. The bipolar structure, crystallized by nuclear weapons and the coalescing of various states around the two superpowers, has undergone major changes, however. Many of these changes are beyond the control of the bipolar system. They are a result of the creation of a variety of new states and what they bring to the system in terms of ideology, policy, and conflict.

Emergence of New States

While Europe was being transformed by World War II, the end of the colonial era began. By the mid-1950s, peoples in Africa and Southeast Asia were either proclaiming their independence from colonial rule or were fighting against colonial powers for independence. By the end of the 1960s, the number of Third World states had increased dramatically, most of them gaining independence out of colonial empires.

Prostrate Europe and the demise of colonialism went hand in hand. This also marked the end of the European-centered world order, which had provided a degree of coherency and order to diplomacy and state behavior, regardless of how one views colonialism. This gave way to a new kind of diplomacy fashioned by new ideologies and Afro-Asian worldviews, changing previously established patterns of state-to-state behavior and relationships.

The magnitude of the new state phenomenon can be seen in the evolution of the United Nations. When it was founded, the organization consisted of a membership of 50 states, the majority Western or Western oriented. By the 1980s 157 member states were represented in the General Assembly, the majority from the Third World.

The proliferation of states also created a fragile stability within both the Third World and in the international order. Most of the new states have yet to develop viable political and economic systems. Indeed independence was accompanied by a host of political, social, and economic problems. While many of these were the result of years of colonial rule, most of the current problems can be placed at the doorstep of indigenous governments. Corruption, mismanagement, and struggles for power exacerbated the problems within most states and left them in constant political turmoil. States with comparatively stable systems were generally those with personalistic, dictatorial, or military rule. There seemed to be little room for democracy.

Increasing Potential for Third World Conflict

In the main, indigenous elites who had gained power were unable to develop the necessary infrastructure or ideological cohesion to establish reasonably stable and effective political systems. Ethnic hatreds, economic dissatisfaction, and social tensions often burst into bloody internal conflicts such as the civil war in Nigeria and regional outbreaks in India. Since the mid-1950s, virtually every region in the Third World has been inflicted by a variety of internal conflicts, some as a result of colonial rule and others as a result of struggles between indigenous elites, which in turn created conditions for intervention by third powers. Many of these struggles evolved into revolutionary and counterrevolutionary war: the Mau Mau rebellion in Kenya, the French in Indochina, the British in Malaysia, and more recently Americans in Vietnam, Castro in Cuba, contras in Nicaragua, the struggle against Vietnamese forces in Kampuchea, and the anti-Marxist revolutions in Angola and Mozambique. The international security situation has become complex and dangerous, and nothing seems to have emerged to replace the earlier European world order. Indeed, even the superpower bipolar structure has faded as new centers of power have emerged, creating a more pluralistic power structure. In addition to the rise of a number of regional powers (Indonesia, Nigeria, India), some small states have been able to exert international power through the support of terrorist groups (Libya) or by deliberate decisions to engage in war in contiguous areas (Vietnam in Kampuchea). This has become more complicated by the use of terrorism by a number of major religious and ethnic groups in the Middle East (Shiite Moslems). Similarly, the United States, the Soviet Union, Britain, and France have been involved in conflicts (Vietnam, Afghanistan, the Falkland islands, Chad, and Beirut). More states have acquired or have developed a potential for acquiring nuclear weapons. The world, in short, seems to have developed into a chaotic, anarchic, and increasingly dangerous place. And in this world, many Third World states became critical flash points.

US Political-Military Posture

For the United States, these changes have had an important impact on its ability to initiate policy and respond to the changing security environment. Not only have changing domestic forces (Watergate, the civil rights movement, the apparent resurgence of Congress, and the War Powers Act, to name a few) created constraints and limitations on US policy and strategy, but foreign challenges (Vietnam war, US hostages in Iran, terrorist bombings in Beirut, the Soviet invasion of Afghanistan, the skyjacking of TWA flight 847, and the struggles in Central America) have revealed the inadequacy of the US political-military posture and use of power.

Equally important, many US policy makers, elected officials, and the media have not come to grips with the nature and character of the changed international security environment, nor have most Americans been able to develop a realistic view of the Third World. Indeed it seems that the United States views the Third World through conventional lenses with a military fixation on Europe, while the most serious problems affecting US national interests are developing in the Third World. Although there are signs of change, the US political-military posture remains rooted in conventional perspectives and big battle scenarios.

According to a prominent British military historian,

> Most strategic scenarios today are based on the least probable of political circumstances--a totally unprovoked military assault by the Soviet Union, with no shadow of political justification, on Western Europe . . . It need hardly be said that hostilities breaking out elsewhere in the world are likely, as they did in Vietnam, to arise out of political situations involving an even greater degree of political ambiguity in which readiness to initiate nuclear war would appear even less credible.[4]

The Soviet Union has not hesitated to exploit tensions and instability in the Third World to further its own goals, particularly in its relationships with the United States. The Soviet Union was instrumental in developing and maintaining Marxist-Leninist regimes in Angola, Ethiopia, and Mozambique on the African continent. Additionally, it has played an important role in maintaining Marxist-Leninist regimes in Nicaragua and Vietnam, indicating the extent of Soviet effectiveness in exploiting situations and strategic capability in non-European areas. The use of proxy forces and surrogates, particularly Cuba, allows the Soviet Union to project its power with minimum risk. Abetted by its willingness to use military forces in contiguous areas (Afghanistan) and the large number of *Spetsnatz* forces (special forces), Soviet strategy seems geared to challenge the United States and the West, albeit indirectly in most instances, in areas where the Soviet Union sees a decided advantage or where a power vacuum exists or is developing.[5]

While the attention of the United States seems fixed on the European continent, parts of the Middle East, and on US-Soviet strategic capabilities, conflicts and challenges in the Third World have become increasingly serious for US national security.

THIRD WORLD SYSTEMS

Virtually the entire Third World consists of states that are in the process of development and change. Much has been written about the process, yet there is a great deal of disagreement on what this means in terms of individual states. There is general agreement that *development* means the drive to establish a modern economy, and *change* refers to the creation of modern political and social systems. This is an oversimplification; in reality development and change are inextricably linked and involve complex relationships among all sectors of a society and its institutional growth. But the distinction between change and development does focus attention on the specifics of politics separate from economics. More important, such distinctions make the study of modernization more manageable and comprehensible in trying to understand the pattern of emerging Third World forces.

Most states in the Third World are in various degrees of change and development, ranging from changing social and economic systems to a change in belief systems, individual behavior, expectations, and government institutions. Over the past two decades, most states in the Third World have been going through deep and dramatic alterations in their total cultural and political life as they drive for modernity.

Few states today do not aspire to modernity. One authority has concluded,

> The day of rulers who were indifferent to the archaism of the society which they governed has almost disappeared. The leaders of nearly every state—both the old established states as well as the new states of Asia and Africa—feel a pressing necessity of espousing policies which will bring them well within the circle of modernity. Much of the opposition which they en-

counter among their politically interested countrymen contends that they are not modern enough. Many traditionalists are constrained to assert that only by cleaving to the essence of older traditions can a genuine and stable modernity be attained.[6]

Although written almost two decades ago, this passage describes the essence of the modernization process and the internal pressures and potential for conflict it generates. Little has changed over time except that the issues and problems may now be even more challenging and dangerous. Not only are the states in Africa and Asia facing problems of modernity, but the same is also true with most states in the Southern Hemisphere of the Americas.

Diversity of Third World States

The blanket use of the term *Third World* tends to obscure the great differences among states, suggesting the notion of a mass of states sharing common problems and political-cultural systems. To the contrary, not only do most states differ in degrees of development and rates of change but also in resources, religions, ethnic and racial groups, languages, geographic scope, and population. In the Southern Hemisphere of the Americas, for example, Christianity prevails; Hinduism, Buddhism, and Islam characterize most of Asia. In Africa, Islam and Christianity exist side by side, at times in uneasy relationships.

Initially much of the conflict within Third World states was between indigenous independence movements and colonial systems. Most of the internal conflicts today, however, are among various indigenous elites contending for power. Many of these conflicts are between groups following Marxist-Leninist ideologies and those with non-Marxist, nationalistic, democratic, and socialist ideologies. These ideological issues, the East-West conflict, and the external aid and assistance required for modernization have internationalized Third World problems. As some argue,

These societies live in wildly different physical and social environments, displaying radically different attitudes and modes of conduct, and their governments pursue very different policies. But the diverse components of the Third World do indeed share one characteristic. This is not poverty, stagnation, exploitation, brotherhood, or skin color; it is the receipt of foreign aid. The concept of the Third World and the policy of official aid are inseparable. Without foreign aid there is no Third World.[7]

The dependence of the Third World on external aid is not a one-way street. A number of Third World states and regions are important to the security interests and power positions of the superpowers. Yet it is the drive to modernity that creates the conditions for external aid and exposes Third World states to external forces. These are the same factors that are at the roots of Third World instability and conflict.

Issues of Modernity

Much has been published on the issues of modernity, its roots and consequences.[8] A thorough understanding of these matters will surely require a serious reading of the literature. Our purpose here, however, is not a study of development and change but rather what specific issues precipitate conflicts within the Third World and how these may affect US national security. Only those issues of modernity that have a direct bearing on US security interests will be addressed.

Three fundamental issues face virtually all Third World states: who should rule, who profits (what kind of economic system should be established), and the nature of the social order. All of these are intended to be bound, rationalized, and legitimized by ideology.

Who Should Rule?

Who should rule? This is a perennial political question, made more serious by the nature of developing systems. During the years following independence, primarily in the 1950s, elites that organized independence movements and challenged the existing system, usually colonial, were given the mantle of leadership, most often by the colonial system they challenged. Algeria, Indochina, Africa, Ghana, Nigeria, and Kenya are cases in point. In Algeria, General Charles de Gaulle, after taking power under the Fifth Republic, turned power over to the Algerian nationalists, whom the French had been fighting for several years.

The euphoria that followed on the heels of independence in the Third World faded with the realization that the quality of life and good government that was promised did not arrive. Instead the sweeping away of colonial restrictions on political activity seemed to spur the growth of a variety of contending elites. Some governing elites adopted an authoritarian posture and co-opted or destroyed those who opposed their rule. Some states developed personalistic regimes; the leader became the fount of all power and legitimacy, effectively eroding the credibility of opposition. For some states, personalism led directly to dictatorial rule, with security forces terrorizing the populace to maintain law and order. Other states went through a period of internal strife as elites struggled against each other in order to grasp the reins of power. Still other states fell into such chaos that the military stepped in to establish order and stayed to rule. Africa illustrates many of these internal conflicts.

Africa's colonial masters left behind parliaments and prime ministers, but just a generation later, half the 50 member countries of the Organization of African Unity are run by the military, and strongmen rule in others. Parliaments are still elected after pitched campaigns in a few countries, but they then offer little debate and no opposition.[9]

In most Third World states, political power is the highest prize, one that leads directly to wealth, status, and even more power. Access to the political arena is seen as the crucial element in achieving individual as well as group success. Equally important, most elites in the Third World see political power as the only way to shape their own society and to challenge external intrusion and internal strife. As the late Kwame Nkrumah wrote, "Seek ye first the political kingdom and all things shall be added unto you."[10] It is no wonder that in the conflict between elites and individuals struggling for political power in the Third World, there is the urgency of totality. "Who rules" becomes a life-and-death struggle.

Who Profits?

Those in political power play a crucial role in shaping the economic system of the state. Part of the drive for independence was based on the idea that once achieved, independence would spur economic growth and a better quality of life for all. This did not happen. Indeed the departure of colonial civil servants, the withdrawal of financial support from the mother country, and, most important, misdirected economies put into place by indigenous governments left a number of former colonies in dire financial straits with declining economies. For many new states, problems became even worse later. In deposing indigenous rulers, new governing elites usually found that the national treasury was in a sorry state and the economic structure fragile. In the 1960s, several Third World states found themselves sitting on an ocean of oil, changing their economic and political power dramatically, but these were exceptions to the rule.

As most authorities point out, Third World economic systems eventually reflect the character of political rule and the attitudes of the governing elite. During the immediate independence period or the period following the overthrow of indigenous governments, economic policy tended to be more or less pragmatic as the new elite attempted to respond to the expectations of the people.

Increasingly, however, the economic system was shaped to the ideological precepts of the governing elite.

Africa is a prime example of the problems of governance and the relationship between politics and economic systems. The eroding political and economic position of Africa as a whole, combined with the ideological confrontations fostered by East-West issues, creates conditions that are likely to lead to even more problems. One authority has noted, "As African countries extend their government controls and the means of production fall under government ownership, the material well-being of their inhabitants will further decrease . . . The condition of the masses in all likelihood will deteriorate steadily."[11] Many other Third World states developed similar patterns.

Although some authoritative systems have allowed a degree of economic capitalism, it is highly problematical whether this will lead to more liberal political systems. Recent changes in The People's Republic of China in this respect have led to much speculation about the nature of changes in that political system. To presume, however, that the Marxist-Leninist system established in China since 1949 will fundamentally alter because of some economic shifts defies historical evidence. The New Economic Policy temporarily instituted in the Soviet Union in the 1920s was followed by an onslaught against those who benefited most by the policy.

Thus, any ruling elite seeks a high degree of congruence between economic and political systems. The philosophical roots underpinning the political and economic systems are inextricable.

Emerging Social Systems

Social system usually refers to the pattern of relationships between individuals and groups and the relative status given to particular roles. Political power and the character of economic systems are closely intermeshed with the social system. The evolution of a middle class, urban dwellers, factory workers, and an educated public has much to do with how individuals and groups achieve political power, how power is transferred, and the degree to which the people are involved in political decisions. Additionally, modernity is based on the presumption that social systems change to provide social mobility, access to wealth, and a better quality of life. Equally important, social divisions and the sharpness among various social classes have political impact, as Jefferson and Hamilton noted and as Marx and Lenin later proclaimed. Socio-economic class empathy and compatibility are critical to democracy, as is the maintenance of a large middle class and social mobility. To Marxist-Leninist ideology, social class and class struggle are fundamental. These views and principles are inextricably linked with the nature of the political and economic systems.

Traditional Third World systems provide clearly defined social structure and roles that are legitimized by custom, religion, traditional norms, or a combination of these. In developing systems, traditional rules are challenged by modern ideas and different relationships and social roles; for example, social mobility replaces ascribed status. Contradictory social forces are one element contributing to instability. To compound the problem, one or another modern element (for example, new social classes or stress on individuality and socioeconomic mobility) challenges not only traditional structures but each other. The political system and its ideological basis ultimately demands a compatible social system as well. It follows that the questions regarding the nature of emerging social systems are closely linked to the questions of who should rule and who profits.

Ideology

Identifying ideology as part of the general character of Third World states is a difficult undertaking because of the various interpretations of even the most coherent ideologies and their modifications as they apply to various Third World systems. Nonetheless, it is important to understand the role that ideology plays in the current context of Third World systems.

Decolonization resulted in the rise of a variety of ideologies, most of which reflected a mix of socialism, nationalism, democracy, sovereignty, and anticolonialism. Elites coming to power as a result of the overthrow of indigenous systems, such as in China, Vietnam, and Nicaragua, followed a Marxist-Leninist ideology at the outset and claimed this as the basis for rule. Others turned to traditionalism (the Khomeini regime in Iran) or an eclectic form of socialism-democracy (Tanzania). As one authority writes, however, "neither liberal-democratic nor Communist outlooks fit easily into most Third World countries. Their choice between them will depend . . . upon which side offers the most in their own terms, and, above all, on which side they think is going to win."[12]

Although many Third World states try to adopt an ideological posture that leans neither toward the West nor the Soviet Union, a number of states tend to see some good in the Marxist-Leninist view because of its apparent rationalization for rule by a self-perpetuating elite. Others tend to adhere to a Western or neutral view for philosophical and economic reasons. The lack of ideological cohesion in many Third World states (with the exception of Marxist-Leninist systems) adds to their vulnerability to external forces. Again, Africa provides examples:

> In Africa there is little or no capacity to deter outside interference in local disputes, despite the expressed general desire of African leaders to avoid a new wave of foreign intervention and domination. Strongly divisive forces also keep regionalism at bay.[13]

Regardless of how one views the Third World, ideology is a major component in legitimizing and rationalizing a nation's system of rule and links it with economic and social systems. Without a cohesive and effective ideology, Third World states face serious internal incongruence among institutions, leadership, and legitimacy, complicated by the politicization of religion (making religion an ideology, as in Iran).

In sum, most states in the Third World are now in political turmoil, with fragmented ideologies, declining economies, and ineffective governing institutions. These are the prime ingredients for internal strife and conflict. Ironically the major exceptions to ideological fragmentation are states that have adopted a Marxist-Leninist ideology and the governing mechanism evolving from this ideology. India is considered by some as one of several exceptions. It does not adhere to Marxist-Leninist ideology, and at the national level there is a relatively cohesive ideology. But this has not prevented ideological fragmentation at the state and local levels. China may also be another exception.

There are signs that governing elites are coming to power in a number of Latin American states who are committed to non-Marxist ideologies (Brazil and Argentina). Whether these signs are indicative of a growing trend remains to be seen.

A number of questions, however, remain unanswered. Why should the United States be concerned with the Third World? What are the stakes, if any? Should the United States become involved? If so, in what way? What are likely to be the consequences of US involvement in the Third World?

EVOLUTION OF US THIRD WORLD POLICY

Until the 1970s, America's relationships with most of the Third World were at a distance. The United States did not see any particular interest or pressing issues related to the Third World. Any matters that did arise were usually handled through the colonial power and later through the former mother country. For example, most US relationships with black Africa were handled through Paris or London. The same general pattern was followed in dealing with Indochina and Malaya.

There were exceptions to this policy. The Middle East became an increasingly important policy area for the United States with the creation of Israel. Additionally, US involvement in the Philippines at the turn of the century (the Spanish-American War) and until the end of World War II was viewed by many as a colonial relationship. The US role in the Southern Hemisphere during the first part of the twentieth century was also considered by many as a form of hegemony over Latin and Central America. Indeed, the uneasy relationships between the United States and a number of Southern Hemisphere states today is a result of the historical US-Latin American experience. Nonetheless, the bulk of the developing world with its colonial structure remained largely outside the immediate interests of the United States. This began to change after World War II.

The expansion of communism and the Vietnam War are critical reference points for US involvement with the Third World. Although US economic aid and assistance far outdistanced military aid to Third World states, it is military power (or its inadequacy) that has left an impression on the Third World.

In the main, US policy has been inconsistent, at times incoherent, and lacking in staying power. There are a number of reasons for this, much of which can be traced to the lack of understanding regarding the nature of the Third World and misunderstanding of revolutionary and counterrevolutionary conflicts. To this must be added the character and policies of various US administrations, political partisanship between Congress and the executive, and the opinions and attitude of the public.

From the late 1940s to the mid-1960s, there seemed to be little change in the worldview held by most Americans. Containment, the Soviet threat, and nuclear weaponry occupied most of the intellectual community, policy makers, opinion leaders, and the media. US excursions into the Third World, aside from the Middle East, were viewed as temporary, transitional, and on the periphery of major US interests. The US-European-Japanese connection became the triad for a future world order and the basis for an effective counterforce to communist expansion, according to many. Under the impact of various events, however, US views began to change.

Vietnam War and Its Aftermath

The Vietnam War marked a major change in US views of the world and of itself, with important consequences regarding Third World relationships. Although there is still much to learn from the Vietnam experience and much remains to be analyzed, there are a number of observations that are well founded.

First, the US withdrawal from Vietnam and the subsequent defeat of the South by the communist forces from the North in 1975 forced a reassessment of US capability to conduct successful military operations in the Third World. For many policy makers, Vietnam was a sure sign of the decreasing utility of military force, creating a "never-again" syndrome: never again should the United States become involved in a Vietnam-type situation. It also seemed to indicate that the United States was lacking in national will and political resolve to become militarily involved and to sustain this involvement. This apparent lack of staying power was not lost on the Soviet Union, US allies, and many Third World leaders.

Second, the US military also seemed to recoil from its experience in Vietnam. Immediately following Vietnam, the military turned its attention with a vengeance (so it seemed) back to Europe and big battle scenarios. The drive toward electronic battlefields, sophisticated weaponry, organization, and training turned to European modes of warfare—not that the US military had departed seriously from its conventional view of warfare, even in Vietnam. Counterinsurgency and unconventional warfare became almost extinct in military circles, marking a dramatic turnaround from the early 1960s with President Kennedy's call for counterinsurgency capabilities.

Third, those in policy-making positions, elected officials, and the media reacted even more violently. In what seemed to be a period of self-flagellation, many Americans damned their government's arrogance of power, perceived militarism, and the immorality of policy. The never-again syndrome came into full play in domestic and international politics. Congressional reaction seemed to ensure that any future president would have one hand tied behind his back should he try to commit forces without congressional approval. Only a few dared to claim that US actions in Vietnam were an important, if unsuccessful, effort and that different strategy and tactics might have changed the outcome. More important, only a few saw the long-range implications of the retreat from Vietnam.

Fourth, events in the Third World seemed to reflect a trend favorable to Soviet policy and power projections. Although many argued that this surely was not sufficient cause to panic, the fact was that such trends also indicated a dangerous level of instability within a number of Third World states. This was a situation that the Soviets were in a position to exploit. For better or for worse, the Iranian revolution toppled the shah, Somoza was deposed in Nicaragua, and the Soviet Union, with its surrogates and proxies, sustained Marxist-Leninist regimes in Angola, Ethiopia, and Mozambique. Later North Vietnam began to extend its regional influence by invading Kampuchea to sustain its own handpicked regime there. It seemed that the correlation of forces, a term used by the Soviets to assess the geopolitical power balance, had turned in favor of the socialist camp.

Thus, from the beginning of the 1970s to their end, the United States was searching for a meaning to Vietnam and developed policies to avoid future similar situations. Policy and strategy became cautious, hesitant, and increasingly rhetorical. Proclamations of human rights, regardless of its high moral plane, had little impact when not backed by effective political-military policy and action. Withdrawal from Vietnam also had its impact on the military, which went through a difficult period. Its combat effectiveness was reduced for lack of adequate financial resources, and the quality of personnel became increasingly poor as the volunteer military was unable to attract an adequate number of high school graduates and a military career became unattractive for many. The vast number of Americans, particularly those in the middle class, distanced themselves from the military.

The Turning Point

The 1979 invasion of Afghanistan by Soviet forces was a turning point in the US political-military posture. Although earlier events had triggered some reassessment of the US role, it was the invasion of Afghanistan that crystallized a different view of Soviet intentions for many in the Carter administration. The direct use of almost 100,000 Soviet combat forces in the invasion revealed the nature of the Soviet system in a way that earlier exhortations could not. The invasion also destroyed the arguments of some in the United States claiming that Soviet leaders had become reasonable and restrained. Even with attempts by the Carter administration to soften US policy toward the Soviet Union and project a moralist human rights policy, Soviet incursions into the Third World appeared ominous. Addressing the state of US-Soviet relationships, President Carter in 1978 stated,

> There also has been an ominous inclination on the part of the Soviet Union to use its military power—to intervene in local conflicts with advisors, with equipment and with full logistical support and encouragement for mercenaries from other Communist countries, as we can observe today in Africa. This increase in Soviet military power has been going on for a long time. We do not desire to intervene militarily in the internal domestic affairs of other countries, nor to aggravate regional conflicts. And we shall oppose intervention by others.[14]

Combined with the taking of US hostages in Iran by the newly formed Khomeini regime, the Soviet invasion of Afghanistan seemed to leave little doubt that the United States needed to take a firm stand and rethink its policy and strategy. Unfortunately, it had neither the intelligence system nor the political-military capacity to oppose Soviet intervention. Even the attempt to rescue the Iranian hostages later failed, further embarrassing the United States as well as its military. To many Third World states and US allies, these events seemed to confirm US impotence with respect to the Third World.

Although other domestic and international factors affected America's relationships with friends and adversaries, this overview illustrates how during the recent past US confidence and ability to deal with world events, particularly those in the Third World, have eroded. With its military in a low state of effectiveness, still suffering from the Vietnam syndrome, and enamored with moralist rhetoric, the United States was increasingly viewed as a paper tiger. In no small measure, this posture and how it has been perceived by those in the Third World has contributed greatly to the increased potential for conflict outside Europe. Although those in the Middle East have responded to their own peculiar set of forces, the rest of the Third World seems to be at the mercy of Soviet power projections and revolutionary challenges.

The Soviet invasion of Afghanistan combined with the taking of US hostages triggered a growing reaction against these cautious and hesitant US policies. During the final year of the Carter presidency, a relatively large defense budget was voted into place—a turnaround from the previous three years. The 1980 presidential election campaign and its outcome were the true indicators of a changed posture, not only toward the Soviet Union but the Third World as well. Throughout the election campaign, there was an underlying theme that demanded a resurgence of power combined with a growing confidence in what the United States could and should do. Ronald

Reagan was elected in no small measure because of his ability to communicate this confident view.

A NEW REALISM

The first part of the 1980s was characterized by a different US political-military policy and strategy toward the Soviet Union and the Third World. Military forces were given high priority. Efforts were made to reshape America's view of itself regarding the Vietnam War; Vietnam veterans were finally given a proper place in society, albeit a decade after the fact. Most important, a new policy and strategy was put into place. Counterinsurgency in Third World conflicts again became a legitimate concern for military professionals and civilian policy makers. These conflicts were initially labeled low-intensity conflicts, a term covering the gamut from terrorism to Vietnam-type situations.

In the early 1980s, US peacekeeping forces were dispatched to the Middle East where terrorist attacks took scores of American lives, including the lives of US Marines. These events, among others, focused increasing attention on developing a US counterterror capacity and underscored the need for a coordinated response to low-intensity conflicts. One result was the creation of the First Special Operations Command in the US Army whose principal mission was special operations, which became the term preferred over *low-intensity conflict*. The successful operation in Grenada seemed to signal a new era of US power, yet nagging problems remain. US capacity to conduct unconventional conflicts is still uncertain. Moreover, new factors complicate US policy and strategy in Third World states. These have to do not only with US-Soviet relationships but also with the changing role of Third World states in international security. These have become important enough to demand a reformulation of US policy and strategy for unconventional conflicts.

US SECURITY INTERESTS

The increasing interdependence of the world and the internationalization of the East-West and North-South dynamics are important enough to broaden US interests in the Third World. Several other important factors make US interests in the Third World more pressing and challenging than in the past.

Geopolitical

Geopolitical factors—or, as these have become known to some, geostrategic factors—associated with some Third World areas are critical to US interests. The term *geopolitical* refers primarily to strategic location and in particular strategic location with respect to US interests. Central America and Cuba are geopolitically important because of US dependence on major sea-lanes through the Caribbean. Much of the sea traffic for supplying European-based forces, as well as forces of the Western allies, moves out of gulf ports in the southern United States through the Caribbean. Adversaries in control of land bases in Central America and Cuba could make it extremely difficult to maintain a logistical link with European based forces over these sea-lanes.

The East Coast of Africa, particularly the Horn of Africa (Ethiopia, Somalia, and Djibouti), is important as a jump-off point and base for influencing events around the Red Sea, as well as the Middle East in general. Although less important now than in the past, the tip of the African continent, South Africa, is important for its naval facilities and possible use as a base for power projection into the Indian Ocean area; Diego Garcia plays an important role in this regard.

Asia also has obvious geopolitical importance. South Korea serves as a major friendly land base and is a major countervailing power balanced against North Korea and the Chinese mainland. Taiwan holds a similar, if less important, geopolitical position. Clark Field and Subic

Bay in the Philippines are important bases for US air and sea forces in the Pacific. In the 1985 annual report to Congress, the secretary of defense stressed the importance of the Philippines:

> The United States and the Republic of the Philippines are bound by the Mutual Defense Treaty of 1951 and the Military Bases Agreement (MBA) of 1947. U.S. military facilities in the Philippines play a key role in projecting American power in the western Pacific, East and Southeast Asia, and into the Indian Ocean.[15]

Encompassing the east coast of Africa, the Middle East to India and the Indian Ocean and extending to Indonesia, the western coast of Australia to the tip of southern Africa, Southwest Asia (SWA) has become a critical geopolitical component in US security interests. The importance of this area was underlined by the activation of the U.S. Central Command (an evolution from the Rapid Deployment Force) with primary responsibility for Southwest Asia.[16]

The importance of Southwest Asia was pointed out by the secretary of defense:

> It is our policy to support the independence and territorial integrity of friendly countries in this politically unstable region and to prevent a further spread of Soviet domination. In addition to our interest in the security of several friendly countries in the region, the fact that one-third of the free world's oil supply is produced in SWA makes the area vital to the interests of the United States and its allies.[17]

A number of other geopolitical regions in the Third World are important to US policy and strategy, but those already identified serve to point out the importance of geopolitics.

Energy and Mineral Sources

Although US dependence on Middle East oil has diminished considerably since the 1973 oil embargo, it remains critical for many Western allies. Ensuring that the Suez Canal, the Gulf of Suez, and the Red Sea remain open for sea traffic is important not only for oil supplies but for maintaining sea communications with Israel. The Persian Gulf has an equally critical geopolitical importance, particularly US and Western access to a number of important states, as well as to oil supplies.

Mineral resources are critical to United States national interests (Table 1-1). The United States imports almost all of its cobalt and an important portion of its titanium needs from Zaire and Zambia. Both minerals are necessary in the production of jet engines. Other imported minerals important to US security interests are bauxite from Guinea, copper from Namibia and Zaire, and chrome from Zimbabwe.[18]

Political-Psychological Factors

Political-psychological factors, which refer to the values, beliefs, and norms of the US political system, are difficult to relate directly to US interests in the Third World, but in the long run, they may be the most important consideration. Governments in democratic systems are not expected to be all encompassing, subsuming all individuals and other systems—religious, economic, and social. Government is intended to be limited, responsible, representative, and sensitive to the demands of the people.

Ideally democracies expect the behavior of their diplomats, soldiers, and other political actors to adhere to the norms of democracy. They also presume that others should behave in the same manner. Thus, it is difficult for Americans, and other democratic peoples in general, to deal realistically with systems whose worldview, ideology, and norms are in direct contrast to those of democracy.

Table 1-1
Strategic Minerals Imported by the United States
*(Selected Listing)

```
Diamonds--------------------------------------------100%
    from South Africa, Zaire, and Britain

Colombium-------------------------------------------100%
    from Brazil, Canada, and Thailand

Manganese-------------------------------------------99%
    from South Africa, Gabon, and France

Cobalt---------------------------------------------95%
    from Zaire, Zambia, and Canada

Tantalum-------------------------------------------94%
    from Thailand, Malaysia, and Brazil

Platinum------------------------------------------91%
    from South Africa, Britain, and
    the Soviet Union

Graphite------------------------------------90%
    from Mexico, China, and Brazil

Chromium--------------------------82%
    from South Africa, Zimbabwe,
    and the Soviet Union

Tin---------------------------79%
    from Thailand, Malaysia,
    and Indonesia
```

*This does not include a variety of other minerals of which the United States imports from 50 to 75% of its needs, i.e., Nickel, Zinc, Rutile, and Tungsten.

- -

Adapted from Casper W. Weinberger, *Annual Report to Congress, Fiscal Year 1985* (Washington, D.C.: U.S. Government Printing Office, 1984) and "Foreign Metals—an Achilles' Heel for U.S.," *U.S. News and World Report*, March 18, 1985.

In terms of the Third World, noninvolvement on the presumption that self-determination and control over internal affairs is a basic principle of international equity and state sovereignty, directly reflects these democratic ideals. Involvement is deemed legitimate if it is for the purpose of supporting self-determination, state sovereignty, and international justice. To be sure, these idealistic notions of involvement and noninvolvement have been distorted and misused time and again, but they still provide important criteria for judging democracy and policies of democratic systems.

Much has been made of a state's staying power. Although such a concept can be overworked, there seems to be little question that the ability of a state, once it is involved in a certain area, to maintain its policy posture and coherency over a length of time is important to the power and prestige of that state and to those with which it is associated. Thus, the ability of a state to project its power to defend its legitimate interests, including support and assistance to like-minded systems over the long haul, is critical in influencing other states. This staying power is a function of national will and political resolve. With respect to Third World areas, until very recently the United States has generally been perceived as lacking staying power.

It is to the advantage of the United States to live in a world that functions primarily through peaceful state relationships and peaceful resolution of conflicts. Although one can easily argue that all states seek such a world, it is a fact that values, ideologies, and behavior among and between states differ. States whose ideology is rooted in participatory politics, justice and fairness evolving from or closely related to the Judeo-Christian heritage or other similar religions, and a commitment to reasonable and rational resolution of disputes, with a nonexpansionist and nonthreatening posture, serve US interests best. These goals are idealistic, to be sure, but worthy of pursuit.

The values and ideology of the United States expressed through its policy goals are best secured through a world order supported by states with a degree of commonality of purpose. This does not mean they must emulate the United States. It does mean that, at a minimum, such states should realistically support sovereignty, self-determination, and nonexpansionism and aim toward openness. Only by openness can systems reduce mistrust and develop realistic linkages as the basis for peaceful competition.

US POLICY ISSUES: THE USSR AND THE THIRD WORLD

US policy has not been completely consistent or practical at times. It ebbs and flows between success and failure; internal forces and the role of individuals and the public expose questionable behavior and policies; and walls have been erected beyond which administrations fear to tread or tread at the risk of political suicide. All of these factors make the relationships between the United States and the Soviet Union, as well as between the United States and other authoritarian or dictatorial systems, asymmetrical. Although nondemocratic systems can pursue policies by a variety of means, there are a number of constraints, limitations, and countervailing forces inherent in a democracy that create significant checks and balances to governmental performance and policies. The contrast between democracy and authoritarian-dictatorial systems in this respect is sharp and clear.

These considerations are extremely important in a world arena in which the internationalization of ideological conflicts reflecting political systems whose values, beliefs, and moral-ethical patterns differ considerably has fragmented the world into contending groups of states. These confrontations and struggles are dangerous because they evolve primarily from different and contradictory values and belief systems, making compromise and understanding difficult.

In this type of international environment, the Third World stands particularly exposed to the influence of external powers. Any intrusion by an external power in the Third World can easily lead to the establishment of a base —political, ideological, psychological, diplomatic, military, and economic. The nature of the external power's system in such circumstances can lead to use of this base to influence the direction and evolution of other states.

Although there may be disagreement regarding the long-range impact and the number of successes and failures, there appears to be agreement among scholars and policy makers that the Soviet Union has developed policies and strategies whose purpose is to gain influence in Third World areas. In this respect,

> It is clear that Soviet involvement in the Third World is antagonistic to Western interests in general and to US interests in particular. There is a consensus represented here that an underlying purpose of Soviet activity in Asia, Africa, and the Middle East and Latin America is to undermine US influence in favor of the Soviet Union. Thus, in this arena the cold war continues.[19]

Such competition and power projection would normally be accepted as a traditional mode of state behavior that is similar to the nineteenth century geopolitical game. But the contemporary period is more dangerous and challenging to the West, and the United States in particular, because the competition is no longer taking place within any generally accepted sense of world order (the rules of the game) and because the means include unconventional conflict and terrorism. This is not a one-sided perspective. Marxist-Leninist as well as other non-democratic systems perceive the struggles in the international field as part of a long-range struggle to determine who will win. Such systems have an inherent fear of democracy (as practiced in the West, particularly by the United States) reflecting an ancient bias that democracy is mob rule: chaotic, anarchic, and leading ultimately to the undermining of the state, ruling elite, and social order.

CONCLUSIONS

Combined with geopolitical and energy supply considerations, critical philosophical issues make the Third
World the contemporary battlefield, even more compelling than nuclear confrontations and European confrontations between the United States and USSR. Since the
1970s, a war has been in progress between contending
ideologies in an area that has yet to institutionalize its
system and legitimize its ideology: the Third World. This
war is not of trenches, front lines, and masses of men in
uniform struggling against each other on bloody battlefields. Rather, this is a war of subtleties, nuances, intimi-
dation, fear, political mobilization, terror, and revolution
—at times bloody but most times characterized by psychological warfare, political maneuvering and mobilization, disinformation, deception, assassination, and terrorism. It is a war whose outcome is more a result of intelligence systems, covert operations, and political leadership,
cadres, and ideology than conventional troops locked in
battle.

It is a war that is difficult for most Americans to
comprehend and engage in; indeed, many do not or refuse
to recognize that there is a war. The very nature of such
wars—with their protractedness, lack of clearly identifiable enemies, obscure boundaries, and political-psychological character—is contrary to the essence of democracy.
A number of Americans argue that such a situation is not
war but one of peaceful competition between states. These
views are based on idealistic notions of democracy, which
according to the argument apply equally as well to US
policy in the Third World.

US policy makers must be concerned, of course, about
Soviet policy, intentions, and power projections in the
Third World, but US policy and strategy must also chart a
course independent of Soviet policy; otherwise the US
posture will be dictated by Soviet initiatives and not by
purposeful US goals. Even if the Soviets and their
surrogates were not in Africa, Latin and Central America,

or Asia, the United States would still be faced with a number of serious and complex policy issues, the most serious of which is response to Third World conflicts.

The fact that few democracies exist and modernity tends to increase the potential for internal conflict in many Third World states makes it essential for US policy and strategy to consist not only of developmental aid, favorable trade and investment but also diplomatic, political, and military aid (if necessary). Moreover, US involvement in one form or another over time may lead to active military engagement. Thus, contingency plans should include the possibility of active military support of counterrevolutionary systems, as well as support of revolutionaries struggling against Marxist-Leninist or dictatorial regimes in the Third World.

A number of conflicts occurring in the Third World promise to have important implications for US security. Without advocating military commitment, it is still essential for the United States to plan for such contingencies. And in so doing, it must understand and respond to the challenges of unconventional conflicts.

This new type of war, the new battlefield, is one in which the West, including the United States has much to learn. Even while acknowledging that a capacity must be developed for Third World conflicts, many in the United States view these through conventional lenses, both militarily and politically. The United States has yet to develop a long-range political-military policy and strategy to respond to the new battlefield. These unconventional conflicts have a nature and character that differ considerably from the conventional battlefields and big battle environments for which most US military forces are postured. To develop an understanding of these new wars, we need to examine Third World conflicts and specifically their primary form—revolution and counterrevolution.

NOTES

1. Hugh Mulligan, *No Place to Die: The Agony of Vietnam* (New York: William Morrow, 1967), p. 318.

2. Stuart A. Herrington, *Silence Was a Weapon; The Vietnam War in the Villages, A Personal Perspective* (Novato, Calif.: Presidio Press, 1982), p. 23.

3. Quoted in Colin Legum, *Pan-Africanism: A Short Political Guide*, rev. ed. (New York: Praeger, 1965), p. 13.

4. Michael Howard, *The Causes of War and Other Essays*, 2d ed., enlarged (Cambridge, Mass.: Harvard University Press, 1984), p. 112.

5. Roman Kolkowicz, "Military Strategy and Political Interests: The Soviet Union and the United States," ACIS Working Paper No. 30 (Los Angeles: University of California, Center for International and Strategic Affairs, January 1981), p. 34. The author states, "There is little doubt that the Soviets are committed to gradual, non-provocative but sustained exploration of vulnerable regions of the Third World as targets of opportunity."

6. Edward Shils, *Political Development in New States* (The Hague: Mouton and Co., 1965), p. 7.

7. Peter T. Bauer and Basil S. Yaney, "Foreign Aid: What Is at Stake?" in W. Scott Thompson, ed., *The Third World: Premises of U.S. Policy*, rev. ed. (San Francisco: ICS Press, 1983), p. 117.

8. See, for example, Monte Palmer, *Dilemmas of Political Development*, 3d ed. (Itasca, Ill.: F. E. Peacock Publishers, 1985), Gabriel Almond, *Political Development* (Boston: Little, Brown, 1970), Gabriel A. Almond and G. Bingham Powell, Jr., *Comparative Politics: A Developmental Approach* (Boston: Little, Brown, 1966), and Everett E. Hagen, *On the Theory of Social Change* (Homewood, Ill.: Dorsey Press, 1962).

9. June Kronholz, "Africa's Political Map: A Gloomy Landscape of Coups, Strongmen," *Wall Street Journal*, October 31, 1983, p. 1.

10. Kwame Nkrumah, *Ghana: The Autobiography of Kwame Nkrumah* (Camden, N.J.: Thomas Nelson and Sons, 1957), p. 163.

11. L. H. Gann and Peter Duignan, *Africa South of the Sahara: The Challenge to Western Security* (Stanford, Calif.: Hoover Institution Press, 1981), p. 99.

12. Max Beloff, "The Third World and the Conflict of Ideologies," in Thompson, p. 32.

13. Catherine Gwin, "Introduction: International Involvement in a Changing Africa," in Colin Legum, I. William Zartman, Steven Langdon, and Lynn K. Mytelka, *Africa in the 1980s: A Continent in Crisis* (New York: McGraw-Hill, 1979), p. 1.

14. Remarks of President Carter at Wake Forest University, Winston-Salem, North Carolina, March 17, 1978, White House press release.

15. Caspar W. Weinberger, *Annual Report to Congress, Fiscal Year 1985* (Washington, D.C.: Government Printing Office, 1984), p. 219. In 1986 the internal problems in the Philippines and the rising resistance to then President Ferdinand Marcos caused some US policy makers to consider Guam or Saipan, among others, as alternatives to US bases there.

16. For a general discussion of security issues in this area, see Iqbal Singh, "US Defense Policy and Power Projection in Southwest Asia" (Washington, D.C.: Washington Institute for Values in Public Policy, 1984).

17. Weinberger, p. 210.

18. See, for example, Congressional Budget Office, *Strategic and Critical Nonfuel Minerals: Problems and Policy Alternatives* (Washington, D.C.: Government Printing Office, August 1983).

19. Joseph L. Nogee, "The Soviet Union in the Third World: Success and Failures," in Robert H. Donaldson, ed., *The Soviet Union in the Third World: Success and Failures* (Boulder, Colo.: Westview Press, 1981), p. 447. See also R. Craig Nation and Mark V. Kauppi, eds., *The Soviet Impact in Africa* (Lexington, Mass.: Lexington Books, 1984).

2

Revolution and Revolutionary Systems

Revolutions and counterrevolutions are the stuff of most Third World conflicts. These kinds of conflicts are not the same as conventional ones. They differ in purpose, strategy, and doctrine from the kinds of conflicts that most Americans have experienced.

In the immediate post-World War II period, most revolutions occurred against colonial systems by those seeking independence. More recently, revolutions have taken place (and continue to do so) against indigenous governments. The United States and a number of other Western states have become involved in such conflicts; examples are the United States in support of the Greek government against communist forces, and later in Vietnam, Great Britain in Malaya, and France in Indochina and Algeria. Although there have been some noted counterrevolutionary successes, in the main the United States and the rest of the West have had a great deal of difficulty responding to revolutionary challenges to existing indigenous systems. The reasons are many, ranging from the ineffectiveness of indigenous systems, external support for revolutionaries, hesitancy and caution on the part of Western states, to the very nature of revolution itself. One of the most important reasons for US difficulty in responding to revolution has been the lack of understanding of revolution and the costs and consequences of counterrevolution.   This in no small way reflects misjudgments and misperceptions about the Third World and unconventional conflicts.   Further, this also stems from a misinterpretation of the Vietnam experience.   The result is an inability to develop policy, strategy, and institutional capability to respond to unconventional conflicts and Third World issues.

One of the first tasks for US policy makers and serious students is to develop a historical sense of the nature and character of revolutions.   This will help provide the necessary intellectual breadth for a critical and balanced analysis of US involvement in Vietnam and what the future may hold with respect to the role of the United States in Third World conflicts.

Most contemporary revolutions are built on anti-Western ideologies that tend to accept, if not adopt, Marxist-Leninist philosophy.   Marxist-Leninist class analysis and conflict, combined with its historical explanations regarding exploitation of the masses and the repressiveness of nonpopularly elected governments, provide an apparent relevancy to conditions in many Third World states.   When combined with Maoist revolutionary policy and strategy, Marxist-Leninist philosophy seems to provide a guide to successful revolutionary conflicts in the Third World.   The Iranian revolution is the major exception, based as it was on a fundamentalist Islamic movement.[1]

Yet the United States and France can trace their heritage to their own revolutions, with their own revolutionary purposes and philosophies.   For many in the West, these revolutions provide the basis for nationalistic ideologies: equality, liberty, and freedom.   The nature and character of modern revolution in the Third World, however, differs from the classic revolutions of the past: the storming of the Bastille in the French Revolution and the Minutemen at Old North Bridge in Concord in the American Revolution.   These earlier revolutions have little resemblance to the peasant-oriented or religious fundamentalist revolutions of the contemporary period.   Thus the study and analysis of contemporary revolutionary conflict is more important for US policy makers than attention to the classic revolutions. Yet there is much in US history that is relevant to contemporary problems—perhaps not the American Revolution as such but American experience as a counterrevolutionary force. Current policy makers, however, seem to concentrate on immediate policy issues and operational guidelines, with hardly any attention to past experience or to the contributions of theorists. Such an approach fosters an unrealistic policy and strategy that in the long run usually leads to ineffective and inadequate responses.

In this chapter, we will examine some of the major theoretical works on revolution.[2] Although the focus will be primarily on the contemporary period, some attention is given to revolutions in the pre-World War II period to the degree they can assist in understanding the present. Conclusions will be drawn regarding the American perspective and how this affects contemporary policy and strategy. The purpose is to develop the historical and intellectual groundwork for understanding current US counterrevolutionary policy rather than developing an encompassing theoretical interpretation of revolutionary phenomena. This latter aim would require a serious study of the literature.[3] (A review of the conceptual basis for US involvement in Vietnam is discussed in a later chapter.)

A critical study of theories, approaches, and policy must be undertaken with caution, though, particularly for those whose perspective evolves from the comfort of a classroom. Burton notes,

> Among the greatest enemies of the next revolution are the academic theorists who write about the last one. This is particularly the case where the authors involved are sympathetic to the persons or the ideologies of the revolutionaries. Lessons which are too neat and principles which are too vague are generalized from the exploits of some revolutionary hero, whose failures are explained away. "Models" of revolution are produced.

Thus we have a Leninist, a Maoist and a Guevarist model whose contemporary Western adherents indulge in abstruse and often irrelevant arguments.[4]

CONCEPTS OF REVOLUTION

There are many concepts describing revolution in the literature, reflecting the variety of academic disciplines and the differences among the purposes of the scholar, the policy maker, and the revolutionary. This has led to a variety of categories, labels, and definitions, such as revolutionary war, people's war, civil war, internal war, wars of national liberation, insurgency, guerrilla war, and a variety of counterparts, including counterinsurgency and counterrevolution. Recently a number of US civilian and military policy makers have used the terms *special operations* and *low-intensity conflicts*. (It is interesting to note that *special warfare* and *special operations* were terms used in the early 1960s as the United States geared up for Vietnam.) A close reading of the literature and study of operational experience reveals three key concepts for understanding revolution and counterrevolution: guerrilla war, insurgency, and revolution.

Guerrilla War

Guerrilla war, or literally, "little war," was coined in the nineteenth century during the Napoleonic invasion of Spain. A number of authorities use the term in the contemporary context. According to Laqueur,

> The old term "guerrilla warfare" has been used in this study because there is no better one. Newer theoretical concepts such as "modern revolutionary warfare" or "people's war" can be of use only with regard to a few countries and applied elsewhere they are misleading; not all guerrilla movements are led by a monolithic political party, or a Communist party, or are either a people's war or a war of national liberation.[5]

Another author, in analyzing the organizational and ideological character of the Vietcong in South Vietnam, provides a more encompassing definition, using the term *revolutionary guerrilla warfare:*

> Revolutionary guerrilla warfare should not be confused with older concepts of a similar nature, such as irregular troops in wartime disrupting the enemy's rear, or with civil war . . . rebellion . . . revolution . . . or partisan warfare. . . . Revolutionary guerrilla warfare as practiced in Vietnam was a way of life. Its aim was to establish a totally new social order. . . . The object was not the ordinary violent social protest around the world with which we sympathize because they reflect inadequate living standards or oppressive and corrupt governments. Revolutionary guerrilla warfare was quite different. It was an imported product, revolution from the outside; its stock in trade, the grievance, was often artificially created; its goal of liberation, a deception.[6]

As a result of the contemporary international security situation, guerrilla warfare has taken on broader meaning. It now encompasses some elements normally associated with revolution and others linked to insurgency. The term *revolutionary guerrilla warfare* is used by some as a convenient method to bridge the apparent gaps among various concepts of guerrilla war.

Insurgency

The term *insurgency* tends to confuse the efforts to differentiate guerrilla warfare and revolution. Nonetheless, it has a standing of its own. According to a Department of the Army definition, insurgency is

> a condition of subversive political activity, civil rebellion, revolt, or insurrection against a duly constituted government or occupying power wherein irregular forces are formed and engage in actions, which may include guerrilla warfare, that are designed to weaken and overthrow the government or occupying power.[7]

One author suggests that the term *insurrection* should be limited in its usage to armed violence in "initial stages of movements of opposition to government," noting that the terms *rebellion* and *revolution* should be employed only when a "substantial portion of the armed forces of the established government" must be used in defense:

> In this sense an insurrection may be thought of as an incipient rebellion or revolution still localized and limited to securing modifications of governmental policy or personnel and not yet a serious threat to the state or the government in power.[8]

Ignoring traditional definitions, another authority studying the Vietnam War writes,

> The point to be stressed is that the war has always remained basically an *insurgency*, boosted by infiltration and aided, to a certain but limited extent, by both invasion and raids. . . . *People's Revolutionary War* is therefore by nature a civil war of a very sophisticated type and using highly refined techniques to seize power and take over a country. The significant feature of it, which needs to be recognized, is its immunity to the application of power.[9]

Thus, for some, insurgency is an integral part of revolution. Some stress the military dimension as an indicator of insurgency progress, and others focus on the political-social role, which they believe is a more important part of the conflict.

Revolution

It seems clear that a number of characteristics of guerrilla war and insurgency are intermingled, not only in the literature but in operational terms. Although there may be a great deal of overlap between these terms (and many authors use *guerrilla war* and *insurgency* synonymously), there are important distinctions. Guerrilla war is associated primarily with armed conflict limited to a tactical dimension; revolution is a political-social phenomenon; and insurgency is somewhere between the two. These general differences can be the basis for a sharper delineation of the three concepts. Clarity in using these terms is important, since the way each is perceived and interpreted has direct bearing on the policy, strategy, and operational doctrine designed in response to them.

Revolution is defined by one scholar as

> an acute, prolonged crisis in one or more of the traditional systems of stratification (class, status, power) of a political community, which involves a purposive, elite-directed attempt to abolish or to reconstruct one or more of said systems by means of an intensification of political power and recourse to violence.[10]

The term *revolution*, like *guerrilla war*, may be used by different persons to denote different things. Examining various definitions of revolutions and revolt, one author concludes,

> We simply cannot isolate from the extraordinary diversity of history a single denominator that is common to and valid for all of these situations and would stand for structure. On the other hand, if we are to understand the phenomenon of revolution, we must take into account the entire society that produces it and not isolate a factor—political, social, or economic—as if it alone were the ultimate and determining one. We must look at all of them together and in relation to one another in order to see the true conditions under which revolt and revolution have been possible and fomented.[11]

Some divide revolutions into various categories. One author differentiates between political and social revolutions, defining social revolution as

> rapid, basic transformations of society's state and class structures; and they are accompanied and in part carried through by class-based revolts from below. Social revo-

lutions are set apart from other sorts of conflicts and transformative process above all by the combination of two coincidences: the coincidence of societal structural change with class upheaval; and the coincidence of political with social transformation.[12]

Another scholar, examining various case studies, defines revolution as follows:

A revolution happens, then, when a set of revolutionaries with quite complex ideas succeed in arousing in vast masses of men already deeply discontented with the prevailing order a sufficient sense of their own superior political and moral capacity to justify the masses in struggling to destroy the prevailing (and to some degree social) order and replace it with the political control of the revolutionaries.[13]

Finally, in an important work on the American, French, and Russian revolutions, Arendt observes,

The modern concept of revolution, inextricably bound up with the notion that the course of history suddenly begins anew, that an entirely new story, a story never known or told before, is about to unfold, was unknown prior to the two great revolutions at the end of the eighteenth century ... to any understanding of revolution in the modern age is that the idea of freedom and the experience of a new beginning should coincide.[14]

These observations and studies are examples of the attempts to categorize, define, and analyze revolution and the various terms associated with it. Clearly there is a great deal of disagreement, confusion, and misinterpretation of the meaning and concept of revolution.

From this general review, we can identify the most salient points, attempt to clarify these, and refashion them into a simpler framework and concept of revolution. Admittedly this simplification may not satisfy the need for comprehensiveness and analytical precision usually demanded in scholarly circles. Nonetheless, it may be more useful from the policy perspective by clarifying and making more manageable the concepts of revolution. This may be adequate to develop operational dimensions and a real world approach to the understanding of the political and social, as well as other challenges, associated with the Third World and unconventional conflicts. Also such a simplification does not necessarily substitute in analytical research terms for the search for comprehensive approaches and analytical precision that has been going on within scholarly circles.

Counterrevolution is fundamentally a reaction to revolution. If counterrevolution is to be effective, it must be based on conceptual clarity of the meaning of revolution. This makes it essential to establish an operational and clear concept of revolution.

Operational Concept

Bernard Fall offers a useful concept of revolution and guerrilla warfare that is the basis for this study:

> Just about anybody can start a "little war" (which is what the Spanish word guerrilla literally means), even a New York street gang. Almost anybody can raid somebody else's territory, even American territory, as Pancho Villa did in 1916 or the Nazi Saboteurs in 1942. . . . But all this has rarely produced the kind of revolutionary ground swell which simply swept away the existing government.[15]

In developing the political-social dimensions of revolution and distinguishing it from guerrilla war, Fall states,

> It is . . . important to understand that guerrilla warfare is nothing but a tactical appendage of a far vaster political contest and that, no matter how expertly it is fought by competent and dedicated professionals, it cannot possibly make up for the absence of a political rationale.[16]

As Thompson points out,

> Revolutionary war is most confused with guerrilla or
> partisan warfare. The main difference is that guerrilla
> warfare is designed merely to harass and distract the
> enemy so that the regular forces can reach a decision in
> conventional battles. . . . Revolutionary war on the other
> hand is designed to reach a decisive result on its own.[17]

Using Fall's observations combined with Thompson's strategic view, a reasonably simple operating definition for revolution can be designed. First, revolutions are a fundamental challenge to the existing political order and to those who hold power.[18] Second, revolution envisions a major change in the social order. Third, armed conflict is an important characteristic of revolution but is not necessarily the most important ingredient for revolutionary success. Fourth, successful revolutions are usually based on the effectiveness of revolutionary leadership, political cadres, and ideology.

This conceptual design serves as a working framework to study and analyze the revolutionary phenomenon, which encompasses a number of components: causes of revolution, the nature and character of revolutionary systems, revolutionary leadership and organization, and doctrinal issues. It can also be argued that the revolutionary phenomenon must include counterrevolutionary considerations, since these are virtually inseparable from revolution.

Only through this kind of analytical process can there develop an understanding of the nature of revolutionary warfare, its long-range challenge to the United States, and an appreciation and understanding of the complexities and difficulties of counterrevolutionary warfare. Only through such a study can realistic assessments be made of America's counterrevolutionary experience, the Vietnam War, the current US political-military posture, and what needs to be done for the future.

CAUSES OF REVOLUTION

The causes of revolution are complex and multidimensional. There is disagreement among authorities on the subject, and a wide variety of issues and grievances are part of the revolutionary phenomenon: socioeconomic grievances, alienation from the political system, ethnic hatred, envy, elite divisiveness, and external intervention to defeat in war.

The most that can be said about causes of revolution is that there are many and they are varied; however, there seems to be general agreement that systems striving to modernize provide the most fertile ground for revolution. As such, most causes of revolution are associated with problems of economic modernization and political change. These generate grass-roots-level grievances and lead to disagreement within and among the elite.

The complex and broad nature of the modernization process leads to difficulties in trying to pinpoint specific revolutionary causes. Analysts must study virtually an entire society: its political, economic, psychological, social, and religious characteristics. Because of the complicated linkages among all of these sectors within a state, identifying the causes of revolution is difficult. Nonetheless, a variety of authors propose many approaches and theories regarding causes. Without attempting to categorize these precisely, which in itself may falsely suggest that there is precision involved, it may be best to focus on three major approaches that include key causes of revolution: the universalistic approach, the performance-oriented approach, and the multiple causation approach.

Universalistic Concepts

Universalistic concepts are primarily general theories that purport to explain all types of revolutionary phenomena. They include those who have identified socio-economic conflicts as causes of revolution, relative deprivation, and systems disequilibrium. Most of the literature by this group tends to be at a high level of generalization and disciplinary sophistication. Although excellent in their own right, these works probably have minimum utility to the immediate concerns of policy analysts. Additionally, much of the published literature in this group is aimed at the scholarly or academic audience and rarely finds its way into the layman's world. Nevertheless, universalistic theories and approaches are important for providing an intellectual as well as theoretical dimension in analyzing revolutionary phenomena. Such dimensions must be included in the policy analyst's thinking if one hopes to provide long-range policy and strategy guidelines. Equally important, by careful study of the universalistic literature, one is more likely to develop a broader understanding of revolution and a more critical basis for analyzing the policy of revolutionary and counterrevolutionary political actors.

The works of Karl Marx, Ted Gurr, and Chalmers Johnson are representative of the wide range and variety of conceptual perspectives that are part of the universalistic group.[19] These works have a common relationship focusing on fundamental disorders within the political-social system. This generally holds true even though the reasons claimed for the instability of political-social systems may be triggered by different causes, such as class conflict, perceived deprivation, and loss of elite control.

Performance-Oriented Approach

The literature in this group, which some categorize as middle-range theory, is performance oriented. Middle-range theory neither claims to be applicable to all cases, nor does it necessarily limit itself to one specific case.[20] Most of the literature in this group rests on the premise that ineffective government and grass-roots grievances are the basic cause of revolution. The interdependence of these themes is emphasized.

As grass-roots grievances emerge and grow, the government is unable to respond effectively, resulting in the further growth of grievances to a critical mass precipitating revolution. Examining the effectiveness of government has broad-ranging implications since this involves linking causes of revolution with a whole range of government activities: how government functions, the efficiency of its various institutions, the capability of the ruling elite, the impact of government policies, the legitimacy of government, the level of support provided by the people, and the nature of the political system itself. It is on this last consideration that performance-oriented approaches merge into universalistic approaches.[21]

Multiple Causation Approach

Not only is there a lack of agreement among authorities regarding revolutionary causes, there is serious criticism of most existing views on revolutionary causes. This is particularly true for those who advance a monistic view (that is, a singular cause of revolution). One authority writes,

> there is much truth in these monistic theories. The thing that makes it difficult to accept any of them as a complete explanation, in general, is that such a variable result as a revolution, even a revolution primarily political, has many social, economic and intellectual implications that can hardly come from a single cause, whether it be socioeconomic, like the Marxist theory, or biographical-psychological, like the conspiracy theory, or the ethical-epistemological, like the Sorkin theory.[22]

The author argues that "for a more satisfactory explanation of revolutionary change, one has to look to multiple causation."[23] Multiple causation, however, creates difficult and complex problems, requiring identification and analysis of relationships between causes and an understanding of the impact of individual causes, as well as their cause-and-effect relationships to the totality of revolution—a difficult charge for even the most accomplished researcher and authority on revolution. Thus, the multiple causation theory develops dimensions that virtually defy policy application and manageable data analysis, except at a very general level. In this respect, Skocpol observes,

> In historical revolutions, differently situated and motivated groups have become participants in complex unfoldings of multiple conflicts. These conflicts have been powerfully shaped and limited by existing socioeconomic and international conditions. . . . And the revolutionary conflicts have invariably given rise to outcomes neither fully foreseen nor intended by—nor perfectly serving the interest of—any of the particular groups involved.[24]

In a pointed reference to multiple causations, Laqueur concludes, "The very asking of the question, 'Why do men rebel?' implies a great many assumptions about both human nature and the perfectibility of society."[25]

In sum, causes of revolution are multiple but generally develop from grass-roots grievances, socioeconomic disparity, gaps between elite powerholders and the rest of society, or attempts to change power relationships within the system. Compounding the problem is the fact that each of these causes may develop because of a number of historical animosities or from a variety of ineffective government institutions. Making matters more complex is the fact that each revolutionary cause may include bits and pieces of virtually every other cause.

In brief, identifying causes of revolution regardless of the approach taken remains a baffling problem to most experts. A number of causes can be identified and have been examined in the literature and by policy makers. The problem is that monistic approaches or even those that attempt to link several causes do not get at the totality of the revolution or focus on the linkages between one or more causes and how one may trigger the other. This is compounded by the contemporary situation in which external forces—revolution by export or by international terrorism—may trigger revolutions. Perhaps the most reasonable, if incomplete, explanation is that revolutions can be triggered by ineffective governments, with all that this implies, including ineffective policies, inadequate resource allocation, ineffective security and intelligence instruments, and incapable rulers. Thus, it would seem that reasonably effective governments are the mainstay of counterrevolution. The study of revolutionary systems, therefore, may be the most productive in terms of understanding revolutionary phenomena and in designing appropriate counterrevolutionary policy and strategy.

REVOLUTIONARY SYSTEMS

The literature on revolutionary systems concentrates on four areas: revolutionary leadership, organization, ideology, and doctrine (strategy and tactics). The amount of attention given to one or the other element varies according to the author's approach and purpose. These range from broad historical pieces to the study of revolutionary systems in the post-World War II period. The number of works on revolutions in Indochina and Vietnam are an increasingly large part of this latter group.[26] More recently, studies have been published on Central America.[27] Most of these studies follow a similar pattern, focusing on leadership, organization, ideology, and doctrine.

Revolutionary Leadership

Much has been written about revolutionary leadership. The volumes by Kerkvliet and by Gott are particularly valuable in the study of this subject.[28] Kerkvliet provides a detailed case study of the Huk rebellion in the Philippines immediately following World War II, with attention to the participants and sympathizers. Following a similar approach, Gott studies and compares the revolutions in Guatemala, Venezuela, Colombia, Peru, and Bolivia.   Some of the most useful books are those by revolutionaries themselves, including Che Guevara, Mao, Carlos Marighela, and Troung Chinh.[29]   Shaw's compilation of Mao's original works is particularly useful.

The general theme common to most of these books is that revolutionary leaders and the command structure must evolve or appear to evolve from the revolutionary situation characteristic of the particular system.   The leader had to project an image of firmness, courage, and compassion combined with a personal linkage to the countryside. Successful revolutionary leadership rests on the leader's ability to establish personal authority and project an image of one who is able to control, supervise, and direct the leadership structure. Leadership style is an important part of the leader's effectiveness. Style refers to the way the leader carries out his duties and how he treats and deals with subordinates and others.

Additionally, the quality of middle-level leaders in no small measure is directly linked to the top revolutionary leaders, since the middle-level revolutionary cadres provide the grass-roots-level contact and direction to revolutionary activities.

Mao Tse-tung's revolutionary system in Yenan Province well illustrates the basis for successful leadership. White's description provides a textbook-like view of the Chinese communist leadership structure in the 1930s and the basis for its success:

> This is one of the things I learned firsthand in Yenan as I searched for history: revolutions are made by intellectuals.   Not all intellectuals are revolutionaries.   But if the intellectuals can weave their ideas about what bothers ordinary people, they can ensnare and mesh them together.   If they are shrewd enough to describe conditions to workers and families so that simple people recognize what is cramping them or destroying them— then they can mobilize these people to change things, to kill, to hunt, to die, to be cruel, with the moral absolu-

tion that intellectuals can always give simple killers and terrorists.[30]

Another important theme is the connection between leaders and the people. Guevara makes a point of this in his own experience:

> Let me say, with the risk of appearing ridiculous, that the true revolutionary is guided by strong feelings of love. ... Our vanguard revolutionaries must idealize their love for the people, for the most hallowed causes and make it one and indivisible. They cannot descend, with small doses of daily affection, to the terrain where ordinary men put their love into practice.[31]

Billington notes, however, that revolutionaries must also stand above the common man and focus on the inner drive of the revolution:

> This is not a story of revolutions, but of revolutionaries: the innovative creators of a new tradition. ... At center stage stood the characteristic, nineteenth-century European revolutionary: a thinker lifted up by ideas, not a worker or peasant bent down by toil. ... This "elite" focus does not imply indifference to the mass, human suffering which underlay the era of this narrative. It reflects only the special need to concentrate here on the spiritual thirst of those who think rather than on the material hunger of those who work.[32]

Although Billington does study other elements of the revolutionary system, for him these are secondary to the focus on the revolutionary personality.

In a similar vein, Wolfenstein's earlier work on revolutionary personality is an important contribution to the literature.[33] Studying Lenin, Trotsky, and Ghandi, Wolfenstein applies a psychopolitical framework in an attempt to explain the development of revolutionary personality. It follows that maturation and socialization combined with some dramatic event turned the individual against the existing system to such a degree that there was created a resolve and a commitment to establish a different or new system.

Although there are relatively few studies on middle-range and grass-roots-level revolutionary leaders and cadres, several works are worthy of note, particularly the study of the Huks by Kerkvliet. The author identifies three levels of leadership in the Huk organization: local, middle, and national or top-level leaders.[34] The local leaders "were usually peasants themselves who knew intimately the predicaments fellow peasants faced. Their goals were also generally restricted to the immediate concerns of most villagers.[35] The national or top level leaders were mostly "urban intellectuals, bureaucrats, lawyers, and other professionals who were sympathetic to the peasant's plight. . . . The most noticeable leaders of this type were several national officers and theoreticians in the Philippine Communist Party (PKP)."[36] Similar observations can be found by the study of other revolutionary leaders: Fidel Castro, Guevara, Mao, Lenin, Cabral, Taruc, and Father Torres.

A recent study on revolutionary leadership is William Darryl Henderson's *Why the Vietcong Fought*.[37] The work is a study of the motivation and cohesion within the People's Liberation Army (PLA) in South Vietnam, with insights into the caliber of political and military leadership at the small unit level. Basing his conclusions on research of previous wars by several scholars, especially Pike, and on interviews of captured PLA personnel, the author concludes that

> the political and military cadre both were shown as loyal party members, with the military cadre as being more of a technician supporting the furthering of party goals. . . . It cannot be concluded that the PLA was completely successful in creating an army comprised of "good communist soldiers." However, the cadre did motivate and control the "human element" to an unprecedented extent, allowing the PLA to endure the disintegrative effects of sustained combat and hardship during the 1965-

1967 period, which resulted in the ultimate control of the battlefield.[38]

Although the concern of most revolutionary leadership is to develop popular support, experience shows that revolutions usually involve the mobilization and participation of a minority of the people. The popular view that revolutions are movements by masses of the people is a myth:

> When we talk about mobilization for revolution of workers, peasants, or the middle classes, we are talking about a small minority of activists within each of these categories. . . . What is at issue for any revolutionary movement, then, is the extent to which the active minority of one social class is able to ally with the active minorities of other social classes. . . . But it should be made clear . . . that just as government in a stable society is the affair of a minority, so is revolution.[39]

Stressing the importance of the role of minorities, the author goes on to say, "A revolution involves minorities fighting minorities. And if the revolutionaries have any advantage over the loyalists, it probably begins with the revolutionaries' greater intensity of commitment to their cause."[40]

In sum, the legitimacy of the revolution and the probability of its success is directly related to the ability of the leadership and cadre to identify with the people and their grievances. Equally important, the ideology, strategy, and doctrine must be compatible with the expectations of alienated groups. Interestingly, Guevara violated many of these principles as he tried to create a revolution in Bolivia, which ultimately led to his death.

In addition to the relative scarcity of works on grass-roots-level revolutionary leadership, there is a serious lack of attention to the intelligence function. The need for adequate intelligence is frequently noted in the literature on revolution and counterrevolution and is stressed in policy-oriented studies, but rarely is the role of intelligence spelled out in sufficient detail. Few authors provide a study of how intelligence systems are established and how intelligence is collected, analyzed, disseminated, and used by revolutionaries or counterrevolutionaries. The works by Shackley, Gazit, and Handel and the series by Godson are major exceptions, as are several works regarding the US role in Vietnam.[41] Nonetheless, given the fact that much of the success of revolution and counter-revolution rests on the effectiveness of the intelligence effort, the lack of systematic and comprehensive studies of the intelligence network is surprising.

Revolutionary Organization

Successful revolutions require an organization capable of providing command and control, recruits, resources, operational supervision and execution, and effective intelligence. As is the case with studies on intelligence, much work needs to be done in analyzing revolutionary organizations. Although Mao, for example, provided considerable examination of various aspects of revolutionary organization, he rarely provided a systematic and analytical view. More useful studies are those by Cabral, Fall, Pike, and Thompson.[42]

The volume by Pike is especially valuable. Analyzing the Vietcong organizational structure, he provides a comprehensive picture of a revolutionary organization. Local revolutionary organizations were linked directly to the National Liberation Front Central Committee and High Command. In descending order were interzone central committees, zonal central committees, provincial central committees, and district central committees. Each level had its equivalent armed element. The District Central Committee established revolutionary structures in villages within its area of responsibility. The village organizations included a variety of committees, cadres, functional associations, and links with hamlets. It was the duty of the village to provide logistical, administrative, and manpower support to the district committees and their equivalent local armed units.[43]

Henderson's work also provides a useful view of Vietcong organization.[44] After reviewing the revolutionary structure and studying the motivations of the various members of the Vietcong, the author concludes that it was organization that was critical to revolutionary success in South Vietnam. He notes that the soldiers of the PLA fought well in the face of overwhelming enemy firepower and hardships because their "behavior was shaped by three strong forces: (1) party organization and ideology; (2) the cadre-leaders; and (3) a primary group of soldiers with strong homogenous values."[45]

In Malaya during the 1950s, similar patterns of revolutionary organization emerged, although they were not as well developed or pervasive as the Vietcong. In Malayan villages, communist cells and supporters provided the political and logistical support for the revolution. At the local level also, armed elements at platoon and company strength conducted military operations. At the district level, company and battalion-strength units under control of district committees carried out military operations. District committees, in turn, were under the control and supervision of the revolutionary committee.[46]

There is a close linkage between revolutionary organization and doctrine. Bell notes,

> The structure of each revolutionary organization is as likely to determine the choice of strategy of national liberation as to be determined by it. The same is true in part of the nature of the cause, the timing of the revolt, and the ideological considerations of the rebels.[47]

The revolutionary situation (causes) and the nature of the existing regime are critical determinants of the kind of revolutionary organization, strategy, and ideology that emerge. For example, colonial systems and their handmaidens are likely to preclude a swift coup d'état or mass urban uprising. They are more likely to generate a long period of revolutionary organization building and mobilization leading to a protracted war. Interestingly, the nature of the revolutionary phenomenon and the authoritarian and encompassing nature of Marxist-Leninist systems in both the developed and developing world make it highly unlikely that successful revolutions can be undertaken in such systems without extraordinary support from external forces.

Ideology

Although revolutionary ideology may appear to be a clear component of revolutions in general, upon closer examination it too presents a complex and at times a confusing picture. For example, Marxist-Leninist revolutionaries rarely publicize their cause or philosophy in clear communist terms. Rather, public causes are usually based on the specifics of a particular revolutionary situation and proclaimed in two ways. In universal terms, these causes are blended in with such concepts as freedom, liberty, and nationalism. At a parochial level, the causes are stated in terms clearly recognizable by local people, such as landownership, taxation, and fair treatment. Burton points out,

> Speeches, writings and tactics contemporary to the actual fighting of the revolutionary war (not later rationalizations) show two outstanding common characteristics. They involve appeals to the collective pride and individual greed, and they are voiced in national terms by men who are of the people. Above all, the leaders of revolutionary wars have understood, not abstract theories culled from books, but the populations they sought to influence.[48]

Although communist parties do not (or have not) necessarily initiate all revolutions, particularly in Latin America and Africa, they often try to capture revolutions as they progress, especially if success seems assured. Thus, revolutions may begin on a nationalistic, noncommunist basis, only to be co-opted by communist organizations later (the Philippines). Moreover, many revolutionary political structures may initially consist of a nationalistic mix of noncommunists and communists, although the armed element may be predominantly communist controlled (El Salvador in the 1980s). As a revolution progresses and becomes institutionalized, the military element may become closely linked with communist revolutionary leadership, eventually displacing noncommunist elements. To be sure, there are revolutions in which the ideological basis is clear (for instance, Vietnam). Yet it is more likely that only later in a revolution does Marxist-Leninist ideology become clear, as in Cuba and Nicaragua.

Revolutionary leadership, organization, and ideology are inextricable. This relationship flows out of a variety of patterns. The legitimacy of revolutionary leadership and organization is contingent on the effectiveness of the ideological appeal, its link to societal issues, and the character of the existing political system. At the same time, the specifics of a particular revolutionary situation condition and influence the effectiveness of the revolutionary appeal. In turn, the revolutionary organization provides the channels for command, control, and communications through which the ideology is nurtured and articulated. It follows that the revolutionary organization and the character of the ideology must be congruent. It is unlikely that a realistic and effective ideology based on democracy and freedom can be institutionalized if the revolutionary organization is clearly structured in authoritarian lines, with little concern for developing an effective representative ruling base over the long term.

In the contemporary period, ideological effectiveness is usually achieved by referring to universally recognized notions of freedom, liberty, and nationalism. These in turn are linked to specific grievances of the local area, such as landownership, repressive taxation, and heavy-handed government. The effectiveness of the ideological appeal is also dependent on revolutionary organizations attuned to such appeals. Most important, successful revolutionary leaders are able to link all of these and shape their leadership style accordingly. In the process, it is often difficult to detect Marxist-Leninist directions until later in the revolutionary process. In the light of the ideological basis of American democracy and its own revolutionary experience, it is difficult for many Americans not to have sympathy for what they perceive as nationalist revolutions striving for freedom and justice.

Strategy and Doctrine

Although many revolutions begin as a nationalistic mix, revolutionary strategies and doctrines usually reflect a Marxist-Leninist, Maoist, or Cuban pattern, or a combination of all three. For many, Marxism-Leninism provides the intellectual and philosophical basis for revolutions in general, although the strategy and tactics of Marx-Lenin may be inappropriate to the situation in most Third World states. For instance, the more recently proclaimed ideology of liberation theology is based on interpretations of the humanistic needs of downtrodden people according to a Marxist-Leninist equation, using intellectual and theological distortions virtually to equate Christianity with Marxism-Leninism. The appeal of liberation theology to Christians in the Third World as a revolutionary ideology to correct injustices without mention of the injustices it brings, which may be even greater in the long run, is, according to some, neither liberation nor theology.[49]

The Maoist perspective, basing much of its strategy on broad interpretations of Marxism-Leninism, has a distinctive Asian dimension peculiar to the Chinese revolution. The Maoist three-stage theory of revolution is seen in one form or another in many revolutionary doctrines as the Maoist rules on revolutionary behavior. In Mao's view, protracted war passes through several stages:

> The first stage covers the period of the enemy's strategic offensive and our strategic defensive. The second stage will be the period of the enemy's strategic consolidation and our preparation for the counter offensive. The third

stage will be the period of our strategic counter offensive and the enemy's strategic retreat.[50]

The preliminary to all of this is the need to penetrate society and establish close linkages to the people. Thus, from mobilizing the people and conducting political-psychological warfare, the first stage can evolve. Similarly, after the third stage, victory is achieved by capturing the government. Subsequently, the revolution is consolidated, which means that counterrevolutionaries are rounded up and neutralized, and the revolution is institutionalized throughout the government structure.

Mao was not a theoretician but an organizer and operator. His concern was to explain the process of revolution in China first against the Japanese and then against the Kuomintang. Mao's views are not contained in a single comprehensive work but are scattered throughout various tracts and spread over a number of years.

The Soviet and Chinese revolutions differed from each other. The Soviet revolution tended to follow the Marxist-Leninist view of class struggle against the aristocratic and bourgeoisie elements. In this light, the concept of class relates directly to a proletariat conscious of its working-class status and aware of the relationships of the working class to the owners of property and ruling elite. As such, the focus is on urban areas.

While Marxist-Leninist views regarding revolutions are focused on the urban masses, who strike directly at the heart of the government, such as the storming of the Winter Palace, the Maoist approach has its roots in the countryside among the peasantry. Thus, the Soviet revolutionary process first aims at capturing the government (mass urban uprising) and then using the instruments of government to expand and institutionalize the revolution throughout the countryside. The revolutionary process captures the inner part of the system first and then moves to the outside—the countryside.

In contrast, Mao saw the revolution as beginning within the peasantry in the countryside, isolating the major cities, and cutting off the government from the peasantry. Using the countryside as a base, the revolutionaries captured the cities as the final act. The revolutionary process thus moves from the outer to the inner part of the system.

The Cuban *foco* theory, although apparently discounted by some American specialists, remains relevant in some of its major strategic as well as tactical principles. The *foco* theory is based on the view that a small group of revolutionaries, combining the role of political cadre and armed fighters, could penetrate a political system and be the base for starting a revolution. The *foco* theory, evolving out of the peculiarities of the Cuban situation, has all of the elements of general revolutionary principles of Marxism-Leninism as well as Maoism. Based on the view that "the guerrilla fighter is a social reformer," Guevara based his revolutionary organization on the *foco*.[51] In summing up this approach, one writer observes,

> According to Che, a nucleus of from thirty to fifty determined men can establish and consolidate a revolutionary guerrilla *foco* in any country of Latin America, providing they have the cooperation of the people and a perfect knowledge of the terrain upon which they will be operating.[52]

There are also a variety of urban revolutionary strategies that are contemporary variations of the Marxist-Leninist pattern, but urban revolutionary warfare tends to be discounted by many as a strategy for overthrowing existing systems. Most argue that revolutionaries cannot succeed by concentrating solely on the major urban areas because this usually means striking at the strength of the existing system. Success by employing such a strategy will occur only if there develops an effective coalition of various socioeconomic classes opting for revolution and generally supported by the existing military system.

While it can be argued that strategic principles outlined in Marxism-Leninism, Maoism, and *foco* theories are generally applicable to most contemporary revolutions, this should not confuse ideological principles with strategy and doctrine. One can adopt Marxist-Leninist, Maoist, or *foco* strategies without necessarily accepting the ideological principles behind them.

SUMMARY

The study of revolutions and revolutionary systems provides a broad panorama of concepts, theories, approaches, and causes, none of which is totally accurate or complete. Although there are general principles of revolution that are universal to all societies, each political-social system has its own unique characteristics that defy generalizations. The successful revolutionary system is one that is led by those who understand the importance of the universal principles and who can interpret these in a way appropriate to their own societies. Equally important, the leadership structure and the effectiveness of the revolutionary command system are in no small part a function of how well these principles can be explained to the people in terms that are meaningful to their own condition. The fact that the revolutionaries are in a position to challenge and proclaim, without necessarily governing the entire system or providing policy results affecting the entire state, gives them an advantage difficult to overcome by the existing system.

The existing system playing the role of counterrevolutionary, therefore, is in a difficult position. Not only must it govern, but it must respond to problems of economic modernization and political change and at the same time try to maintain security in the countryside and defeat a serious challenge. For the United States, this is a particularly difficult problem, because as an intervening state in support of an existing system, its problems are compounded by the nature of democracy.

NOTES

1. Hannah Arendt, *On Revolution* (New York: Viking Press, 1965); Crane Brinton, *The Anatomy of Revolution,* rev. and expanded ed. (New York: Vintage Books, 1965); S. N. Eisenstadt, *Modernization: Protest and Change* (Englewood Cliffs, N.J.: Prentice-Hall, 1966); Theda Skocpol, *States and Social Revolutions: A Comparative Analysis of France, Russia, and China* (Cambridge: Cambridge University Press, 1979); Lawrence Stone, "Theories of Revolution," *World Politics* 18 (January 1966); Jack A. Goldstone, "Theories of Revolution: The Third Generation," *World Politics* 22 (April 1980).

2. Much of the material in this chapter is taken from Sam C. Sarkesian, "American Policy on Revolution and Counterrevolution: A Review of the Themes in the Literature," *Conflict* 5, no. 2 (1984):137-84.

3. Thomas Greene, *Comparative Revolutionary Movements* (Englewood Cliffs, N.J.: Prentice-Hall, 1974); Bard E. O'Neill, William R. Heaton, and Donald J. Alberts, eds., *Insurgency in the Modern World* (Boulder, Colo.: Westview Press, 1980).

4. Anthony Burton, *Revolutionary Violence: The Theories* (New York: Crane, Russak, 1978), p. 1. See also Barbara Salert, *Revolutions and Revolutionaries: Four Theories* (New York: Elsevier, 1976), p. 5, in which the author writes: "One of the problems that is immediately gleaned from an analysis of these four theories—as well as from any overall survey of the literature on revolutions—is that there is no consensus about the object of the study: that is, there is no single definition of 'revolution' that is adhered to by all analysts. This means that general theories of revolution may not be at all comparable since these may actually be analyzing different sets of events."

5. Walter Laqueur, *Guerrilla: A Historical and Critical Study* (Boston: Little, Brown, 1976), p. x. See the distinction made between revolution and revolt in J. Bowyer Bell, *On Revolt: Strategies of National Liberation* (Cambridge: Harvard University Press, 1976), pp. 3-9. See also François Sully, *Age of the Guerrilla* (New York: Avon Books, 1970), and J. Bowyer Bell, *The Myth of the Guerrilla: Revolutionary Theory and Malpractice* (New York: Alfred A. Knopf, 1971). Although both authors use *guerrilla* to label revolutions, insurrections, and similar conflicts, Bell makes a point of identifying the modern version as guerrilla-revolution.

6. Douglas Pike, *Viet Cong: The Organization and Techniques of the National Liberation Front of South Vietnam* (Cambridge: MIT Press, 1967), pp. 32-33.

7. Department of the Army, *Special Warfare* (Washington, D.C.: Government Printing Office, 1962), p. 8.

8. Frederick L. Schuman, "Insurrection," in *Encyclopedia of the Social Sciences* (New York: Macmillan, 1968), p. 116.

9. Sir Robert Thompson, *No Exit from Vietnam* (New York: David McKay, 1969), p. 45 (Emphasis added).

10. Mark N. Hagopian, *The Phenomenon of Revolution* (New York: Dodd, Mead, 1974), p. 1. See also Jacques Ellul, *Autopsy of a Revolution* (New York: Alfred A. Knopf, 1971), in which the author examines various meanings of revolution in a historical context. Among other things, Ellul concludes, "Our lengthy exploration of 'definitions' was an effort to grasp an experience, not a word, and to interpret it intelligently" (p. 299).

11. Ellul, pp. 27-28.

12. Skocpol, pp. 4-5.

13. John Dunn, *Modern Revolutions: An Introduction to the Analysis of a Political Phenomenon* (London: Cambridge University Press, 1972), p. 15.

14. Arendt, pp. 21-22.

15. Bernard Fall, *Street without Joy: Insurgency in Indochina 1946-63*, 3d rev. ed. (Harrisburg, Penn.: Stackpole, 1963), p. 356.

16. Ibid., p. 357.

17. Sir Robert Thompson, *Revolutionary Wars in World Strategy, 1945-1969* (New York: Taplinger, 1970), pp. 16-17.

18. See, for example, Dunn, pp. 1-23.

19. See, for example, Karl Marx, *The Communist Manifesto (1848)* and *Critique of the Gotha Programme* (New York: International Publishers, 1938); Chalmers Johnson, *Revolutionary Change* (Boston: Little, Brown, 1966); and Ted Gurr, *Why Men Rebel* (Princeton: Princeton University Press, 1970).

20. For a definition of middle-range and other theories, see Jack C. Plano and Robert E. Riggs, *Dictionary of Political Analysis* (Hinsdale, Ill.: Dryden Press, 1973), pp. 101-2.

21. Brian Crozier, *The Rebels: A Study of Post-War Insurrections* (London: Chatto and Windus, 1960).

22. Louis Gottschalk, "Causes of Revolution," *American Journal of Sociology* 50, no. 1 (1944): 1-8.

23. Ibid. See also Hagopian, p. 185. Noting the multiplicity of causes, the author writes that "while each revolution is unique, certain causal features are common enough to merit special comparative emphasis." According to the author, "This outlook tends to rule out monistic explanation and even to greet with skepticism claims that this or that feature is the 'decisive' cause of all or some revolutions."

24. Skocpol, pp. 17-18.

25. Laqueur, p. 386.

26. A number of such works have already been cited. To these should be added such works as Stanley Karnow, *Vietnam; A History* (New York: Viking Press, 1983); Stuart A. Herrington, *Silence Was a Weapon: The Vietnam War in the Villages—A Personal Perspective* (Novato, Calif.: Presidio Press, 1982); and Michael Maclear, *The Ten Thousand Day War—Vietnam: 1945-1975* (New York: Avon Books, 1981).

27. See, for example, John A. Booth, *The End and the Beginning: The Nicaraguan Revolution* (Boulder, Colo.: Westview Press, 1982); T. S. Montgomery, *Revolution in El Salvador* (Boulder, Colo.: Westview Press, 1982); and Robert S. Leiken, ed., *Central America: Anatomy of Conflict* (New York: Pergamon Press, 1984). Several recent books on Central America reflect sharply different views ranging from the pro-Sandinista to the anti-Ortega regime postures. See, for example, Omar Cabezas, *Fire from the Mountain: The Making of a Sandinista*, trans. Kathleen Weaver (New York: Crown, 1985); Lester D. Langley, *Central America: The Real Stakes* (New York: Crown, 1985); and Shirley Christian, *Nicaragua: Revolution in the Family* (New York: Random House, 1985).

28. Benedict J. Kerkvliet, *The Huk Rebellion: A Study of Peasant Revolt in the Philippines* (Berkeley, Calif.: University of California Press, 1977), and Richard Gott, *Guerrilla Movements in Latin America* (Garden City, N.Y.: Anchor Books, 1972).

29. Che Guevara, *Guerrilla Warfare* (New York: Vintage Books, 1969); Kwame Nkrumah, *Handbook of Revolutionary Warfare* (New York: International Publishers, 1969); Carlos Marighela, *For the Liberation of Brazil* (Baltimore: Penguin Books, 1971); and Truong Chinh, *Primer for Revolt: The Communist Takeover in Vietnam* (New York: Praeger, 1963).

30. Theodore White, *In Search of History: A Personal Adventure* (New York: Harper and Row, 1978).

31. Jay Mallin, ed., *"Che" Guevara on Revolution: A Documentary Overview* (New York: Dell, 1969), p. 4.

32. James H. Billington, *Fire in the Minds of Men: Origins of the Revolutionary Faith* (New York: Basic Books, 1980), p. 3.

33. E. Victor Wolfenstein, *The Revolutionary Personality: Lenin, Trotsky, Gandhi* (Princeton: Princeton University Press, 1966).

34. Kerkvliet, pp. 262-66.

35. Ibid., p. 262.

36. Ibid., p. 263. See also Jean Larteguy, *The Guerrillas: New Patterns in Revolution in Latin America*, trans. Stanley Hochman (New York: Signet Books, 1970), p. 15, in which the author states, "In Guatemala, the country of the six hundred colonels, there was fighting in the streets. Assassination attempts and kidnappings were everyday affairs. As in almost all countries on this continent, the university was a rebel citadel. The children of the large landowners, of the colonels, of the politicians, were the ones directing the fight against the abusive and anachronistic privileges enjoyed by their families."

37. William Darryl Henderson, *Why the Vietcong Fought: A Study of Motivation and Control in a Modern Army in Combat* (Westport, Conn.: Greenwood Press, 1979).

38. Ibid., pp. 120-21.

39. Greene, pp. 48-49. See also Arthur Campbell, *Guerrillas: A History and Analysis* (New York: John Day Co., 1968), pp. 279-80.

40. Greene, p. 47.

41. Theodore Shackley, *The Third Option: An American View of Counterinsurgency Operations* (New York: Reader's Digest Press, 1981), and Schlomo Gazit and Michael Handel, "Insurgency, Terrorism and Intelligence," in Roy Godson, ed., *Intelligence Requirements for the 1980's: Counterintelligence* (New Brunswick, N.J.: Transaction Books, 1980), pp. 125-28.

42. Richard Handyside, ed., *Amilcar Cabral, Revolution in Guinea* (New York: Monthly Review Press, 1969). See also previously cited works of Guevara, Fall, Pike and Thompson.

43. Pike, pp. 210-31.

44. Henderson.

45. Ibid., pp. 119-20.

46. Sir Robert Thompson, *Defeating Communist Insurgency: The Lessons of Malaya and Vietnam* (New York: Praeger, 1966), p. 30.

47. Bell, *On Revolt*, p. 186. See also Campbell who writes "We shall see examples of guerrillas bringing about political conditions favourable to themselves without the final development of regular forces, as in Cyprus and Cuba in 1959 and in Algeria in 1961, but in each case there were other considerations both within and without the area of operations which helped to bring about these favourable conditions" (p. 3).

48. Burton, p. 3.

49. See, for example, "Development and Peace: A Multicolored Socialism at the Service of Communism," in *Crusade for a Christian Civilization* 13, no. 1 (1983): 5-40.

50. Shaw, p. 146.

51. Harris, p. 4.

52. Ibid., p. 42.

3

Counterrevolution and Counterrevolutionary Systems

For many Americans, counterrevolution conjures up images of authoritarian systems bent on repression and reaction against the so-called progressive forces of revolution. While revolution is seen as an effort to achieve human rights, liberty, and justice, counterrevolution is viewed as opposition to all of these good goals. Yet the very opposite may be the case. It is generally true that the use of *counter* in the term *counterrevolution* indicates a response to or against something. As such it is a reactive posture and policy, and for many, a reactive policy is viewed negatively.

This underlying view is characteristic of studies on counterrevolution and is partly the reason that the study of counterrevolution lags behind those of revolution, particularly study of counterrevolutionary systems. Part of this also stems from the fact that the study of counterrevolution focuses on existing systems, and these are included in the studies of political systems in general. Since most Third World systems are hardly democratic in the Western sense, many Americans see them through tarnished lenses. In brief, for many, revolutions with their proclamations of equality, justice, and freedom are presumed to be better than any existing Third World system, except those established by post-World War II revolutions. Few people see counterrevolution as a separate subject from revolutions. That is, revolution and counterrevolution are seen as almost inseparable concepts and phenomena.

For Americans trying to understand revolutions, this creates difficulty in at least three respects. First, the lack of serious attention to the specifics of counterrevolution as a separate concept tends to limit intellectual and theoretical depth, diminishing serious analytical and comparative approaches. Second, distortions regarding revolutionary and counterrevolutionary relationships and processes develop. Third, a marked degree of confusion emerges regarding the role of third powers (intervening powers) with respect to their support of counterrevolutionary systems. All of these make it difficult to develop policy insights into the counterrevolutionary process. They tend to focus attention on the revolutionary system without adequate attention on the strategies, policies, and programs required to prevent or defeat revolutionary systems, except in the most general sense.

Studies of the counterrevolutionary systems that do exist can be classified into several groups according to approach and focus.[1] There are works that study revolutionary change and view counterrevolution as part of the same phenomenon; the approach is based on a synthesis of the two phenomena. There are studies of counterrevolutionary elites (elites of existing systems) as the basis for generalizing about counterrevolutionary systems and their effectiveness. Finally there is a large body of literature on the United States as a counterrevolutionary force in the context of the Vietnam War. This last group will be treated separately in following chapters.

REVOLUTIONARY AND COUNTERREVOLUTIONARY SYNTHESIS

The synthesis approach is the effort to link and analyze counterrevolution by viewing it as a logical reaction to revolutionary phenomena. This is primarily an action-reaction perspective. Several authorities focus on the role of revolutionary systems: their operation and ideological posture as the basis for examining the response by counterrevolutionary systems. A common subject is the study of the effectiveness of the instruments of the state, their credibility, the legitimacy of the state, and the quality of the counterrevolutionary elite.

The major thrust of these works is on broad historical descriptions of revolution, with attention to counterrevolution as an adjunct to revolution. This pattern appears consistent with the views of Lenin, who wrote:

> It is not enough for revolution that exploited and oppressed masses should understand the impossibility of living in the old way and demand changes. It is essential for revolution that the exploiters should not be able to live and rule in the old way. Only when the "lower classes" do not want the old way and when the "upper classes" cannot carry on in the old way—only then can revolution triumph.[2]

Similarly, Dunn writes that "a revolution happens, though, only if this process of political struggle does lead to the collapse of social control by the existing political elite."[3] Thus, the revolutionary struggle is viewed against the background of the effectiveness of the counterrevolutionary system. At the same time, however, Taber cautions that counterrevolution is a distinctly different political-military operation: "The counter-insurgent cannot win by imitating the insurgent, because he is alien in the revolutionary situation, and because his tasks are precisely the opposite of the guerrilla."[4]

In an attempt to break out of the revolutionary-counterrevolutionary linkage, one authority states that "counterrevolution is an oppositionist political response to an imminent, early, or advanced revolution."[5] He goes on to classify counterrevolutions as follows:

> A counterrevolution may precede the actual outbreak of the revolution—a preemptive counterrevolution; or it may occur almost concomitantly with it—a reactive counterrevolution; or it may be deferred until the revolution has become rather firmly established—a delayed counterrevolution.[6]

There are those who argue, nonetheless, that the task of counterrevolution is primarily to counter the revolutionaries in a step-by-step advance through the revolutionary process, only in the opposite direction. Thus, the counterrevolutionary must drive the revolutionaries backward through each phase of the revolutionary process. But some see counterrevolution as a strategic and tactical operation in its own right that needs to be pursued not in response to the revolutionaries but as a measure of effective government.[7]

COUNTERREVOLUTIONARY ELITE

The ruling elite of counterrevolutionary systems are usually studied as a group or major political actor rather than as individuals in leadership positions with certain leadership patterns, motivations, and beliefs. In many cases, those in ruling positions tend to be viewed as evil, while those in revolutionary positions are seen as good. This is particularly the case in some of the current literature in the United States, partly because of the ideological bent of a number of authors and partly because of lingering themes that revolutions follow the American pattern based on the theme of democratic systems struggling against repressive ones.

In earlier periods, ruling groups in many Third World states were colonialists; in others, they were traditional elites. In the independence era, indigenous elites came to power and occupied positions of authority in existing and later counterrevolutionary systems. With the rash of military coup d'états and military governments, some scholars viewed military officers as a group and studied their motivations as ruling elite.

Chorley, for example, examined the role of national armies as a counterrevolutionary force. She writes, "Whatever government or party has the full allegiance of a country's armed force is to all intents and purposes politically impregnable."[8] She argues that an army officers' corps will react against revolution because in most cases the position of the corps is linked to regime survival. Equally important, the attitude and behavior of the lower ranks of the army in most revolutionary situations is determined by the officer corps and is likely to reflect regime values. This is, according to the author, partly a consequence of the semi-isolation of the army from the mainstream political grievances of the general society. The major problem for the counterrevolutionary system according to Chorley is to sustain and control the army.

In Latin America, counterrevolutionary systems were in the main controlled by landowners and/or the military officer class.[9] Thus most peasants and disaffected individuals saw the existing systems as instruments for the protection of the ruling class, with little sensitivity toward or sympathy for the mass of people. Yet a number of these systems were not totalitarian nor were they necessarily repressive governments. They were not, to be sure, liberal democracies or fully participatory systems, but in a number of cases, Third World states were trying to establish the basis for democracy. Many Third World systems have a high potential for revolution, in no small part as a result of the drive for modernity and the difficulties encountered in trying to adjust governing structures to the de-

mands triggered by modernity. This creates internal instability, a drive for security on the part of the governing
elite, and even more internal resistance—a catch-22
situation for all practical purposes.[10] The more the state
drives toward modernity, the more instability is created
and the more likely it is that new elites evolve to
challenge those in power. Not only do these actions and
reactions create instability, they are just as likely to expose
the existing system to the influence and manipulation of
external forces.

History seems to show that when the counterrevolutionary elite are Marxist-Leninist and the system is based
on Marxist philosophy of governance, they have rarely
been overthrown by revolutionaries. It follows, therefore,
that a serious study of the counterrevolutionary elite is an
important step in understanding the nature of revolution
and counterrevolution. This is particularly important in
correcting the variety of distortions that tend to frequent
the literature regarding democracy, the Third World, and
US involvement in counterrevolution.

In brief, the demands of modernity, the relatively short
period of time in which Third World states have existed
as independent states, and the dynamics of internal and
external forces tend to drive such states toward authoritarian forms of rule, particularly when faced with revolution. Yet such forms are far from being institutionalized
and legitimized, even by members of the ruling elite. In
many cases, these systems are a far cry from modern
totalitarian systems. Third World systems are vulnerable
to change and can be influenced by internal and external
forces. In this respect, it is reasonable to ask, why not by
democratic forces aimed at establishing a democratic, non-
Marxist, and nonexpansionist system?

EXTERNAL FORCES AND GEOPOLITICAL CONSIDERATIONS

One of the most important characteristics of contemporary revolution and counterrevolution is the role played

by external forces or, more specifically, third powers. The nature of contemporary international politics, particularly with respect to ideological conflict, fragmentation, and problems of governance in many Third World states, provides ample opportunity for power projection by superpowers and even lesser powers. This includes commitment of forces in support of various systems; examples are the United States in Vietnam, France in Chad, the Soviet Union in Afghanistan, and the Soviet and Cuban involvement in Angola and Ethiopia. Perhaps an even more challenging form is third power support of revolutions: involvement of communist states in support of revolutionaries in El Salvador is an example.

Geopolitical considerations, although playing a secondary role to other major considerations, need to be understood in the context of third power involvement. For example, even as late as 1985, there were still those in the United States who argued that Soviet involvement in Afghanistan was the same as US involvement in Vietnam. Yet even a cursory look at the geopolitical aspects of the situation should be enough to dispel such notions. Afghanistan is contiguous to the Soviet Union, while Vietnam is thousands of miles from US shores. The political-psychological issues and geopolitical relationships differ considerably in each case. Moreover, the historical relationships and the policies of the two superpowers with respect to Afghanistan and Vietnam also differ. Finally, the nature of the Soviet system as contrasted to the US system dictates differing policies. Those who argue about such similarities also attempt to make the case of equating Soviet purposes and operational doctrine with US involvement in Vietnam. This is the most glaring error, as any serious study of the character and nature of the US and Soviet systems easily reveals. In this respect, geopolitical considerations and external (third power) involvement are linked.

External Forces

The focus of inquiry here is on third power impact within the indigenous conflict area. The most direct and visible third power role is usually as a major counter-revolutionary force. Distinctions need to be made, however, between the colonial and contemporary periods. In the immediate post-World War II period, colonial powers were usually placed in a counterrevolutionary role. In the contemporary period, third powers have frequently become involved in support of existing indigenous systems.

A number of excellent studies examine the colonial role, including particularly the British role in Malaya and the French in Algeria and Indochina.[11] The views of anticolonial revolutionaries provide particularly useful insights on such struggles. For example, Mondlane addressed the struggle against the Portuguese in Mozambique:

> On the military front, the Portuguese face all the problems of a regular army combating a guerrilla force and a foreign army of occupation fighting in a hostile territory. ... The political aspect is of even greater importance, for the struggle is essentially a political struggle in which the military is only one aspect. To justify their presence, the Portuguese must affirm that their army is defending Mozambique against outside aggression. Yet such a posture is impossible to maintain persuasively, for the FRELIMO forces are, without exception, composed of Mozambicans, whereas the Portuguese army is almost entirely composed of Portuguese troops and numbers little more than one thousand puppet African soldiers among its ranks.[12]

Fall provides similar insights into the French role as a counterrevolutionary force, as do studies on the British role in Malaya.[13] The French failed; the British were reasonably successful. Such comparative studies are especially useful for studying counterrevolutionary policies and strategies and the reasons for success or failure. They are also important in analyzing US involvement in Vietnam.

Recently some scholars have argued that the introduction of third powers into a revolutionary situation tends to expand internal political violence and serves to create a neocolonial condition eroding support for the indigenous system, as in US involvement in South Vietnam and El Salvador. The other side of the coin is that third powers have also become involved on the side of revolutions, creating an even more difficult problem for counterrevolutionary systems (for example, US support of the "contras," Cuban involvement in Nicaragua and Nicaraguan involvement in El Salvador or support of terrorist groups by Libya and Iran). This is not necessarily a new phenomenon. What is new is that much of this external triggering of revolution can be traced to the Soviet Union and its surrogates, including Cuba and East Germany.

Geopolitical Considerations

With few exceptions, little serious attention has been given to geopolitical factors in revolution and counterrevolution in the literature and even less in assessing strategy. The exceptions are usually the work of revolutionaries or those that include geopolitical elements as part of a general study of broad policy issues. Geopolitical factors are generally included in works studying the character of military combat, but these tend to be focused at the tactical level, with scant attention to geopolitical factors as they affect policy and strategy.

In terms of tactical geopolitical considerations, there are excellent works on Malaya and Indochina. With respect to French Indochina, for example, Fall writes,

> Special geopolitical conditions may bring about a situation particularly favorable to the sustenance of a revolutionary war. Probably the most important such condition is the existence of what—for want of a better term—I call an active sanctuary. . . . An active sanctuary is a

territory contiguous to a rebellious area which, though ostensibly not involved in the conflict, provides the rebel side with shelter, training facilities, equipment, and if it can get away with it—troops.[14]

In the 1950s, General Matthew Ridgway placed great importance on the geopolitical considerations of counter-revolutionary conflict. It is important to recall that Ridgway's book is not on revolution or counterrevolution but more specifically on his own military career spanning service in Europe and Korea and as the US Army chief of staff. With respect to the proposed US intervention in Indochina in support of the French in 1954, Ridgway noted that an army team of experts was sent to the area to assess its military character:

> The area, they found, was practically devoid of those facilities which modern forces such as ours find essential to the waging of war. Its telecommunications, highways, railways—all the things that make possible the operation of a modern combat force on land—were almost non-existent. Its port facilities and airfields were totally inadequate, and to provide the facilities we would require a tremendous engineering and logistical effort.[15]

The lack of serious study of geopolitical factors has been part of a larger problem: that of US strategic thought on counterrevolution. Lately there has been some attention on geopolitical factors from a strategic level. This is particularly the case in discussions about the Soviet role in Afghanistan as compared to the US role in Vietnam, as well as third power roles in distant areas, such as Nicaragua and Africa. The relationship between geopolitical factors and third power involvement is a necessary calculation in designing third power policy and strategy and in determining levels of logistical support required for the conflict area. Although these may be closely associated with military dimensions, those who study revolution and counterrevolution must also consider it as a part of third power calculations from the political and psychological perspective, particularly since this is an important element in assessing staying power.

WHO IS WINNING?   WHO IS LOSING?

The most difficult problem in analyzing revolution and counterrevolution is in charting the direction of progress and determining the likely outcome. Most conventional criteria—the amount of real estate occupied, the number of battles won, body count, enemy weapons taken, prisoners captured—may not be true indicators of who is winning and losing. The focus of revolutionary-counterrevolutionary conflicts is in the political-social milieu, which needs to be assessed with political-psychological measures. These are usually based on a variety of subjective conditions, most of which cannot be measured precisely.

In brief, trying to measure the progress or outcome of a revolution is similar in scope to the problem of trying to measure government effectiveness. It necessitates measuring systems' effectiveness, policy impact, and behavior and the attitudes of leaders and members of the ruling elite. Social scientists have been trying for years to develop reasonably accurate indicators of these factors in peaceful industrial systems, yet even here conclusions, approaches, and theories are unconvincing to many. Imagine the difficulty of trying to do this in developing systems involved in revolutionary and counterrevolutionary conflict.

. This does not mean that studies, assessments, and reasonable analysis cannot be made of such conflicts. But this work requires an intellectual disposition and sophistication based on broad understanding of revolution and deep insights into the culture and history of the area in which such conflicts take place. Conclusions based on such analysis must be constantly challenged, assumptions about revolution questioned, and the policy of third powers as well as those of the counterrevolutionary system critically reviewed. If these stand up to close scrutiny, then the basis for developing sound policy and strategy exists. Unfortunately, in the United States and the West in general, this kind of analysis has been the exception rather than the rule. As a result, analysis of revolutionary progress that tries to determine who is winning and who is losing can (and has) become enmeshed in subjectivity, misguided intuitiveness, pseudo-empirical models, and a confusing array of multiple indicators. This confusion is compounded by the fact that such conflicts usually include a variety of unknown causations and unanticipated directions. Most of the literature on revolutionary-counterrevolutionary progress reflects this confusion. Nevertheless, the literature must not be ignored; it can be used as a starting point to develop understanding of conflict progress and the uncertainties of measurement. If progress cannot be measured accurately, at least we need to develop insights on why this is so.

Complicating the attempt at realistic analysis is the fact that much of the literature addressing conflict progress tends to follow a zero-sum game approach: whatever the revolutionaries win, the counterrevolutionaries lose; when the revolutionaries progress, the counterrevolutionaries recede, and vice-versa. The problem with such an approach is that it is based on the presumption that the entire country or state is under a government whose presence and control are everywhere. Therefore it follows that loss of control by the government in one area is immediately translated to a gain of control by the revolutionaries. But in actuality, in many outlying areas there is little, if any, government presence, much less control. The fact that Third World systems are in the process of development places many outlying areas at the margin of government control. For all practical purposes, therefore, such areas are not necessarily lost by anyone; they are simply there to be won. In fact, the inability of revolutionaries to strike at the strongest part of the state may also be an indicator of their initial weakness—where the zero-sum game is hardly relevant.

There is nevertheless a degree of truth in the proposition that revolutionary progress, particularly if it continues and increases in momentum, poses an increasingly dangerous challenge to the counterrevolutionary system. Initially it may be best for the existing system not to attempt to counter every revolutionary move in outlying areas since this can dissipate resources and expend a great deal of energy with minimal or no results. It is even conceivable that revolutionary strategy is aimed exactly at deliberately drawing out counterrevolutionary forces into the least populated areas so that revolutionary forces can concentrate on the most populated areas.[16]

It may be best for the counterrevolutionary system to consolidate its strength, assess the scope and seriousness of the challenge, develop realistic policy and strategy, and aim at the heart of the revolutionary system at a time and place most propitious to counterrevolutionary strategy. This policy and strategy must be based on an understanding of the indicators of revolutionary and counterrevolutionary patterns and an appreciation of the complex relationships between winning and losing in such conflicts. Such sophistication is rarely a result of conventional perspectives.

Some of the most valid indicators are generally those that are political in nature and indicate government effectiveness. These include the success of tax collection efforts in the countryside, the number of youth in school, the effectiveness of land reform programs, the amount of agricultural output, and the ease of travel. In terms of the political-psychological dimension, the attitude of the mass of people regarding the "mandate of heaven" of the existing government (that is, the legitimacy of the existing system and its ruling elite) is a crucial indicator. This is a difficult aspect to measure. It is linked closely to indicators noted previously, along with the kind of support, implicit or otherwise, given to the system by traditional groups (religious, peasant, landowners), as well as those in the modern sector.

Historical Perspectives and Case Studies

The literature and various policy approaches on conflict progress can be grouped into two categories: classical revolutions from which theoretical formulations can be studied and case studies of a modern genre from which specific indicators can be identified and a general policy template designed.

In the main, historical studies base their analysis on histories (cases) of various revolutions.[17] Historical studies of the purely theoretical are not included in this category. Such studies concentrate heavily on the philosophy, psychology, and at times metaphysics of revolution.

In historical studies, revolutionary progress tends to be viewed primarily in terms of governmental ineffectiveness. There is an inextricable association between revolution and counterrevolution in which revolutionary progress is indicated by the ability to develop the rudiments of governing structures to which the existing system is unable to respond.

Reflecting on her study of the French, Russian, and Chinese revolutions as they might apply to the contemporary period, one author concludes,

> All of these have broad resemblances to the French, Russian, and Chinese revolutions. They occurred in predominantly agrarian countries, and they became possible only through the administrative-military breakdown of preexisting states.... The key to successful structural analysis lies in a focus on state organizations and their relations both to international environments and to domestic classes and economic conditions.[18]

Close study of the many case studies of post-World War II revolutions and counterrevolutions reveals numerous assessments of reasons for success or failure. For example, in studying the relative success of the Philippine government against the Huks, Brigadier General Lansdale writing in 1962 concluded,

The Huks had analyzed the people's grievances and made the righting of these wrongs into their slogans. And the change came when Ramon Magsaysay became Defense Minister. He was from the people, loved and trusted by them. He and the army set about making the constitution a living document for the people. As they did so, they and the people emerged on the same side of the fight. The Huks lost support and had to go on the defensive.[19]

Kerkvliet notes that there were three reasons for the failure of the Huks and the parallel success of the Philippine government. The first he identifies as "general weariness among peasant rebels and their supporters in Central Luzon."[20] The second reason was "government reforms." The third, and perhaps most important, reason was that the "peasants in Central Luzon liked Magsaysay ... because he had personal contact with villagers and because the military became less abusive under his leadership."[21]

Other books attempt to provide a general counterrevolutionary policy template based on phases or various levels of counteraction against the revolutionaries. Although such studies may vary in terminology and labels, they have similar themes stressing the need for aggressive counteractions based on policy and strategy following phases and a systematic application of political-military pressures.

While studying non-Marxist revolutions, two authors comment on counterrevolutionary strategy:

Policies designed for dealing with prolonged Marxist revolutionary insurrections may be inappropriate or unnecessarily costly for non-Marxist secessionist movements. The student or analyst who has recognized this will be led to inquire under what circumstances reform is or is not important and what it means for the situation he is examining.[22]

Many historical and case studies that try to provide a policy template for examining revolution or counterrevolution usually focus on a Maoist phase approach or some variation of it. Although the Maoist approach may not be applicable to all Third World revolutions, it does provide general guidelines for such conflicts. The Marxist-Leninist perspective, however, may be more appropriate for urban-based revolutions and conflicts because they are linked to class struggle. Nonetheless, general principles of Marxism-Leninism regarding conflict, change, and class struggle are interpreted and applied by many revolutionaries to their own Third World situation, ignoring the Marxist-Leninist disdain for the peasantry.

Summary: The   Counterrevolutionary Dilemma

How can you tell who is winning? In the latter part of the Vietnam War, a small number of Americans were finally beginning to ask that question. To the frustration of many, the answer proved elusive. As this study points out, trying to identify clear indicators of progress in revolution and counterrevolution is exceedingly difficult for a variety of reasons, primarily because we are dealing with attitudes and loyalties and with political and social phenomena. Even in the most developed countries, these are not easy matters to measure with precision. If progress is very difficult to measure, trying to predict outcomes is virtually impossible. One scholar concludes, "Despite a voluminous literature . . . the explanatory power of the postulated theories remains low and the predictive power virtually non-existent."[23]

Perhaps the best that can be said regarding approaches, theories, and models aimed at determining progress and predicting revolutionary phenomena are contained in observations by Bell. Examining why rebels against British rule succeeded or failed, he concludes,

> The rebels with the most subtle and complex analysis, with organizations fashioned for special purposes, with a grasp of reality unhampered by theoretical considera-

tions, and most of all with a reasonable if not rigorous estimation of British assets and liabilities fared best. The simple, the short-sighted, the ideological bound, the theorists, and the gunmen did less well; but even then the cost to the British to close down the flawed revolts was considerable.[24]

This does not mean that one should forgo the study of revolutionary and counterrevolutionary linkages, nor does it suggest that there is no utility in trying to assess progress or outcomes. An intelligent analysis of the revolutionary environment and counterrevolutionary challenge requires a deep understanding of the revolutionary process and the problems of modernity. Although these may not provide the specifics of progress, they will help reduce misinterpretation of information and thus avoid wrong policy options and inappropriate strategy.

SUMMATION AND CRITIQUE

A realistic study of revolution and counterrevolution cannot view each of these separately. Their interrelationships and action-counteraction dynamics make it extremely difficult to study one without understanding its inextricable relationship to the other. Yet for the sake of manageability and order, the analysis of revolution and counterrevolution usually has been separated into two distinct areas of study.

A number of conclusions can be drawn from this overview. The clearest is that revolution and counterrevolution are complex and multidimensional phenomena that cannot be understood by monistic or single theme approaches or theories. There is no easy way to analyze such conflicts. Policy and strategy are considerably affected by these complexities.

The roots of revolution and counterrevolution are deeply entrenched in the political-social system; their causes are multiple. A certain mix of causes may distinguish one revolution from another. Yet most revolutions also have certain common factors, ranging from ineffective government to peasant disaffection.

The evolution of Third World states, characterized by the challenges of modernization, make most of them highly vulnerable to revolutionary challenge. The drive to modernity triggers deep changes from the old to the new in virtually every sector of society. Existing institutions are challenged, new ideologies are introduced, new social and political roles evolve, different economic patterns emerge, and a different and more encompassing political environment is created. All of these changes and developments are likely to create a high degree of instability. The existing government will find it quite difficult to manage all of these changes, creating a situation in which contending elites develop. Of particular danger to the existing system is that after a period of time, the instability and frustration created by the drive to modernity may convince emerging elites that the best and quickest way to change the system is through immediate and dramatic means. In the process, a revolutionary environment is created.

Revolutions in the immediate post-World War II period were aimed primarily at the colonialist powers. Thus, England, France, and the Netherlands, for example, were faced with revolutions whose objective was independence. There were some exceptions; the Greek conflict in the late 1940s and the Philippine struggle against the Huks are examples. In contrast, revolutions in the contemporary period have been aimed primarily at indigenous systems, such as in South Vietnam, El Salvador, Nicaragua, and Iran. The current period is also characterized by the role of third powers (external powers) supporting revolutions or counterrevolutions. This development has internationalized revolutions so that they rarely can be perceived realistically as solely internal affairs.

What compounds the problem for researchers, policy makers, and indigenous governments is that there is little agreement regarding the nature and scope of the challenge. Those studying revolution and counterrevolution disagree as to definitions, concepts, and causes. The very nature of revolution makes it particularly difficult to identify in its early stages. Thus most systems faced with revolutionary challenges respond initially with military force and in an ad hoc fashion.

Many people in the United States tend to perceive contemporary revolutions and counterrevolutions in terms of the American or French revolutions or the Soviet revolution. Although these may provide some broad analogies, they rarely provide the strategy or doctrinal roots of the contemporary revolutions, though the Iranian revolution may be the major exception. One must look to the Chinese revolution for these principles and to variations that evolved into the Cuban approach. While much has been said of urban guerrilla warfare, this is not the all-encompassing political-social phenomenon of revolution that is common to the contemporary period.

From the perspective of the United States and other democracies in general, response to revolutionary and counterrevolutionary conflicts is particularly difficult and challenging. Because of the American view of war and the democratic policy-making process, among other things, many political actors and policy makers in the United States misperceive the nature of revolution. They tend to see these through conventional lenses or by the study of classic revolutions. Further, policy makers and military professionals are not necessarily helped by the complex and theoretical nature of many American studies of revolutions and counterrevolutions.

There will always be those who advocate certain policies and strategies as clear and sure steps for successful counterrevolution, but charting the progress, much less predicting the outcome, of such conflicts is extremely difficult. Yet it is also clear that without a serious study of theories, definitions, concepts, and explanations, it will be difficult to address the issues of contemporary revolutions and counterrevolutions with any understanding. Without a historical sense that derives from serious study, it is unlikely that policy makers, either civilian or military, will be able to design effective US counterrevolutionary policy and strategy.

COUNTERREVOLUTION: GENERAL GUIDELINES

The dynamics of revolution create the context within which counterrevolutionary policy and strategy need to be designed. Counterrevolution is in the main a response to revolution; that is, it tends to be a reactive policy that is forced on the existing system. There is a degree of truth in the statement that a reasonably effective political system precludes any serious revolutionary challenge.[25] A revolutionary challenge is a degree of proof of the ineffectiveness of the existing system.   It follows that the best counterrevolutionary policy and strategy is to establish effective government and the programs necessary for government to ensure eventual control over its own territory.

Although this appears to be a relatively simple approach to the problem of revolution, actually it requires that difficult choices be made and that scarce resources be committed to make government more effective.   No government, even those in the most developed systems, has enough resources, time, and energy to do everything. Thus, priorities must be established to counter the most serious and challenging revolutionary strategies.   This cannot be done without understanding the nature and character of revolution and the specifics of the revolutionary challenge within the conflict area.

An understanding of revolution must be combined with an understanding of the society within which the revolution is occurring.   Thus the counterrevolutionary system must try to identify the causes of the revolution, its leadership, and its specific strategy. Only once this is done, no matter how imperfectly, can effective strategies be formulated and implemented.   However, the best counterrevolutionary policy and strategy are not those based on reaction to revolution but those that are based on effective government and reasonable response to the political-social issues within society. This should be done as a principle of government long before any revolutionary impulses emerge in the system. If it is done reasonably well, there will be few if any revolutionary conditions created. Such an approach, however, requires an enlightened governing elite whose understanding of the politically acceptable goes beyond the superficialities of public rhetoric or Marxist-Leninist distortions. Unfortunately, there are few such elites, and in a number of instances those that do emerge tend to be overwhelmed by opposing elements.

Counterrevolution: Models and Approaches

There appears to be no particular model or strategy of counterrevolution except perhaps the need for the government to demonstrate its determination and capacity to win while providing a legitimate framework within which the grievances of the people can be addressed and their aspirations pursued. The existing system must not only prevent the revolution from growing, but it must implement political, social, economic, and psychological strategies designed to create a government-controlled revolutionary movement against the revolution—in essence, a revolution within the revolution.

Doing this requires a nonrepressive quality to be institutionalized within the existing system—a large group of committed leaders and administrators who are sensitive to the people and reasonably effective and humane security forces. *Enlightened repression* is a useful, though pejorative, term.

The quality of the national leadership is critical to the success of the counterrevolutionary effort. As history has shown, one individual can make the difference; Magsaysay in the Philippines' efforts against the Huk rebellion in the 1950s is a case in point. In addition, the system must conduct an effective psychological warfare campaign

aimed at both its own people and the revolutionaries, responding to some of the most serious grievances, perceived or otherwise.

All of this must be combined with a strategy that is
aimed toward long-range policy goals and one that em-
ploys means that do not seriously violate the basis of
legitimacy and credibility. These factors can create a perception on the part of the populace that the existing system offers the best opportunity to achieve a better life. In
other words, the momentum in achieving and maintaining legitimacy and control must remain on or shift to the
side of the existing system. How US policy and strategy
are affected by these considerations is the focus of later
chapters.

Counterrevolutionary Strategy

The strategic plan must include both short- and long-
term considerations. In the short term, it may be that
military measures are the most important, since security
is an immediate problem. In the long term, political and
economic measures prevail. Political and psychological
strategies must be the major priorities in the overall
strategy.

A former chief of staff of the US Army has written that

> the counter insurgent's task is to maintain the estab-
> lished order while in fact waging war against the insur-
> gents who are spread among the population. The coun-
> ter insurgent is thus restrained against the use of force
> which would normally be acceptable against a com-
> pletely hostile population. The arms of the government
> must be long enough to reach out to all of the people,
> firm enough to give them support, and strong enough
> to protect them from coercion and outside influence.[26]

The author goes on to say that an effective response to
revolution rests on

> a close integration of the political, economic, informa-
> tion, security, and military branches of the government.
> ... One must constantly keep foremost in mind that
> military action is only part of counter insurgency and
> that a well-integrated "team" can often compound a
> military success or minimize a failure.[27]

Written in the early 1960s, these words remain relevant. Their importance lies in the fact that they convey
an American perspective, although such perspectives
were (and are) rarely implemented realistically in counterrevolutionary policy and strategy.

In the Malayan conflict, the same points were emphasized by one authority on the subject:

> Communist influence can exist largely because of the
> absence of civil administration and government control
> in the areas concerned. This is basic in all Communist-
> dominated rural areas in all developing countries, and is
> a crucial point in planning counter-measures against the
> Communist-led "National Liberation Struggle" to over-
> throw any government that is not Communist. No
> amount of military pressure can succeed unless it is
> carried out hand in hand with the introduction of gov-
> ernment administration in the areas concerned.[28]

In sum, there is no sure strategy for counterrevolution
except better government, which can be interpreted in a
variety of ways by a variety of people and leading to
different policies, strategies, and concepts. The goal of any
existing system in the conduct of counterrevolution is the
same: defeat of the revolution. However, strategies must
have their roots in the particular circumstances of the
country concerned. Equally important, the character of
the counterrevolutionary system has much to do with the
kinds of strategies that can be pursued. For example, a
Marxist-Leninist system is not likely to feel bound by
democratic constraints.

The broadening of the revolution and the ability of the
revolutionaries to move to higher phases of struggle have
their parallel impact on counterrevolutionary strategy.

With the movement of the conflict from lower to higher phases, the costs for the counterrevolutionary system also increase but at disproportionately higher levels. While the revolution may advance from a lower to a higher phase arithmetically, the costs for the counterrevolution increase geometrically. The reason that counterrevolution is increasingly more expensive in materiel and personnel is that revolution creates a synergistic effect, combining the dynamics of revolution with the societal grievances and inherent instability of society, thereby developing a threat that is considerably more than the sum of its parts. For example, the appearance of a revolutionary unit in an area that was previously secure requires that the counterrevolutionary system commit not an equal unit but at least five to ten times more units in order to protect the numerous government activities that are threatened: officials, teachers, bridges, transportation lines, tax collectors, buildings, and critical population centers. Additionally the government must make some effort to mount offensive operations against the revolutionary unit. Expansion of the revolution also increases perceptions that it is gaining momentum and succeeding. In turn, counterrevolutionary supporters increase their demands for protection and government effectiveness.

In its role as a third power in support of a host state, the United States also faces these problems. As the revolution expands, it is likely that the counterrevolutionary system (host state) will require an increasing amount of aid and assistance. This leads to the distinct probability of increased US involvement. (See Chapters 7 and 8.)

Studying revolutionary and counterrevolutionary conflicts separate from broader conflicts can create distorted impressions of the nature of international security and lead to errors regarding proper response to unconventional conflicts. It is important to appreciate the nature and character of the whole range of conflicts in the international field.

NOTES

1. This chapter is based, in general, on Sam C. Sarkesian, "American Policy on Revolution and Counterrevolution: A Review of the Themes in the Literature," *Conflict* 5, no. 2 (1984).

2. V. I. Lenin, *"Left Wing" Communism, An Infantile Disorder* (New York: International Publishers, 1940), p. 66.

3. John Dunn, *Modern Revolutions: An Introduction to the Analysis of a Political Phenomenon* (London: Cambridge University Press, 1972), p. 15.

4. Robert Taber, *The War of the Flea: A Study of Guerrilla Warfare Theory and Practice* (New York: Lyle Stuart, 1965), p. 21.

5. Mark N. Hagopian, *The Phenomenon of Revolution* (New York: Dodd, Mead, 1974), p. 341.

6. Ibid., p. 350.

7. John J. McCuen, *The Art of Counter-Revolutionary War* (Harrisburg, Penn.: Stackpole, 1966). See also Douglas Blaufarb, *The Counterinsurgency Era* (New York: Free Press, 1977); David Galula, *Counterinsurgency Warfare: Theory and Practice* (New York: Praeger, 1964); and John S. Pustay, *Counterinsurgency Warfare* (New York: Free Press, 1965).

8. Katherine Chorley, *Armies and the Art of Revolution* (London: Faber and Faber, 1973), p. 16. See also John Ellis, *Armies in Revolution* (New York: Oxford University Press, 1974), and D. E. H. Russel, *Rebellion, Revolution and Armed Force: A Comparative Study of Fifteen Countries with Special Emphasis on Cuba and South Africa* (New York: Academic Press, 1974).

9. Richard Gott, *Guerrilla Movements in Latin America* (Garden City, N.Y.: Anchor Books, 1972).

10. Paul M. Kattenburg, *The Vietnam Trauma in American Foreign Policy, 1945-75* (New Brunswick, N.J.: Transaction Books, 1980), pp. 324-25.

11. See, for example, Joseph Buttinger, *Vietnam, A Dragon Embattled*, 2 vols. (New York: Praeger, 1967); Michael Clark, *Algeria in Turmoil: A History of the Rebellion* (New York: Praeger, 1959); John Talbot, *The War without a Name: France in Algeria, 1954-62* (New York: Alfred A. Knopf, 1980); Richard L. Clutterbuck, *The Long, Long War: Counter-insurgency in*

Malaya and Vietnam (New York: Praeger, 1966); Oliver Crawford, *The Door Marked Malaya* (London: Hart-Davis, 1958); Bernard B. Fall, *The Two Viet-Nams: A Political and Military Analysis,* 2d. rev. ed. (New York: Praeger, 1967); J. M. Gullick, *Malaya* (New York: Praeger, 1963); Jean Lacoutre, *Vietnam: Between Two Truces* (New York: Random House, 1966); and Sir Robert Thompson, *Defeating Communist Insurgency: The Lessons of Malaya and Vietnam* (New York: Praeger, 1967).

12. Eduardo Mondlane, *The Struggle for Mozambique* (Baltimore: Penguin Books, 1969), pp. 141-42.

13. Bernard B. Fall, *Street without Joy: Insurgency in Indochina, 1946-63,* 3d rev. ed. (Harrisburg, Penn: Stackpole, 1963). See also Buttinger, 2:787.

14. Fall, p. 357.

15. Matthew B. Ridgway, *Soldier: The Memoirs of Matthew B. Ridgway* (New York: Harper and Brothers, 1956), p. 276. See also Arthur Campbell, *Guerrillas: A History and Analysis* (New York: John Day, 1968), pp. 282-84.

16. Hung P. Nguyen, "Communist Offensive Strategy and the Defense of South Vietnam," *Parameters* 14, no. 4 (Winter 1984):3-19.

17. See, for example, Dunn; Gerard Chailiand, *Revolution in the Third World* (Baltimore: Penguin Books, 1978).

18. Theda Skocpol, *States and Social Revolutions: A Comparative Analysis of France, Russia, and China* (Cambridge: Cambridge University Press, 1979), p. 291.

19. Brigadier General Edward G. Lansdale, "Guerrilla Warfare," *Newsweek,* February 12, 1962, quoted in Fall, *Street without Joy,* p. 356.

20. Benedict J. Kerkvliet, *The Huk Rebellion: A Study of Peasant Revolt in the Philippines* (Berkeley, Calif.: University of California Press, 1977), pp. 236-37.

21. Ibid., p. 238.

22. Bard E. O`Neill, William R. Heaton, and Donald J. Alberts, eds., *Insurgency in the Modern World* (Boulder, Colo.: Westview Press, 1980), p. 282.

23. Robert S. Leiken, "The Salvadoran Left," in Robert S. Leiken, ed., *Central America, Anatomy of Conflict* (New York: Pergamon Press, 1984), pp. 119-20.

24. J. Bowyer Bell, *On Revolt: Strategies of National Liberation* (Cambridge: Harvard University Press, 1976), p. 191.

25. See, for example, Hagopian.

26. Clutterbuck, pp. viii-ix.

27. Ibid., p. ix.

28. C. C. Too, "Some Salient Features in the Experience in Defeating Communism in Malaya, with Particular Regard to the Method of the New Villages," (paper given at the International Seminar, Communism in Asia, June 9-25, 1966, Onyang, Korea), p. 3.

4

The Conflict Spectrum:
Wars in the Contemporary Period

Although revolutionary and counterrevolutionary conflicts have been an important part of the world landscape over the past two decades and are likely to continue to remain so for the foreseeable future, their impact cannot be properly examined outside of the total international security environment. These kinds of conflicts must be analyzed in the context of the broad conflict spectrum. A broad view of conflicts in general, particularly in terms of US political-military capability and conflict characteristics, helps in understanding the relationship of revolution and counterrevolution to US political-military policy and strategy and to other types of conflict. Equally important, it can help to clarify our understanding of revolution and counterrevolution and sharpen the focus on the long-range impact of such conflicts.

OVERVIEW OF CONTEMPORARY CONFLICTS

The fact that an increasing number of states possess nuclear weapons not only complicates the study of conflicts but adds a destructive dimension and escalation factor that cannot be discounted, even when the focus is on revolution and counterrevolution. There is no assurance that once a conflict begins, even one at the lowest scale of intensity, it will not trigger a broader conflict and ultimately lead to escalation involving major powers. It is against this backdrop that revolutions and counterrevolutions must be assessed. Of all of the major differences between the conflict environment of the past and that of the present, this is one that stands out.

It is argued that aside from the nuclear component, conflicts in the contemporary period are evolutions from the past. While there is a certain amount of truth in this, it is oversimplified and misleading. The nature of the international world today is quite different from the pre-World War II period; it is more complex and contentious, with all that these mean for international security, particularly because of nuclear weapons. Moreover, the technological age has had a major impact on the nature of nonnuclear conflicts, making them increasingly destructive and technologically oriented. An example is the technological drive within the US military for capability in an electronic battlefield; it has developed tactical computers, precision-guided munitions, shoulder-mounted ground-to-air missiles, and a highly complex command, control, and communications system. The variety and complexity of weapons available today at the lowest tactical level, that of the infantrymen, provides firepower and destructiveness that would have been unimaginable to their World War II and Korean counterparts. There is no reason to believe that other major and lesser powers are not developing similar capabilities.

Much of this same sophisticated weaponry is also available to revolutionaries and terrorists. For example, terrorists have access to missiles, and there is a growing fear that even nuclear and biological weapons will be available in the future. Revolutionaries are able to acquire many of the most modern weapons through the world arms market or through third states. Given the nature of world arms traffic, it is likely that many revolutionaries may be able to arm themselves as well as and even better than the armies of existing governments.

These developments have created an environment in which patterns of interdependency exist among various types of conflicts. Combined with the dynamics and characteristics of contemporary international politics, the conflict spectrum is now fundamentally different than it was during the immediate post-World War II period or even the past decade.

Figure 4-1 shows the general categories of conflicts according to intensity as conceived by US policy makers in the contemporary period.[1] The spectrum is not intended to show actual intensity of conflict on the ground. Rather the various categories and levels of intensity are designed to be policy and strategic indicators. Even the lowest-scale involvement can create situations in which the individual soldier is engaged in high-intensity conflict. It makes little difference to the individual involved in a firefight that the political-military policy of the moment is defined as low-intensity conflict. For the individual, it may be a life-and-death struggle.

At the lowest end of the spectrum are noncombat political-military operations (at least this is the assumption for the initial involvement). Shows of force, for example, are usually based on the presumption that a flotilla of warships maneuvering offshore will signal a particular state that the stakes involved in a particular issue have been visibly raised beyond the diplomatic table. Economic aid and assistance as well as certain levels of military aid also raise the stakes between donor and recipient state to a higher level than in normal state-to-state relationships.

At the other end of the conflict spectrum is the ultimate in war, major nuclear conflict. Little needs to be said about the character of such conflict since there exists a great deal of literature about it, despite some wide-ranging disagreements on causes and outcomes of such conflicts. There is little disagreement that such conflicts are likely to embroil the whole world and are all encompassing in that the distinctions between noncombatants and combatants,

Figure 4-1
Contemporary Conflict Spectrum

Noncombat	Special Operations	Conventional	Nuclear
Shows of Force	Unconventional Conflicts Terror-Counterterror Revolution Counterrevolution	Limited-Major	Limited-Major

<---------Most Likely Contingencies------>

<-----------Degree of U.S. Capability--------------------->

<----Adequate------Poor to Adequate---------Adequate to Excellent--->

between cities and military targets, almost disappear. The totality of such conflicts is what makes them so frightening.

While the extremes of the conflict spectrum are reasonably distinct and provide relatively clear boundaries, it is in the vast middle range between them that boundary difficulties and interdependence exist to a degree that raise fears of escalation and superpower confrontation.

Conventional Wars

Although the war experience of the present generation of Americans has its roots in the Vietnam War, the intellectual basis for such experience and for the perception of wars rests in the conventional wars of the past, particularly World War II. This does not mean that Vietnam has not had an impact, but its major impact is a result of the gap between the expectations and realities of war. The expectations of most Americans are rooted in a conventional and Western concept of war that evolves from the Clausewitzian notion of combat between armies and the destruction of the enemy's military might. Even with experience since World War II, the concepts of combat remain fixed in such notions. These wars have common characteristics, though they may differ in degree, depending on the level of intensity.

In the opinion of many experts, major wars of today, particularly nuclear conflict, will be fought primarily by forces in being. That is, the military forces of the United States as trained, organized, and armed are the primary determinants of major war. Many argue that in a nuclear war, the outcome will be determined in relatively short time after its initiation. Some argue that there is the possibility of a long war, even with the use of nuclear weapons. Thus there is a need, they argue, for a mobilization concept: a selective service system and a plan for mobilization of reserves and the American people for a long-term conflict. There seems to be general agreement, nonetheless, that what counts in nuclear war is what is immediately available in both weaponry and military systems.

It is presumed that nonnuclear major conventional wars will follow an updated version of World War II. Skeptics of such a scenario, however, argue that any major conventional conflict will surely lead to the use of nuclear weapons. Yet a number of scenarios focusing on the European landscape are based on conventional combat. For example, the use of precision-guided munitions and the AirLand Battle concepts are based on US conventional war doctrines.[2]

The major characteristics of conventional conflicts include a high degree of mobility, the use of highly destructive munitions, the need for a large logistical support system, and a relatively large reservoir of manpower already in the forces in being and in reserve forces. Additionally, it presumes an industrial capacity to produce modern weapons and increase the production dramatically should a long war occur.

Plans for such conflicts are in many ways designed to deter the outbreak of a major conventional and nuclear war. Much of the planning, forces in being, and development of weaponry are designed to reinforce deterrent strategy. While much of the reasoning behind deterrence has focused on nuclear war, it applies equally to major conventional wars.

About the defense of Europe, for example, one noted European military historian argues,

> By "defend ourselves" I mean defend ourselves in the conventional sense with conventional weapons. . . . It is often argued that no such defence is possible unless we are prepared to turn Western Europe into an armed camp, a proposition that would be true if we intended to fight a total war aiming at the destruction of the Soviet armed forces. . . . Let us remember what we are trying to do. It is to deter the Soviet Union from using military force to solve its political differences. . . . We have to make it clear to our potential adversaries that there can be no easy military solutions.[3]

If there should be a major conventional war or nuclear war in which the United States is involved, it is likely that there will be a total mobilization and general recognition that the nation's survival is at stake. The identification of the enemy and the purposes of US involvement probably would be clear. The role of the military and its purpose in combat would also be clear: the destruction of the enemy armed forces and its capacity to continue the war. With respect to major conventional and nuclear wars, therefore, the US military posture and capability are considerable and firmly established.

Limited conventional conflicts present a different problem. To be sure, many of the characteristics are similar: the use of forces in being supported by reserve forces, if necessary (although reserve forces were not called up during the Vietnam War, for a variety of reasons, primarily because of the political implications). The operational patterns of such wars are likely to be determined by conventional strategy and doctrine. Training, organization, and operational commitment of US forces would not differ greatly from current patterns.

As the United States learned in Korea, however, the purposes of limited conflicts are not likely to be as clear-cut as in major wars. It may be difficult in many instances to identify the US role. That is, for many Americans, policy makers and major political actors alike, the use of the military in combat for limited goals, both political and military, is a difficult concept to accept, much less understand. There is a tendency to commit military forces on the presumption that the mission is clear and can be accomplished. In brief, there is a prevailing attitude that military forces should be committed to go in, "clean up the mess," and get out. This presumes, of course, a general understanding and agreement on what the mess is and how it is to be cleaned out. Equally important is the presumption that it can be cleaned out.

The major characteristics of limited as contrasted to unlimited (major) wars are determined by the fact that the conflict area has geographic limits. Additionally, military targets are also limited, in turn imposing restrictions on the kind of weapons used and also on the tactics employed. During the Korean conflict, for example, there was a general and unstated agreement between the United States and China that the conflict would be limited to the Korean peninsula. The United States tried to avoid targets in China after the Chinese intervention, although major bases for the conduct of the Korean War were located there.

Wars such as Korea are also limited in the number of participants. In the main, the adversaries attempt to limit outside involvement beyond the immediate conflict area for fear of escalation and the possibility of costs beyond the gains in the conflict. This limitation is characteristic of the Iran-Iraq war, which has been in progress since the early 1980s. It was also a characteristic of the Falkland Islands (Malvinas) conflict between Great Britain and Argentina. Thus, policy and strategy are aimed at limiting the war and preventing escalation.

Limited goals and participation, and geographical considerations characteristic of limited wars, complicate US political-military policy since how the conflict is presented to the people affects the political acceptability of the degree to which mobilization, if any, should be undertaken, as well as the basis of national will and political resolve. The nature of limited war suggests that the state involved as a third power, such as the United States, is constrained and limited in the intensity to which it can prosecute the war and in the goals of its political-military policy.

Although the purpose here is not a detailed discussion of US nuclear strategy, it is important to note the existence of a school of thought that accepts the notion of limited nuclear war. In its most recent form, this includes a variety of options.[4] These options are an attempt to avoid an all-or-nothing nuclear response and to provide a strategic counter to the Soviet ability to engage in a variety of nuclear options.

Unconventional Conflicts

At the other end of the conflict spectrum are a variety of unconventional conflicts. There is a great deal of disagreement and debate regarding the concepts, definitions, and categories of such conflicts. At the present time, most conflicts in the middle range of the conflict spectrum are included under the term *special operations*—a misleading term and concept in my view. Noncombat contingencies are at the lowest end of the spectrum (Figure 4-1).

An examination of the general patterns and characteristics of unconventional conflicts clearly shows their important differences from conventional and nuclear wars. To do this properly, however, we need to be clear about the two major types of conflicts within the unconventional category: terror (and its antithesis counterterror) and revolution (and its antithesis counterrevolution). These distinctions, shown in Figure 4-2, are not those generally used in contemporary US political-military policy. What the diagram shows is the way unconventional conflicts should be viewed to clarify the concept and to design a proper response.

Unconventional conflicts are divided into two categories: special operations and low-intensity conflicts. Special operations are those primarily concerned with terror and counterterror. As Figure 4-2 shows, however, this category also includes a variety of highly specialized conventional operations. These are considered conventional because they are primarily operations undertaken by small and highly mobile elite units—for instance, Rangers, whose training is primarily small unit tactics raised to a high level of proficiency. Counterterror operations include not only hostage rescue but hit-and-run raids on suspected terrorist groups and camps. They may also include operating with police forces and involve more than one nation. Such operations follow the patterns similar to special weapons and tactics (SWAT) teams of metropolitan police forces.

Low-intensity conflicts as shown in Figure 4-2 are primarily revolution and counterrevolution and terrorist

Figure 4-2
Revised Conflict Spectrum

Noncombat[a]	Unconventional		Conventional	Nuclear
Shows of Force	Special Operations[b]	/ Low / Intensity	Limited-Major	Limited-Major
	Terror Counterterror	/ Revolution Counter- / revolution		
		/ I,II,III,IV[c]		

```
<-------Most Likely Contingencies----------->

<-------------------Degree of U.S. Capability------------------------->

<---Adequate-----Poor to Adequate----------Adequate to Excellent---->
```

a. Examples are shows of force; economic assistance and aid; low levels of military assistance.

b. Includes hit-and-run raids, hostage rescue, and spearhead operations.

c. Phase I: Combined economic and other non-military assistance and aid; weapons assistance teams, military advisers, police training, military cadres for counterrevolutionary operations. Phase II: Special Forces teams plus phase I. Phase III: Special Forces headquarters and teams, light infantry units plus phases I and II. Phase IV: Light infantry combat role; US ground troops plus phases I, II, and II; Vietnam parallel.

activity directly emanating from these types of conflicts. Revolution and counterrevolution differ from special operations in time, missions, the character and purpose of adversaries, and the demands placed on open systems, among other things. They are a different dimension of unconventional conflicts that require different responses. There are several different components within revolution and counterrevolution that are directly linked to US political-military posture and require different strategies and doctrines. The term *low-intensity conflict* is used as a convenient label to encompass all of these considerations.

The label *low-intensity conflict* clearly reflects the policy directions and boundaries of conflict. These are not conflicts that are necessarily less violent or deadly than conventional conflicts. Rather, the term *low-intensity* characterizes the US political-military posture and the policies, strategies, and doctrine established to engage in such conflicts.

Low-Intensity Conflicts: Revolution and Counterrevolution

Revolution and counterrevolution are major elements included in the low-intensity conflict category. A number of important characteristics of low-intensity conflicts clearly distinguish them from conventional conflicts as well as special operations.

First, these conflicts are asymmetrical. Thus, for a third power, such as the United States in Vietnam, the conflict is primarily a limited one with respect to resources, political goals, and military operations. For the revolutionaries, the conflict is total; they are intent on overthrowing the existing system. Only later does the existing system (counterrevolutionary system) usually recognize and accept the fact that the conflict is a total struggle against the revolutionaries. In some cases, this acceptance comes too late to change the outcome of the struggle.

Second, low-intensity conflicts are most likely to be protracted using unconventional tactics. The nature of revolutionary warfare is focused on the political-social milieu and a variety of complex internal and external forces. Not only are these a result of relatively long-term political-social developments, but they are difficult to resolve by purely military or paramilitary instruments or doctrine. Indeed revolutionaries are likely to strike at the weakest part of the existing system, which tends to be in the political-social realm. At the same time, the revolutionaries attempt to build their own political system within the existing system.

If the existing system cannot be overthrown by a quick coup d'état or a mass uprising, then the revolutionaries are faced with the prospect of conducting a protracted revolutionary war similar to the Maoist struggle in China. This is generally the case. At the same time, the counter-revolutionary system is placed in a position of responding to challenges primarily aimed at ineffective and repressive government. Quick-fix or military solutions are rarely successful.

Third, revolutionary strategy and tactics combine armed conflict with political mobilization and organization. The armed elements of the revolutionary system engage in a variety of unconventional tactics, ranging from hit-and-run raids, sabotage, and assassinations to quick strike conventional operations. These are conducted at a time and place determined by the revolutionaries. The primary purpose is to create conditions that are conducive to revolutionary political organization and to demonstrate the ineffectiveness of the existing government. The existing system is at a distinct disadvantage; it is faced with the prospect of trying to protect everything in order to prove it is an effective government. But as Sun Tzu observed centuries ago, one who tries to protect everything protects nothing.

Fourth, a third power committed to support the existing system is placed in a difficult position. For the United States, this is particularly difficult. Not only does it become engaged in a protracted war, but it is faced with the prospect of supporting a system that is probably involved in a drive for modernity, with all of the pitfalls this entails. The major political actors in the United States, many of whom still suffer from the Vietnam malady, are likely to condition and qualify the extent of US involvement. Additionally, the US military is postured primarily for the high-intensity end of the conflict spectrum and is therefore at a distinct disadvantage if it becomes engaged in unconventional conflicts—particularly revolution and counterrevolution. Compounding the problem are the political constraints and expectations of American society regarding military operations and behavior.

Fifth, as a third power, the role of the United States is complicated by the confusing array of political forces that develop within Third World systems. In order to assist nonauthoritarian elites and groups, the United States must identify them early and be prepared to provide appropriate "non-Americanized" assistance so that such groups have an opportunity to prevent seizure of government power by authoritarian groups. For example, US assistance can be channelled through a friendly third state or by cooperative arrangements with states within a particular region. Further, the United States may simply use diplomacy to convince a third state to undertake assistance without direct US involvement. In a number of past instances, the United States has either intervened too late or has been unable to identify and link with nonauthoritarian elite and groups.

Sixth, the nature of developing systems makes them particularly susceptible to revolution. Most are trying to modernize, which means there is already an ongoing struggle between those supporting change and development and the traditional power groups, as well as between groups following different ideologies. Rarely are such societies democratic in Western terms. They are more likely to be authoritarian and, at best, only partly democratic. To expect anything different is to misunderstand and ignore the nature of the Third World and the problems of modernity.

These conditions make it difficult for the United States as a third power to develop a consensus within the nation as a whole or within its policy-making circles regarding acceptable policy and strategy. Support of systems that are not democratic strikes some as hypocritical. Thus, countervailing forces in the body politic and within the institutions of government have a major impact on what kinds of policies the United States can follow in Third World conflicts.

The same is true with respect to strategy and tactics. The nature of democracy precludes the use of certain means at the strategic level and prevents certain objectives from being pursued as part of national strategy. Examples are the use of weapons of mass destruction in revolution and counterrevolution and the objective of destroying the enemy by whatever means are difficult for any democracy to accept. This is in direct contrast to what is likely to occur in major wars.

Finally, the contrast between conventional and unconventional conflicts is perhaps sharpest in terms of mindsets, mental disposition, and staying power. In conventional conflicts, the perceptions of war, assessments of the enemy, and the whole focus of political-military action are rooted in traditional principles and philosophies. Additionally, the presumption is that such conflicts will occur against similarly postured adversaries. This is particularly clear in the United States, whose experience in war, which includes a variety of counterrevolutionary conflicts, is deeply rooted in European models, the Civil War, and World War II.

This experience has generated a body of literature, military thought, and a professional ethos that rarely acknowledges the existence of a type of warfare that does not necessarily adhere to Clausewitzian notions. It is presumed that training, organization, and doctrine designed for conventional conflicts and its special variations are adequate for any type of conflict along the conflict spectrum. Even in the atmosphere of the contemporary period with its fear of international terrorism and ongoing unconventional conflicts, US policy, strategy, doctrine, and organizational structures are focused on strategic wars (nuclear and major nonnuclear) and on European-type scenarios. This is not surprising given perceptions of who are major adversaries. The problem is that this preoccupation has minimized attention paid to other conflicts to such an extent that it is unlikely that the US political system and its military professionals are in a position to undertake military operations in an unconventional environment. (The exception is Special Forces.)

Terror and Counterterror

Terrorism, both as a strategy and as a tactic, is usually placed at the low end of the conflict spectrum since it rarely is considered to be a high-intensity conflict from the policy perspective. Yet terrorism cuts across many kinds of conflicts and has a number of variations that make it difficult to categorize neatly on one end of the spectrum. Terrorism is part of the larger spectrum of unconventional conflicts.

The purpose of terrorism, broadly defined, is to create fear in a large segment of a population in order to influence a government to accept the demands of terrorists. Using hostages as pawns, terrorists try to affect a larger audience. The key to the terrorist act is the creation of fear, not only by the threat of a particular act but also by the apparent unpredictability and clandestine nature of those involved.

An important part of the terrorist act is gaining access to the mass media in order to publicize the act. For the most part, terrorism is theater. To perform properly, there must be an audience, which includes the public of the target government, as well as the international world. In a study of terrorism and the media, one authority concluded, "The Western mass media through their attention provide the terrorist group with the credibility it might not otherwise have."[5] This was true in the skyjacking of TWA flight 847 in June 1985 and the subsequent 17-day ordeal of 39 American hostages held by Shiite Moslems in Beirut, Lebanon. The media, particularly US television, followed the dramatic events not only by reports from

Lebanon and the Middle East but by reports from Europe, the United States, and the homes of families of hostages. Television became a major participant in the event. Indeed, the terrorists and the Amal leader Nabih Berrih seemed to be in a position to manipulate television in order to publicize the Shiite political message. Television provided direct access to the American people, which the Shiite leader did not hesitate to exploit. Nonetheless, many Americans felt that television coverage of the event was important and necessary.

Although most terrorist acts are similar in their operational patterns, terrorist groups differ in their motivation and source of support. There are terrorist groups whose prime purpose is terror for the sake of terror. Such groups tend to be autonomous and nihilistic and place themselves squarely against the system in an attempt to discredit or destroy it while proclaiming their acts in the name of the "people" for the sake of some vague political cause. The Baader-Meinhof Gang, the Japanese Red Army, and the Symbionese Liberation Army were (and are) examples of such groups.

The second category is revolutionary terror. Terror associated with revolution is a tactic used to further the revolutionary cause. In most instances, such terror is local; it is aimed directly at the existing system in the specific territory that the system controls or occupies. At the same time, such terrorist activity is usually tempered by the realization that success is based on the ability of the revolutionary leadership to win the hearts and minds of the people. It is hardly useful to terrorize the people whose willing support is needed to overthrow the existing system. For example, during the communist revolution in China, Mao was careful to point out the need to restrain terrorist activity and to use it selectively, primarily against government officials, government targets, and staunch supporters of the counterrevolutionary system. Terrorist activity by the Vietcong during the Vietnam War was another example of revolutionary terror. However, even revolutionary terrorism focused on a particular conflict area attempts to influence a larger population through fear—fear that the existing government is incapable and that the best chance for survival is with the revolutionary system.

The final category is state-supported terrorism. This is a particularly elusive category because it is difficult to prove support of terrorists by one state or another. There are strong evidence and strong political indicators, however, that a number of states not only support terrorist activity but provide financial support, training bases, logistics, and even leadership and operational implementation while publicly denying such involvement.

The US government has periodically pointed to Libya's Muammar Qaddafi as a strong supporter of terrorist groups. Indeed, Colonel Qaddafi has publicly proclaimed his support of terrorist operations. The United States has also identified Iran and the fundamentalist Islamic movement as the source of much of the current terrorist activity in the Middle East. The Palestine Liberation Organization (PLO), supported by several states, is well known for its activities in the Mideast, Europe, and Latin America. Syria is also a major source of terrorist activity, the role of President Hassad el Assad in the release of TWA flight 847 hostages notwithstanding. The attempted assassination of the pope implicated the Soviet Union and was further evidence of its support of wide-ranging terrorist activity from Europe to Latin America to South Africa. What is ominous is that there seems to be a loose international network of terrorists, many of whom seem to be operating at the behest of particular states, including the Soviet Union.[6]

State-supported terrorism can also be aimed at the state's own citizens as a control measure. Closed systems such as the Soviet Union are prime examples: the destruction of the Kulaks, the terror against the Ukrainians, and the use of terror against Soviet dissidents in the current period. The use of such terror by repressive regimes, military dictatorships, and personalistic systems has been well publicized in the United States. It also exists in the terrorism inherent in South Africa's apartheid system.

Less well known and obfuscated by some in the United States is state-supported terrorism undertaken by Third World regimes such as Nicaragua under Ortega and Zimbabwe under Mugabe. The terror used by the Nicaraguan regime, for example, is at times subtle and at other times quite clear. Its campaign against the Catholic church, the previously independent newspaper *La Prensa*, the Miskito Indians, and opposition political groups are cases in point. There is strong evidence that the Nicaraguan regime has links to Cuba and the Soviet Union.[7]

At the same time, Nicaragua has engaged in an extensive public relations campaign in the United States to project an image of justice and democracy. Indeed, it is reported that Managua had gone so far as to hire a US public relations firm to help convince Americans of the goodness of the Ortega regime. According to some reports, Nicaraguan representatives and their supporters in the United States are active in trying to mobilize American public opinion against US policies in Central America. Various lobbying groups and special interest groups have been organized and are active in the United States advocating support of the Ortega regime and opposing the Duarte government in El Salvador. Such groups include the North American Congress on Latin America (NACLA), the Washington Office on Latin America (WOLA), the Council on Hemispheric Affairs (COHA), and the Committee in Solidarity with the People of El Salvador (CISPES). Witness for Peace, another advocacy group, has ties with various colleges and universities. Many of these groups provide information to and are linked with various church groups in the United States, as well as to several congressmen. According to some, much of the advocacy of these groups is colored by political biases, disinformation and misinformation.[8]

The issue is not political orientation and advocacy, however, but access. This kind of political-psychological effort typifies the strategy of those engaged in terrorism,

their supporters, and other types of unconventional conflicts: using the instruments of open systems to gain access to the public and to influence the public agenda. At
the same time, open systems are denied real access to the
people and instruments in closed systems such as Nicaragua, Cuba, and the Soviet Union or to a particular
terrorist group.

How can a democratic system such as the United States
respond to and prevent terrorism? The United States is by
nature an open system, and as such terrorists, their supporters, and those engaged in other types of unconventional conflicts can use the basis of the system in an
attempt to destroy it.

The ability of the United States to respond to terrorism
and other types of unconventional conflicts is constrained
and limited by the view the nation has of itself and its
expectations as a democracy. This does not mean that a
democracy cannot find reasonably effective responses. It
does mean that effective response to terrorism requires
that a democracy reexamine its basic values in the light of
the real world and consider the costs and consequences of
various types of responses. Public understanding of the
nature of terrorism, terrorists, and unconventional conflicts is essential.

From this can evolve long-range, effective counterterror policy and strategy resting on three components:
preventive measures, hostage rescue-strike force, and retaliation. There are a number of options in each of these
categories that democracies can undertake effectively
within the bounds of propriety and the rule of law. Some
others require greater latitude but can be controlled, super-
vised, and justified on the basis of democratic survival.

Preventive measures are primarily efforts designed to
gather information and engage in intelligence activities
aimed at all categories of terrorists and terrorism. This
means that there must exist within the United States and
its overseas instrumentalities an intelligence system capable of identifying terrorist groups or potential terrorist
groups, developing patterns of their activities, identifying

individual terrorists by name, including their personality and history, and designing clandestine networks to track and, if possible, penetrate terrorist organizations. Successful preemptive operations are based on such intelligence measures. To do all of these properly, the intelligence system must be highly professional, it must understand the dilemmas of democracy in dealing with unconventional conflicts, and it must have wide latitude to engage in intelligence activities. Indeed, effective intelligence is essential for any effective policy and strategy aimed at all types of unconventional conflicts.

The second capability is hostage rescue and strike force operations. In the simplest terms, this means the ability to undertake military or combined civilian-military operations against ongoing terrorist acts. Examples include the Israeli rescue of Air France passengers at Entebbe airport in Uganda in 1976 and the operations of the British Special Air Squadron (SAS) Regiment in storming the Iranian embassy in London in 1980. In a negative sense, the failure of America's Delta Force to rescue the hostages in Iran in 1979 provided another example of hostage rescue operations.[9] The United States must not only develop and maintain such a capability, but at some stage this must be demonstrated if it is to be credible. Quiet but forceful diplomacy and the involvement of third parties go hand in hand with the possible use of rescue operations.

The third component is retaliation. Although it may be easy for some to demand revenge and retaliation following a terrorist act, it is difficult many times to identify the specific terrorist group, where they are located, or their support base. This does not mean that one cannot retaliate, but it is not simply a matter of striking at somebody, somewhere. Indeed, not to retaliate in some appropriate way against terrorists and their supporters can undermine the entire counterterror effort.

The scope and intensity of the retaliation must be done in a precise way so that the terrorists and their supporters are clear as to the linkage between the retaliatory act and the terrorist activity (for example, the US interception in October 1985 of the Egyptian aircraft carrying four terrorists responsible for the *Achille Lauro* piracy and murder of an American and the US bombing of Libyan bases in April 1986). Retaliatory measures include a wide range of options from diplomatic and economic sanctions to the use of military force.

Only through the effective combination of all three and an effective capability in each can US counterterror policy and strategy be made credible. Equally important, policy and strategy is much more effective if these components are undertaken by multinational efforts. But it must be realized that even the most effective counterterror policy and strategy is not without costs in lives as well as in the quality of open systems.

The basic dilemma for the United States is clear: how far can a democracy go in developing and carrying out counterterror operations without becoming like them? That is, at what point does the United States itself become a terrorist state? There is no easy answer. It is particularly difficult to try to differentiate what actions are acceptable within democratic boundaries from actions that are unacceptable. It may be best to seek answers by recognizing that the highest value is the survival of the democratic system. Democracy has a right to defend itself. Given the traditions of government accountability, responsibility, and commitment to Judeo-Christian values, the United States can surely develop effective oversight, control, and accountability of its political-military instruments, even if allowing them a greater latitude to engage in counterterror and other types of unconventional conflicts. To do anything less is to invite the self-destruct syndrome described by Jean-François Revel and well summed by the statement, "Democratic civilization is the first in history to blame itself because another power is working to destroy it."[10]

The problems in dealing with terrorism and terrorists are the same as those facing open systems in responding to unconventional conflicts across the conflict spectrum.

Although this book concentrates primarily on low-intensity conflicts, most of what is studied and analyzed applies equally to various forms of terrorism.

In developing counterterror capability, the United States has created special operations forces. Additionally, special agencies within the Department of State and the Federal Bureau of Investigation have been formed to study terrorism and develop policies and strategies to respond.[11]

SUMMARY AND CONCLUSIONS

Revolutionary and counterrevolutionary conflicts differ considerably from conventional and nuclear wars, and these differences are reflected in the intensity of conflict and US capability.

The differences between the vast middle range of conflicts and the high and low ends of the conflict spectrum are best summed up by focusing on the key to success in such conflicts. The primary determinant of US policy effectiveness is the quality of the personnel on the ground in low-intensity conflicts, as well as in special operations. This is particularly important in low-intensity conflicts. Although the number of forces, their equipment, and military training are important, these are not usually the critical elements in such conflicts. For example, a handful of US Special Forces personnel were directly responsible for the defeat and capture of Che Guevara's forces in Bolivia. Trained personnel, sensitive to the foreign cultural environment in which they operate, with a deep understanding of the nature of revolution and counterrevolution, placed in critical positions at the planning and operational levels, are much more important than battalions of troops responding to attacks by revolutionary forces.

The nature of the US military profession and the US way of war was summed up by General Weyand:

There is no such thing as a war fought on the cheap.
War is death and destruction. The American way of war
is particularly violent, deadly and dreadful. We believe
in using "things"—artillery, bombs, massive firepower
—in order to conserve our soldiers' lives.[12]

General Weyand went on to say that "the Army must
make the price of involvement clear before we get involved."[13]

The problem is that the outcomes of revolutionary and
counterrevolutionary conflicts may not in the long run be
determined by the amount of firepower or technological
devices but rather by what is taking place of a political and
psychological nature deep within the society. Massive
firepower and technological advantage may actually trigger a more determined response against a third power
such as the United States, especially when such a power is
committed to democratic norms and values.

Moreover, the nature of revolutionary and counterrevolutionary conflicts often means engagement and involvement long before the clarity of the threat can be
conveyed to the people—if it can ever be conveyed. It
may be that a higher-visibility involvement by US forces
may become necessary long before a consensus can be developed within the body politic and before crisis proportions are reached. Indeed, once crisis proportions are
reached in revolutionary and counterrevolutionary conflicts, it may be too late for the United States to become
effectively involved.

In the conflict spectrum, the general characteristics of
the various conflicts have been listed, as have been the
general capabilities of the US political-military posture.
The US political-military posture seems best suited to the
high intensity and the extreme lowest end of the conflict
spectrum. US capability is at its lowest in the middle
range.

Since 1975, the United States has not effectively established itself as a state with the national will, political
resolve, and staying power to grapple with unconventional conflicts and Third World issues (although there

are some signs of change). Yet images of the United States and perceptions of its staying power are critical in influencing and affecting the views of those intent on engaging in unconventional warfare. Even with a vast military instrument, the United States may find itself unable to respond effectively to low-intensity conflicts and engage in special operations because of such images and perceptions.

The United States has had a long and varied history in unconventional conflicts ranging from the pre-Revolutionary period (the French-Indian Wars) to Central America in the 1920s and 1930s. From this experience, it appears that few, if any, lessons have been learned, and in some respects, the wrong lessons have been learned. The high point was the Vietnam War. It provides the immediate historical substance and focal point in examining policy, strategy, and doctrine in the current period. Vietnam was not an aberration of policy but one of a long line of unconventional conflicts in which the United States was involved.

NOTES

1. The conflict spectrum is adopted from Sam C. Sarkesian, "American Policy and Low-Intensity Conflict: An Overview," in Sam C. Sarkesian and William L. Scully, *U.S. Policy and Low-intensity Conflict: Potentials for Military Struggles in the 1980s* (New Brunswick, N.J.: Transaction Books, 1981), p. 6.

2. One of the better short treatments of the AirLand Battle doctrine is Colonel John R. Landry (USA), Colonel Malcolm B. Armstrong (USAF), Colonel Howell M. Estes, III (USAF), Lt. Colonel Wesley K. Clark (USA), and Boyd D. Sutton (CIA), "Deep Attack in Defense of Central Europe: Implications for Strategy and Doctrine," in *Essays on Strategy* (Washington, D.C.: National Defense University Press, 1984). For example, the authors write, "AirLand Battle doctrine attempts to deny success to an aggressor's attack by seizing and maintaining the initiative. . . . Two battles must be fought simultaneously and in close coordination: a forward battle against committed units; and a deep battle against uncommitted forces. . . . While

the doctrine seeks a balance between maneuver and fire-power, it particularly emphasizes maneuver. . . . Because the doctrine focuses on corps operations, it envisions the conduct of the deep battle out to 100-150 kilometers—the limit of the corps commander's area of influence" (p. 36).

For the official statement of the AirLand Battle doctrine, see *U.S. Army Field Manual, FM 100-5* (Washington, D.C.: Department of the Army, August 20, 1982). See also Arie van der Vlis, "AirLand Battle in NATO, A European View," *Parameters* 14, no. 2 (Summer 1984):10-14.

3. Michael Howard, *The Causes of Wars and Other Essays,* 2d ed., enlarged (Cambridge: Harvard University Press, 1984), p. 262.

4. Aaron L. Friedberg, "The Evolution of U.S. Strategic Doctrine," in Samuel P. Huntington, ed., *The Strategic Imperative: New Policies for American Security* (Cambridge, Mass.: Ballinger Publishing Co., 1982), esp. pp. 78-80.

5. Michael J. Kelly and Thomas H. Mitchell, "Transnational Terrorism and the Western Elite Press," in Doris A. Graber, ed., *Media Power in Politics* (Washington, D.C.: Congressional Quarterly Press, 1984), p. 283.

6. See, for example, Claire Sterling, *The Terror Network* (New York: Berkely Books, 1981), and Roberta Goren, *The Soviet Union and Terrorism* (New York: Allen and Unwin, 1984).

7. See, for example, Humberto Belli, *Christians under Fire* (Garden City, Mich.: Instituto Puebla, 1984); Arturo Cruz, "Nicaragua's Imperiled Revolution," *Foreign Affairs* 61 (Summer 1983); and Ricardo Lizano, "A Revolution of Disillusion; Nicaragua's Repression by Another Name," *World Press Review* (June 1983): 37-38; Jim Denton, "Contra Atrocities, or a Covert Propaganda War?" *Wall Street Journal*, April 23, 1985; and Georgie Anne Geyer, "American Protesters Miss Real Issues of Nicaragua," *Chicago Sun-Times*, June 6, 1985, p. 76.

8. See, for example, Georgie Anne Geyer, "This peace witness was mostly witless," *Chicago Sun-Times*, August 13, 1985, p. 35; Mike Sullivan, "La Prensa's 'freedom' only a sham, its editor says," *Washington Times*, December 20, 1983, p. 1; and Joan Frawley, "The Left's Latin American Lobby," The Heritage Foundation, *Institution Analysis*, October 11, 1984.

9. Colonel Charles Beckwith and Donald Knox, *Delta Force: America's Counterterrorist Unit and the Mission to*

Rescue the Hostages in Iran (New York: Harcourt Brace Jovanovich, 1983).

10. Jean-François Revel, *How Democracies Perish* (Garden City, N.Y.: Doubleday, Inc., 1983), p. 7.

11. See Robert M. Sayre, "Combatting Terrorism: American Policy and Organization," *Department of State Bulletin* 82, no. 2065 (August 1982): 1-7.

12. Quoted in Harry G. Summers, Jr., *On Strategy: The Vietnam War in Context* (Carlisle Barracks, Penn.: U.S. Army War College, 1981), p. 25.

13. Ibid.

PART II

The US Political-Military Posture:
The Response

5

Vietnam and After

The Vietnam War has become part of the American psyche. Although more than a decade has passed since the war ended, many Americans are still not sure what it was about or how it happened. Scholars also remain in disagreement about the meaning of events and argue about what could have or should have been done. Even with the belated recognition of the men and women who served in Vietnam, most Americans prefer to put the war behind them and try to forget the trauma of the 1960s and 1970s. Unfortunately, Americans have also forgotten the kind of war that was fought in Vietnam (see Figure 5-1). In this sense it has become a forgotten war.[1] What is important for our study is that the Vietnam experience has added to the misconceptions and misdirections of US unconventional warfare policy, strategy, and political-military posture.

A thorough understanding of the evolution of the US military capability and effectiveness in unconventional warfare requires a serious study of its formative period, 1950-1960, for it was during this period that the United States tried to develop an unconventional warfare capability and established the basis for later Vietnam strategy. It also forms the background for the current US posture.

Throughout the formative period, the subject of low-intensity conflict was completely submerged by the perceived strategic threat from the Soviet Union and later from Mainland China. The atomic and nuclear battlefields were based on a European scenario. This was broadened to include a strategy of massive retaliation against the Soviet heartland should the Soviets engage in aggression anywhere in the world. Flexible response followed as the Soviets developed their own nuclear capability neutralizing the concept of massive US response. US capability in low-intensity conflict must be seen in the context of these strategic concerns and threat perceptions.

The response to low-intensity conflict was fashioned out of the conventional US political-military strategy that had been formed during the immediate post-World War II period. The introduction of atomic and nuclear weapons, Soviet military power and expansion, combined with decolonization, and the rise of communist China changed the international security situation that followed the Korean War. But even with the experience of the Korean War behind them, Americans tended to view the world with a mind-set more appropriate to the World War II era. This posture was reaffirmed by important characteristics of the US political system.

Wars were seen as a struggle between good and evil. Thus, Americans tended to perceive wars as a challenge to democracy and the American way of life, to be met by mobilization of manpower and resources and a drive for total victory. The idea that wars could be fought for limited objectives or for political posturing was far removed from the American mentality.

Moreover, the military is governed by a well-established concept of civilian control. Reaching back to the Founding Fathers, the constitutional provision of civilian control of the military has not been seriously challenged. Indeed, it is well embodied in the military value system. It follows that US military personnel are (and were) expected to perform within the context of democratic rules and norms, with all of the moral and ethical implications

Figure 5-1
South Vietnam

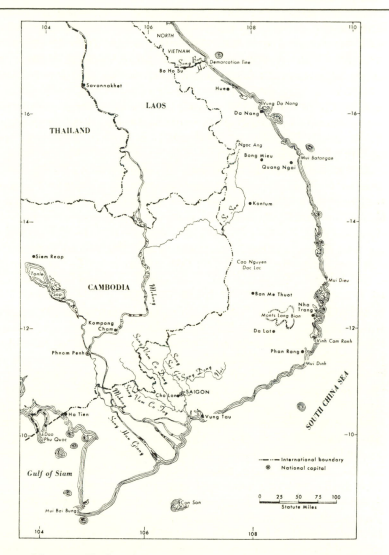

From: Harvey H. Smith, et al., *Area handbook for South Vietnam* (Washington, D.C.: U.S. Government Printing Office, April 1967), p. 14.

these suggest. Thus, the good guy-bad guy syndrome characteristic of World War I and II prevailed, with the United States expected to enter a conflict as the good guy. In such circumstances, it is presumed that the identification of the enemy is clear and that American intentions and purposes are clear. Unfortunately, unconventional conflicts hardly adhere to such democratic notions. In brief, a perceptual lens is used to assess unconventional conflicts (see figures 4-1 and 4-2) leading to policy, strategy, and doctrines that are rooted in conventional organizational postures, conceptual misunderstanding, and doctrinal confusion, all in the context of constraints imposed by the US political system.

Conceptual and doctrinal confusion regarding low-intensity conflict evolves from a number of factors. First there exists a doctrinal view based on the notion that low-intensity conflict is (and was) an amalgam of special operations (Ranger/Commando missions) and special forces-type missions. It is assumed, therefore, that units trained and organized for hit-and-run raids and long-range patrols, for example, can readily undertake all kinds of low-intensity conflict missions. Similarly, many view Special Forces as a "super" Ranger/Commando organization. Indeed, Special Forces traces its lineage to the First Special Service Force of World War II, which in many respects epitomized special operations.

Another component of this doctrinal confusion is the presumption that low-intensity conflict (as originally conceived) is an adjunct to conventional operations. Even when some distinction is made between special operations and Special Forces missions, it is presumed that guerrilla warfare (the initial primary mission assigned to Special Forces) is an adjunct to conventional operations. The most glaring example of this was when the 10th Special Forces was assigned to Germany. Planners in US European headquarters assessed the effectiveness of the 10th Special Forces by the number of men the unit could put on the line. Related to this is the view held by many military men that conventional units organized and trained for the European battlefield were (and are) quite capable of engaging in any kind of conflict anywhere. Thus, little attention was given to the nature of unconventional conflicts or to the kind of mental preparation needed for engaging in them.

In my view, special operations are special types of conventional operations undertaken by highly trained conventional elite units such as Rangers, and include counter terror (hostage rescue) missions and operations such as Grenada. Special Forces should be used primarily for strategic and long range unconventional missions such as revolution and counterrevolution and requires unconventional training, planning, and organization.

Although there has been improvement in the organizational direction and doctrinal development for unconventional conflicts, even as late as 1985 the US military still placed special operation units with Special Forces. The First Special Operations Command at Fort Bragg, North Carolina, includes Special Forces, Rangers, civic action and psychological warfare units, and Delta Force (counterterror unit). Special units from the US Navy and Air Force were designated to serve with the command.

Perhaps the most fundamental issue is conceptual: disagreements and confusion over the nature of and response to low-intensity conflict. Special operations, guerrilla war, insurgency, revolution, counterinsurgency, and counterrevolution are generally conceived of in similar terms, yet they differ considerably in their strategic and tactical dimensions, as well as in their civilian and military components. These conceptual problems, in turn, are reflected in the composition, planning, and training of forces designed for low-intensity conflict.

Many of the conflicts in the Third World and those in which the United States has (and may have) a vital interest are revolutionary in nature. Revolution is more than guerrilla war and insurgency; it is a total war against the existing political system with its main battlefield in the political-social milieu. Political mobilization, psycho-

logical war, propaganda, and terrorism are the major instruments of revolutionary conflicts. Armed struggle is
important, of course, but it is primarily an adjunct to the
major struggle. Political mobilizers and cadres are more
important in the long run than battlefield soldiers. This is
a view that has been and remains difficult for US civilian
and military leaders and officials to grasp.

The formative period institutionalized the doctrinal
confusion and conceptual misunderstanding that exist
today.[2] The hesitancy with which planners approached
the establishment of low-intensity conflict capability reflected the political and military constraints placed on
such operations. Conventional military wisdom, superpower threat perceptions, and lessons of the grand battles
of the past dominated military professionalism. Civilian
policy makers hardly did any better, viewing guerrilla war
and low-intensity conflict as something undemocratic
while expecting to counter such warfare according to
democratic rules and with a conventional military posture. Those few within military and civilian circles who
understood the nature of low-intensity conflict found it
difficult to translate this into realistic policy, strategy, and
organizational capability.

Organizational resistance, conceptual misunderstanding, and doctrinal confusion of the formative period have
yet to be overcome. Not only is this seen in current policy
debates regarding US involvement in Third World areas
but also in the persistent downgrading of those within the
military who are committed to a career in low-intensity
conflict. Finally, there is always the danger that a serious
response to low-intensity conflict will be designed in conventional terms, with all of the mistakes and misunder-
standings of the formative period.

The lessons of the formative period show that, at best,
incremental changes are the most that can be achieved
within military organizations. Such changes are likely to
be closely linked to the underlying traditions and philo-

sophical substance of US democracy. A system committed to the principles of liberal democracy giving birth to a military resting on absolute civilian control and whose military traditions and heritage are based primarily on regulars fighting regulars cannot adapt readily—if at all —to unconventional conflict, particularly to its most challenging form, revolution and counterrevolution. Only when civilian leaders in the United States understand the character of unconventional conflict and this in turn is transmitted to the people can there be an effective conceptual, organizational, and doctrinal adaptation to such conflicts. It is not impossible, but it will be difficult and demanding, testing the moral and ethical fiber of the democratic system.

VIETNAM: THE DEBATE CONTINUES

The 1980s brought a continuing debate on the meaning of Vietnam. Revisionists disagree with traditionalists, and military men still argue among themselves as to what could or could not have been done in Vietnam and the impact of the war on military professionalism.[3] It is still difficult to draw lessons from Vietnam because no one is quite sure what took place there. For the military this has made it difficult to develop tactical guidelines, doctrines, and organizational structures for unconventional wars.

Still, the Vietnam War has had a profound impact on the political-military posture of the United States with respect to unconventional warfare. This impact is most pronounced in the military. It is incorrect to see Vietnam as an aberration of US policy and strategy. The Vietnam experience was only one instance, albeit a major one, of a long list of US involvement in unconventional warfare, including the Second Seminole War (1835-1842), the Philippines War and the Moro Wars (1899-1914), the punitive expedition into Mexico (1916), and the Nicaraguan affair (Sandino Chase, 1927-1935).[4]

LITERATURE ON THE UNITED STATES AND VIETNAM

The amount of literature on US involvement in Vietnam is constantly increasing. Although a great deal of work is aimed at clarifying the major issues, the war remains perplexing to many. Part of this is a result of the varying perspectives by authors who represent different disciplines and ideological positions. This confusion is also due to the complexity of the war itself and the ambiguous circumstances under which the United States became involved. Finally, the contradictory views and positions taken by a variety of elected officials and other major political actors, both military and civilian, have further clouded the issues.

It is important for our purposes to identify several critical areas in the literature that provide reference points for our own study. It must be kept in mind, however, that the intent here is not to try to untangle all the issues—it is unlikely this could be done—or to resolve them once and for all.

There are two major dimensions in the literature of the United States and Vietnam: the impact of the war on the United States and the nations's role as a third (external) power in support of an existing counterrevolutionary system, or, more specifically, the impact of the United States on South Vietnam. Although many works consider both of these dimensions, generally one or the other dimension emerges as the dominant theme.

Morality of US Involvement

The first group of studies generally revolve around the theme that by the late 1960s, many Americans viewed involvement in the Vietnam War as immoral and illegal. The 1968 election of Richard Nixon as President of the United States is seen as the key element in reflecting domestic discontent. Henry Kissinger writes, "For the war had set into motion forces transcending the issues and emotions that went beyond the substance of the debate."[5] This view is reflected in other works. For example, one author concludes that "the main lesson of Vietnam lies at home. Vietnam led directly to Watergate and to the severest constitutional crisis in U.S. history since the Civil War."[6]

There is evidence to suggest that Lyndon Johnson's decision not to seek reelection in 1968 was a direct result of the domestic discontent over the prosecution of the war. In his own work, Johnson provides revealing insights on the constraints and limitations placed on the conduct of the war by domestic political considerations. He admits that the breakdown of consensus led to his decision not to seek reelection.[7]

Some studies deal with the US policy process and decisionmaking. These include attention to such matters as the mind-sets of those in policy-making circles and to the bureaucratic struggles within the Johnson administration regarding policy and strategy.[8] Even works whose purpose was to examine US actions in Vietnam could not ignore what was happening in the United States itself. In this vein, one foreign expert on counterrevolution concluded,

> It was my own view in June, 1968, that the United States had lost the war because all the odds appeared to favour a sell-out, however camouflaged, which would lead to the withdrawal of American forces and a takeover of South Vietnam by the North, with or without transitional arrangements and whether negotiated or not.[9]

This is exactly what took place in the mid-1970s.

An important source on the US policy-making and decision processes is a volume of official papers that have become famous because of the legal events associated with them: the Pentagon Papers.[10] This collection of official reports and memoranda provides an extraordinary view of the internal bureaucratic process and political dynamics that occurred within the various agencies of government during the Vietnam War period. Covering the period from 1945 under President Truman to the Tet offensive in

Vietnam in early 1968, these papers reinforce the view held by a number of observers that the conduct of the war was characterized by misjudgments, misinterpretations, and bureaucratic commitment to a lost cause.

US Military in Vietnam

The literature in the second group is primarily concerned with the military aspect of the war and focuses on the United States in Vietnam. These works are particularly important because they provide views on the role of a third (external) power in support of an existing counter-revolutionary system and thus provide insights applicable to the contemporary period.

An important contribution to the literature is by Summers, a former military professional. Although aimed at strategic issues, it includes observations about the impact of the war on military men and assesses tactical doctrine as well as US policy making.[11] Applying Clausewitzian logic, the author points out that US military operations in Vietnam violated basic principles of war. Time after time, "instead of providing professional military advice on how to fight the war the military more and more joined with the systems analysts in determining the material means to win."[12] As a result, according to the author, little serious attention was given to the strategy for victory and proper tactics.

As if to underscore this issue, the author adds a personal touch. As a US army colonel negotiating with the North Vietnamese delegation in 1975, the author engaged in a conversation with a North Vietnamese colonel. "'You know you never defeated us on the battlefield,' said the American colonel. The North Vietnamese colonel thought about this remark and a moment later replied, 'That may be so, but it is also irrelevant.'"[13]

Many books by civilian and military authors portray the Vietnam War from the level of ground combat.[14] In an early book, one author perhaps anticipated the negative impact on American fighting men when he wrote in 1967,

In no other war have respected voices in the community, people in authority, people of eminence— senators, representatives, clergymen, professors, even some military men—questioned the morality as well as wisdom of our [U.S] intervention and raised grave doubts about our motives. The pacifists and conscientious objectors we have always had with us, but never before have the halls of Congress and the hearing rooms of the Senate Foreign Relations Committee echoed against our involvement, while half a world away 400,000 American troops already are committed to fighting and dying.[15]

In still other works, authors assess the effect of the war on the military. For example, in one study of the US military, the author provides a prophetic insight. He quotes a senior US Army general as saying at the height of the Vietnam War, "I'll be damned if I will permit the U.S. Army, its institutions, its doctrine and its traditions to be destroyed just to win this lousy war."[16]

Authors have pointed out the courage of Americans fighting on the ground and also the peculiar perplexities and dangers they faced. Of particular importance is not only the linkage between what was occurring in the United States and to Americans in Vietnam but also the views of Americans in Vietnam regarding the war. Most Americans in Vietnam did not understand their allies, the South Vietnamese, nor did they understand their enemies or the nature of the war. This is a major theme in one study, which highlights the point by quoting an American soldier stationed in Vietnam:

When we got here, we landed on a different planet. In Germany and Japan, I guess there was a thread of contact, but even when a Vietnamese guy speaks perfect English I don't know what the hell he's talking about.[17]

The consequences of the war on American fighting men in Vietnam are still vigorously debated. During the course of the war, a number of publications addressed this issue on a short-term basis. In the main, most of these works pointed out the difficulties of combat and the problems that were created for American military men.[18] Works appearing in the late 1970s and early 1980s seemed to follow in the same pattern.

Some studies used the Vietnam experience as the basis for critically assessing the military profession as a whole. An important work in this regard is the U.S. Army War College's study of military professionalism.[19] Among other things, this study points out that the war had a major negative impact on professionalism; it motivated some officers to seek career-oriented command and staff positions, other officers fell into the *ticket-punching game,* and a number of officers performed poorly in some combat situations.[20] Ticket punching refers to officers whose primary concern is rapid promotion and prestige positions, even if this means becoming involved in internal politics. Such officers seek to manipulate their careers to obtain the "right" assignments (tickets) and to insure that these are duly noted on their service records (punching). Much of this can be traced to the nature and character of revolution and counterrevolution and the difficulty of translating conventional doctrine and traditional professional expectations into effective counterrevolutionary operations. The unconventional nature of the war, the study concludes, exposed serious professional failings, particularly among the middle and higher-ranking army officers.

One of the most critical military assessments is the report by Major General Peers of the My Lai massacre.[21] Not only did the report reinforce the view of those who held that the war had a largely negative impact on American fighting men, but it also concluded that there was a serious negative impact on US military professionalism. The cover-up of the My Lai massacre by several high-ranking army officers did little for the image of the military officer as a moral, ethical, and thoughtful professional.

In the late 1970s, questions persisted regarding US strategy and tactics in Vietnam. Within the broader context of these questions, the critical analysis of US military professionalism continued. One military writer of the period notes, for example, "Given the eventual outcome of the war, however, one cannot help but experience lingering doubts about the validity of American tactics. . . . The Vietnam War greatly affected the U.S. Army." Noting the questions raised about drug abuse and racial difficulties and their impact on US combat effectiveness, the author concludes that "while such problems are partially attributable to the nature of the fighting in Southeast Asia, they also reveal fundamental problems with leadership, morale and training."[22] In reviewing this aspect of the literature, one comes away with the impression that Vietnam remains complex, ambiguous, and misunderstood within the military profession.

South Vietnamese Society and the US Impact

Studies of South Vietnamese society that relate directly to US involvement also provide important material for assessing US military and political strategy. The cultural context within which revolution takes place directly affects the third power's ability to conduct political-military operations. Effective strategy and doctrine for unconventional conflict require sensitivity to and understanding of the politics and culture of the target area. Thus, an understanding of South Vietnamese history and society was essential for the proper conduct of US operations in Vietnam. Unfortunately, few Americans recognized and understood this.[23]

Studies of Vietnamese society stress the importance of village life and the notion of law to the coherency of society.[24] The breakdown of traditional rule in the villages, the disruptions caused by various government programs, and the impact of the revolutionaries were important factors in the disintegration of peasant society. As the disruption increased, it became more difficult for the South Vietnamese government to rule effectively in the countryside and to prosecute the war. A close reading of such studies provides ample evidence why Americans had such difficulty understanding the Vietnamese culture and political system.[25] The values, experience, and outlook of most Americans provided little empathy for or understanding of Vietnamese peasant life, the family and ancestral networks, and the nature of Buddhist society.

In a book written by a South Vietnamese Buddhist monk, this aspect of the relationship between Americans and South Vietnam is well analyzed. Trying to find a peaceful solution to the Vietnam War, Thich Nhat Hanh traces the historical development of South Vietnamese society and shows how US involvement in the war affected many South Vietnamese:

> The more American troops sent to Vietnam, the more the anti-American campaign led by the NLF becomes successful. Anger and hatred rise in the hearts of the peasants as they see their villages burned, their compatriots killed, their houses destroyed. Pictures showing NLF soldiers with arms tied, followed by American soldiers holding guns with bayonets, make people think of the Indochina war between the French and the Viet Minh and cause pain even to the anti-Communist Vietnamese.[26]

Former high-ranking officials in the South Vietnamese government have added their voices to the growing critical assessment of the US role in the Vietnam War. For example, General Cao Van Vien, the last chairman of the South Vietnamese Joint General Staff, argues that the turning point of the war was the 1973 Paris Agreement, which "was served on South Vietnam like a death warrant." He goes on to note that the stage was set earlier for the defeat of South Vietnam:

> There is no doubt that the South Vietnamese soldier could fight, and he did fight well! But for years he had learned to do things the easy way, taking for granted the needed supplies would never cease to flow and that if he were in any kind of trouble "Big Brother" would always be there to "bail him out." ... So, when the United States shifted its policy to negotiation and began withdrawing

its forces from Vietnam under ... "Vietnamization," the
Republic of Vietnam armed forces were not entirely
prepared to take over, psychologically or physically.[27]

Nguyen Cao Ky, former prime minister of the republic
of Vietnam, is particularly critical of US misunderstanding of Vietnam and revolution and its disregard of
the sacrifices of the South Vietnamese. In a biting narrative, he writes about the 1973 Paris Agreement:

> All of us who witnessed the sellout at the Paris talks had
> no hesitation in believing that it was now only a ques-
> tion of time before the North Vietnamese attacked us.
> They were in no hurry, for each day they waited meant a
> drop in South Vietnamese morale as we watched our
> one-time allies on their way back home—and, to them,
> peace.[28]

Other works written by Americans as well as South
Vietnamese reach similar conclusions regarding the US
impact on South Vietnam.[29] The critical assessment of
the US role in Vietnam by South Vietnamese officials,
civilian and military, sheds considerable light on the differences between allies regarding the conduct of the war.
These differences are even greater when considering the
nature and conduct of the war from the point of view of
the North Vietnamese and the Vietcong.[30] The debate
continues as to the impact of the United States on Vietnam and the proper strategy and doctrine of the US
military.[31]

Summary

The general themes and analysis in the literature on
the United States and Vietnam are critical of US policy
makers. Not only is there little support in the literature
for US strategy, tactics, and the general conduct of the war,
but there are those who argue that US behavior in the war
and the conduct of US personnel on the ground, particu-

larly later in the war, reflected the disintegration of an army.[32]

Some analysts argue that there was little understanding of the war within US policy-making circles. This led to misdirected policy, bad decisions, and improper strategy, thwarting the attempt to design an effective posture to respond to revolution.

Still another view is that because the South Vietnamese government was ineffective and embroiled in internal intrigues, it could never mount a total response to the Vietcong and the North. Moreover, the South Vietnamese military was not capable of undertaking the kinds of operations required to be effective against revolutionary armed forces.

A more encompassing theme is that Vietnamese culture, society, and the political system were so distinct from the American way of life that there was virtually nothing the United States could do short of total war that could have prevented the North from defeating the South. This critique is based on the premise that the nature and character of US democracy precluded conducting the war in a more effective way. Thus, the very means that might have achieved acceptable ends could not be employed because these were contrary to the notion that moral and ethical means are necessarily linked to moral and ethical ends.

Recently another trend in the literature has emerged that focuses on a description of the nature of the combat in Vietnam. Although this focus in not entirely new, its emphasis has become pronounced as an increasing number of books have appeared based on actual combat experience. These books implicitly go beyond simple narrative since their description of US involvement in combat tends to reinforce the other themes in the literature.

Finally, one of the most critical perspectives argues that US involvement in Vietnam was immoral and reflected a bankrupt policy. This perspective directly and indirectly presumes that the US military was an important partner in designing the Vietnam involvement and in conducting an immoral war. Although there is no doubt that there still are questions regarding the practicality, feasibility, and appropriateness of US involvement, it is also true that the US military performed about as well as it has in other wars.

In later chapters, several of these major themes will be the basis for analyzing US policy and strategy for low-intensity conflicts. For the remainder of this chapter, we will view the landscape of US involvement in Vietnam and its aftermath to provide some reference points that will be the basis for a better understanding of the major themes in the literature.

A word of caution is in order. As this overview of the current literature has made clear, the nature and character of revolution and counterrevolution are extremely complex. There is little agreement among those who have studied these matters and who have written about them, including US policy makers, the media, the public in general, and most of those involved in the conduct of political-military operations. Years after the Vietnam War, Americans are still engaged in trying to disentangle the events and determine the causes and outcomes of involvement. The brief overview of involvement that follows is not intended as a substitute for a serious study of the literature on the subject. Nor is it intended as an explanation or definitive discourse. The purpose is to analyze the broad landscape of US involvement in Vietnam as revealed by major reference points in political, military, and domestic politics.

POLITICAL CONTEXT OF THE VIETNAM WAR

Any critical analysis of the United States and the Vietnam War must dig deeply into the political dynamics within the United States over a highly charged and dramatic five-year period, beginning with the assassination of President Kennedy in November 1963 and ending with President Johnson's announcement in 1968 that he would not seek reelection to the Oval Office. Although the

Vietnam War continued for another five years, it seemed to many that the election of Richard Nixon to the presidency in November 1968 was also the signal for a change in posture with respect to Vietnam. Withdrawal with honor and Vietnamization became critical themes.

These tumultuous years have been studied, interpreted, and criticized by a variety of authors. One authority describes the period immediately following Kennedy's assassination in this way:

> The abrupt transition of power began America's most painful decade since the Civil War. It was the genesis of the most questionable conflict of arms in modern history, its dimensions and duration seemingly inexplicable unless first examined through the combustive interaction of several factors. . . . Vietnam plagued Johnson almost from the moment he was sworn in. It destroyed his presidency, drained his enormous vitality, aborted then reversed the fuller democracy for which he had struggled a lifetime.[33]

The roots of Vietnam precede Kennedy, and its final outcome goes beyond the Johnson and Nixon presidencies, but focusing on the Kennedy and Johnson years provides insights into US politics and military posture that carry on beyond Vietnam.

The dynamics of politics had changed with the election of President John F. Kennedy in 1960. After two terms of President Eisenhower, terms that many viewed as maintaining the status quo and quiet, a more aggressive political leadership was emerging at the national level. John Kennedy's personality and character captured the imagination of many Americans, particularly the young. His call for a Peace Corps and civil rights was combined with firmness in dealing with the Soviets. All of the high hopes of a new generation were dashed at Dallas in 1963 with the assassination of the president.

Lyndon Johnson, after being sworn in as president, vigorously pursued enactment of many Kennedy legislative proposals. Civil rights legislation and the beginning of the Great Society programs took shape. It was not until Johnson won the presidency in his own right in 1964 against Barry Goldwater that he placed his own imprint on the office. The Great Society became a major goal for the Johnson administration. Combined with the increasing momentum of the civil rights movement, these developments seemed to portend a new era in politics.

Almost hidden behind the domestic political veil was the growing involvement of the United States in Southeast Asia. Beginning with a 1954 letter from President Eisenhower to Prime Minister Diem of South Vietnam, US involvement grew under Kennedy from economic assistance and low levels of military aid to a US military mission of close to 23,000 personnel by the end of 1963. By the time Johnson came into office, the shape of commitment had become broad and an accepted part of US foreign and national security posture. One authority concludes,

> The American involvement in Indochina began almost imperceptibly, rather like a mild toothache. At the end, it ran through Vietnam and America like a pestilence. Each president based his policies on exaggerated fears, and, later, on exaggerated hopes. Thus, each president left the problem to his successor in worse shape than he had found it.[34]

Although Americans were not actually engaged in direct ground combat operations in 1963, they were becoming the targets of Vietcong attacks in South Vietnam. This changed in August 1964 when the US Senate passed the Gulf of Tonkin Resolution, stating in part, "The United States is . . . prepared as the President determines, to take all necessary steps, including the use of armed force, to assist any member or protocol state of the Southeast Asia Collective Defense Treaty requesting assistance in defense of its freedom." The events leading up to the resolution remain in dispute. US destroyers were engaged in repelling attacks by North Vietnamese torpedo boats in the Gulf of Tonkin. After the second such attack, President Johnson ordered a bombing raid against oil storage depots in Hanoi. The whole incident still sparks debate within the United States not only on the rationality of action but whether the Tonkin Gulf incident took place at all.[35]

The Gulf of Tonkin Resolution paved the way for deepening involvement in Vietnam. Within six months after passage of the resolution, 100,000 US ground troops were deployed in South Vietnam. Thus, in less than a year the situation was first escalated by Kennedy from assistance to extensive involvement and then by Johnson to the beginnings of a war. At the same time, the Great Society programs took off.

Within three years a president who had begun with great expectations to uplift the United States with his Great Society program was mired in Vietnam. Johnson's desire to be remembered for his Great Society was not to be; he became the president directly associated with the Vietnam agony.

For many Americans, the assassination of John F. Kennedy and the war policies of the Johnson administration marked the corruption of US politics, morality, and vision. The expectations of the Kennedy New Frontiers were dashed by his assassination. The visions of a Great Society and an era of civil rights seemed hypocritical side by side with involvement in Vietnam. The apparent inability to resolve the Vietnam conflict, combined with the increasing politicization of the war and polarization of society as a result, seriously tarnished US efforts in Vietnam. Equally important, the impact of attitudes on military men in Vietnam combined with the unconventional nature of the war did much to diminish US military capabilities.

In sum, the politics of the 1960s were a complex mix of morality, immorality, confrontation, irrationality, distorted ideologies, sincere concern about war, political ambition, interest group selfishness, political integrity, concern for the nation, and a spreading distrust of the instruments of government. And even while the politics of the

1960s spilled over into the 1970s, another event took place that seemed to confirm all that was wrong with the US political system: the Watergate affair.

The US withdrawal from Vietnam in 1973 and the defeat of South Vietnam shortly after seemed almost ordained after all of the crises stretching back to the Kennedy assassination. For some, it was a relief to have Vietnam over with, regardless of what it did to the United States. For others, the withdrawal from Vietnam began an agonizing journey down a road that still seems to have no end.

THE MILITARY CONTEXT

US military forces entered Vietnam in strength in 1965 and eventually numbered over 500,000 at the height of the war. The major military effort and the length of time that Americans were involved in combat has given rise to a variety of interpretations and views regarding the military meaning of the war and its impact on the military profession. But there seems to be little agreement even among the experts regarding what it was all about and what it did to the military. Nonetheless, there are some important lessons to be gained, even from a brief view of the military role. This can be seen more clearly if we examine US involvement as a series of phases.

First Phase

US Marines entered South Vietnam in March 1965 followed by the landing of the 173d Airborne Brigade in May 1965. These deployments marked the shift from a US advisory role to active combat. Although the momentum for enlarging the war had begun earlier, it was the military situation in Vietnam in 1964 following the installation of Nguyen Cao Ky as president of South Vietnam that marked the first phase.

In 1964, the Vietcong demonstrated their ability to attack, and in many cases defeat, the South Vietnamese

Army. Battalions of South Vietnamese Army troops in a number of instances were engaged by lesser numbers of Vietcong main force units with the outcome uncertain despite the superior numbers employed by the South Vietnamese. The inability of the South Vietnamese Army to stand up to the Vietcong signaled certain defeat for the Saigon government. Many US observers felt that by the end of 1964, the South Vietnamese were on the verge of defeat, with the Vietcong ready to split the South in two.[36]

By the end of 1964, about 23,000 US military personnel were in South Vietnam. By the end of 1965, US troop strength had increased to 184,000, and US tactics had shifted to active ground combat. By the end of 1965, over 1,300 Americans had been killed and over 6,000 wounded. The war had begun to take on an American character and reverberations were being felt at home.

Because the Vietcong and the North Vietnamese Army (NVA) infiltrators were operating in larger and larger units, the first phase of US ground involvement revolved around large unit tactics. Division-sized units and larger were deployed to prevent the enemy from achieving its objectives of splitting the South in two and from preventing it from destroying the South Vietnamese army.

Massive firepower, large concentrations of troops, and doctrine reminiscent of Korea and World War II were employed. What was new was the employment of helicopters, which provided a mobility to US forces unknown in previous wars. The ability to move large concentrations of troops rapidly from one battle area to another was critical to the initial success of US combat operations. Further, such mobility reduced the need to abide by the ten-to-one ratio in counterrevolution (that is, 10 counterrevolutionary fighters for every revolutionary fighter), at least temporarily. Many experts view that ratio as necessary for any hope of counterrevolutionary success.

The US doctrine of search and destroy was designed to find and destroy the enemy without attempting to capture and hold land. A variety of conventional tactics were used to carry out such operations. It was relatively easy to adapt the conventional US military posture to this initial phase of the Vietnam War. The enemy's use of large units was compatible with the doctrinal view institutionalized within US military circles regarding the organizational posture of an enemy.

The weaknesses in search-and-destroy operations were soon revealed, however. Areas that previously had been cleared were soon reoccupied by enemy units, and attempts were again made to mobilize the area politically against the South Vietnamese government. Counterrevolutionary warfare, it seemed, could not be effectively undertaken or limited to conventional military doctrine and units.

Second Phase: Limits of Americanization

The Tet offensive in 1968 marked the end of the US buildup and the start of a reassessment of the US role. At the time of the offensive, many argued that the communists had handed the Americans and South Vietnamese a major military defeat. Only later was it recognized that Tet was a major defeat for the communists. At the time of the offensive, the images portrayed by the US media of US military men in seeming disarray, fighting against the Vietcong in the heart of Saigon, sent a message of a US and South Vietnamese military defeat. Indeed, the media were the major culprits in conveying the wrong message. According to an authoritative study of the role of the media in Vietnam, "Journalistic laziness led to hasty conclusions about the nature of pacification and the effects upon it—both immediate and long-term—of Tet. Drama and retribution were served, but not dissemination of available facts."[37] The author concluded,

> In overall terms, the performance by the major American television and print news organizations during February and March 1968 constitutes an extreme case. Rarely has contemporary crisis-journalism turned out, in retrospect, to have veered so widely from reality. Essentially, the dominant themes of the words and film from

Vietnam (rebroadcast in commentary, editorials, and much political rhetoric at home) added up to a portrait of defeat for the allies. Historians, on the contrary, have concluded that the Tet offensive resulted in a severe military-political setback for Hanoi in the South. To have portrayed such a setback for one side as a defeat for the other—in a major crisis abroad—cannot be counted as a triumph for American journalism.[38]

The portrayal of this distorted view of the Tet offensive had both short- and long-range political repercussions. In the short term, the Johnson administration began to search for a way out; the military spoke less about winning the war. In the long term, the views on counter-revolutionary warfare, shaped partly by the experience of Tet, reinforced the school of thought that accepted the inability of a democracy to engage successfully in such warfare. Further, Tet showed the importance of psychological warfare in unconventional conflicts.

Actually, Tet was a US military victory. At the same time it showed the resilience of the South Vietnamese people and its army. Yet this is not the message that came across.

Third Phase: Vietnamization

The election of Richard Nixon as president in 1968 was also a signal for a shift in US war policy and strategy. Efforts were turned to making the South Vietnamese military into a more self-sufficient and effective fighting force. The underlying policy was that the South Vietnamese military should replace US ground forces and take on the major role of combat. It was assumed that modern weapons, intensified training, and a shift of military resources to the South Vietnamese military would allow them to take on an expanded role, while US forces gradually withdrew from active combat.

Vietnamization led to U.S. military operations in Cambodia to destroy Vietcong sanctuaries in an effort to ease the pressures within South Vietnam and to lessen the dangers of withdrawing U.S. troops. Although the Cambodian operation lasted only about one month, it generated increasing opposition in the United States and led antiwar groups to assail U.S. policy in Vietnam again.

A year later, in 1971, President Nixon directed that US artillery, air, and helicopter forces support the South Vietnamese Army (ARVN) invasion of Laos. No US ground forces were involved. The main purpose was to cut the Ho Chi Minh trail and delay North Vietnamese offensive operations (Operation Lam Son). The operation almost ended in disaster; some have called it a disaster.[39] Aside from the commitment of insufficient number of ARVN forces, there were high casualties among US air and helicopter crews and among ARVN forces.

In a relatively short period of time, Vietnamization had gotten off to a shaky start, first with the invasion of Cambodia and then with the virtual disaster in Laos. Compounding the increasing stridency of the opposition in the United States was the publication of *The Pentagon Papers*. Aside from exposing the misjudgments regarding the war, the reaction of the administration to the publication of classified documents helped to create the environment that would lead to Watergate.

For the US military, the Cambodian invasion set the final stage for complete withdrawal from Vietnam. During the first part of the Cambodian invasion in 1970, President Nixon had announced that 150,000 US troops would be withdrawn from Vietnam over the next twelve months. By the end of 1972, only about 140,000 US military personnel remained in Vietnam. In January 1973, President Nixon announced that another 70,000 would be withdrawn within four months, leaving a total force of 69,000 Americans.

On March 30, 1972, the North Vietnamese began their spring offensive with 120,000 troops. The president responded with a massive bombing of the North around Hanoi and Haiphong. A few months passed, and the North Vietnamese offensive faltered. It had become clear that neither side could achieve an outright military victory. In the meantime, US ground forces continued their withdrawal.

The active involvement of the United States in the war ended in March 1973 after long and tortuous negotiations that resulted in peace—at least for the Americans. In 1975, after a devastating North Vietnamese offensive, South Vietnam was defeated. The defeat was a result of a number of important factors, several of which had to do with the United States. According to a former South Vietnamese general, not only was the defeat triggered by the decision of the US Congress to cut off most aid to South Vietnam but it was also a result of the Paris Agreements, which weighed heavily against the South, and the general political biases in the United States against the South Vietnamese.[40] The former general writes,

> To the people of the United States and the world at large, the war fought by our side was made to appear as an inhuman and evil war and the government of South Vietnam as an inept and corrupt administration deserving no aid. . . . The American press, many of whose papers were inclined against the war, did not do much to counter this. The cause for which we fought, therefore, was either largely ignored or falsely portrayed. In addition, very vocal antiwar groups in America helped drown out the voices of reason and truth.[41]

THE AFTERMATH

The response immediately following US withdrawal from Vietnam was a turning away from virtually anything that resembled counterinsurgency or a Vietnam-type situation. The Vietnam War became a forgotten war as the US military concentrated almost all of its efforts toward European-type wars. The Special Forces, which had had a major role in organizing mountain tribes (the Montagnards) against the Vietcong and North Vietnamese and in conducting a variety of unconventional operations, became the symbol of what was wrong with the war. Moreover, some elements of Special Forces had operated under control of the Central Intelligence Agency (CIA) in Vietnam, and this seemed to link Special Forces with the distorted images of the CIA.

The concept of Special Forces was not only belittled but was shifting to a more conventional orientation with behind-the-lines operations in conjunction with conventional troops. In the later 1960s there were 13,000 Special Forces personnel. By the later 1970s, this was reduced to fewer than 4,000. Control over Special Forces was fragmented among five different army commands. Finally, the other services had little of their own unconventional capacity other than what had evolved from support of Special Forces in Vietnam. The concept of counterinsurgency and everything associated with it was reduced to little more than a minor military sideline.

THE REAWAKENING

By the end of the 1970s, a number of events had taken place that reawakened interest in Special Forces. Soviet-Cuban involvement in Ethiopia, Angola, and Mozambique and the revolution that began in El Salvador generated a new dimension for US security policy. Coming after what seemed to be a retreat from world engagement following Vietnam, the United States was forced to recognize the threats posed by Soviet power projections and the expansionist efforts of Marxist-Leninist regimes. Another aspect of the new challenge was the increasing patterns of international terrorism. Highlighted by the killing of Israeli athletes at the 1972 Munich Olympics, terrorists seemed to have an almost free hand throughout Europe.

The hostage taking in Iran in 1979 and the Soviet invasion of Afghanistan gave dramatic evidence of a new and more challenging international security situation. Combined with Soviet efforts in Africa, expansion of the revolution in El Salvador, and the threatening posture of the Marxist-Leninist regime in Nicaragua, the United

States was placed in a difficult and exposed political-military position.

The United States had a very limited capacity to respond to these challenges short of military intervention on an unacceptable scale. Indeed, there were those who felt that the United States did not have the capacity to respond even with conventional military means. During the first years of the Carter administration, the defense budget had decreased, and major efforts were made to constrain and limit intelligence activities. The volunteer military system was unable to attract the quantity and quality of personnel that it needed to maintain an effective military force. The US Army had become a "hollow army" according to a former army chief of staff, General Edward C. Meyer. Although the airforce, navy, and marines had less difficulty, they too were going through a difficult period trying to recruit and retain high-quality personnel. Overall, it was a dark period for the military, and many felt the same way about the political-military capacity of the United States.

The Buildup

Since 1980, the capacity of the United States to respond to unconventional conflicts has increased considerably. This is reflected in the number of personnel and units in Special Forces and Ranger battalions. Other services have also taken steps to develop unconventional warfare capacity. Navy SEALS (sea, air, and land teams), Marine Corps reconnaissance forces and special operations squadrons in the air force have expanded and become more skilled in special operations.

The First Special Operations Command includes Special Forces, Ranger battalions, civil affairs, and psychological warfare units. In addition, navy SEALS and air force special operations units work in close coordination with the command. In 1985, Special Forces numbered almost 10,000 men, with reserve Special Forces units numbering over 13,000 personnel. Special Forces were organized into four groups, each with about 1,200 personnel. A fifth group was to be activated over the next three to four years. It was estimated that by 1990 there would be about 12,000 active duty personnel in Special Forces.[42]

There were three Ranger battalions in place (about 600 men each) with a Ranger regimental headquarters. An additional Ranger battalion was also planned. In the air force, over 4,000 personnel were assigned to special operations duties. This was to be increased to 5,800 by 1990. The navy had 1,700, to be increased to 2,700 by 1990. All the services were to increase their logistical and aircraft support accordingly.[43]

One of the first steps taken in 1980 was the establishment of the Intelligence Support Activity, a small, classified intelligence operation designed to collect intelligence and plan for special military operations. According to some, this unit was created without the knowledge "of the Secretary of Defense, the Director of Central Intelligence or Congress."[44] This was preceded by the formation of Delta Force for the express purpose of rescuing the hostages in Iran.

The importance given to special operations by the new administration was made clear in the 1982 *Defense Guidance*, which stated in part, "We must revitalize and enhance special operations forces to project United States power where the use of conventional forces would be premature, inappropriate or unfeasible."[45] The report also pointed out that in an October 1982 memorandum by W. Paul Thayer, at that time the deputy secretary of defense, the importance of special operational capability was reemphasized. The memorandum stated in part, "The revitalization of those forces must be pursued as a matter of national urgency."

Subsequently, a critical step was taken by the creation of the First Special Operations Command in the army and, later, the creation of the Joint Special Operations Agency at the Department of Defense level. The First Special Operations Command was to be the operational element; the Joint Agency was to serve as the planning and coordinating agency for special operations. To assist the Joint Agency, there was established the Special Operations Policy Advisory Group, composed of distinguished retired officers to advise the Joint Agency and the Department of Defense.

Congressional interest in special operations was sharpened by the increased effort of the Department of Defense. One source reported,

> A subcommittee of the House Armed Services Committee has formed a special panel to track improvements in US special operations forces, signifying sharpened legislative interest in that small but important branch of the military.[46]

The revitalization of special operations was also reflected in the Department of Defense budget. In 1975 special operations was allocated 0.001 percent of the department budget; by 1985 this had more than doubled. The fiscal year 1985 defense authorization provided for about $500 million for special operations. It was the intent of the Department of Defense to develop a serious special operations capacity by the end of fiscal year 1990.[47]

The apparent increase in special operations forces angered some groups critical of the Department of Defense. Charges were made that a special operations buildup was likely to lead to US involvement in war. The same critics contend that the special operations forces give the United States military a covert capability that will not only be used but will likely violate existing laws.[48] Nonetheless, most observers felt that there was a need to establish a special operations capability not only to be able to respond effectively but also as a deterrence to others.

By 1985 it was clear that the United States had established a degree of political-military capability in special operations. Of equal importance, the shape of future special operations was becoming clearer, at least to a number of military men. According to one source,

DoD also is bettering SOF (Special Operations Forces) readiness by developing joint command systems, putting more men in special operations units, installing new avionics and fire control gear in SOF aircraft, and stocking more spare parts. . . . The Services are also expanding SOF research and development, while stressing "off-the-shelf" procurement to ensure units get special gear quickly.   And. . . .the Army is forming a General Officer Steering Committee for Special Operations Forces to ensure those units receive high-level management.[49]

In sum, by 1985 special operations and unconventional warfare had not only become fashionable again in the military services, but Congress and a number of policy makers were slowly recognizing the need for such forces. One of the motivations for such developments was undoubtedly the economy associated with special operations. Not committed to costly items and structured into small and mobile units, special operations forces were more economically palatable to Congress and to the public at large than the billions associated with the MX missile and Trident submarines.   For many, US involvement in foreign areas was more acceptable if it was based on the low visibility and short-term duration associated with special operations, although the Grenada operation in 1983 precipitated some criticism on Capitol Hill and among certain groups in the United States.   Even a number of military men contend that special operations are low risk and economical.

The resurgence of special operations capability, however, has not necessarily resolved serious problems of policy, strategy, and doctrine.   Conceptual confusion and organizational ambiguity remain.   Within policy-making circles, there remains a high degree of confusion over the meaning of special operations.   Most people believe it includes everything from counterterror operations and hit-and-run raids to counterrevolution.   At the same time, there is lack of a policy as to when and where to use such forces; missions for the various forces within the special operations concept are unclear. Further, there is lacking a central authority exercising control over all special operations resources. One result is that each service determines its own requirements and missions in special operations. In 1985, for example, the marine commandant "launched a major initiative to sharpen the special operations capability that 'already exists' within the forward-deployed Marine Amphibious Units (MAUs)."[50]

This problem is also reflected in the First Special Operations Command. Not only does this command include units designated for counterterror operations and hit-and-run raids, for example, but also Special Forces whose primary missions are (or should be) in revolution and counterrevolution. These missions differ considerably and require a different set of strategies and doctrine.

Finally, there remains a great deal of resistance within the mainstream military establishment against elite forces and special missions. This has always been a historical fact and seems to be particularly so in the contemporary period. Assignment to special operations forces is not one of the avenues considered useful to advancing military careers. This traditional resistance to special units has blunted the need for distinct organizational styles and doctrines. In sum, the conventional mind-sets and traditional thrust of the US military seem to be affecting the shape of forces designed for unconventional conflicts. This will continue to limit the effectiveness of such forces and has a chilling effect on their professional quality. But this problem goes beyond the military. It is also a characteristic of the US political system as a whole. The combination of military and civilian views makes it difficult to come to grips with unconventional conflicts.

NOTES

1. For a more detailed explanation of Vietnam as a forgotten war, see Sam C. Sarkesian, *America's Forgotten Wars:*

The Counterrevolutionary Past and Lessons for the Future
(Westport, Conn.: Greenwood Press, 1984), pp. 1-20.

2. For assessments of the formative period and its impact,
see Colonel Francis J. Kelly, *U.S. Army Special Forces, 1961-
1971* (Washington, D.C.: Government Printing Office, 1973);
Alfred H. Paddock, Jr., *US Army Special Warfare: Its Origins,
Psychological and Unconventional Warfare, 1941-1952* (Wash-
ington, D.C.: National Defense University Press, 1982); and
Charles M. Simpson III, *Inside the Green Berets, The First
Thirty Years: A History of the U.S. Army Special Forces*
(Novato, Calif.: Presidio Press, 1983).

3. See, for example, John M. Gates "Vietnam: The Debate
Goes On," *Parameters* 14, no. 1 (Spring 1984); Harry G. Sum-
mers, Jr., "Palmer, Karnow, and Herrington: A Review of
Recent Vietnam War Histories," *Parameters* 15, no. 1 (Spring
1985); and General Bruce Palmer, Jr., *The 25-Year War:
America's Military Role in Vietnam* (Lexington: University
of Kentucky Press, 1984); Arthur W. Radford, *From Pearl Har-
bor to Vietnam: The Memoirs of Admiral W. Radford*, ed.
Stephen Jurila, Jr. (Stanford: Hoover Institution Press, 1980);
Harry G. Summers, Jr., *On Strategy: The Vietnam War in
Context* (Carlisle Barracks, Penn.: Army War College, 1981);
and William C. Westmoreland, *A Soldier Reports* (Garden
City, N.Y.: Doubleday, 1976). See also David L. Bender, ed.,
The Vietnam War: Opposing Viewpoints (St. Paul, Minn.:
Greenhaven Press, 1984).

4. In addition to the Vietnam War, the second Seminole
war, the Philippine and Moro wars, and the punitive expedition are examined in detail in Sarkesian. The focus on these
unconventional conflicts rather than others, such as the Indian wars on the Plains and the Nicaraguan Intervention, is
explained in detail.

5. Henry Kissinger, *White House Years* (Boston: Little,
Brown, 1982), p. 288.

6. Paul M. Kattenburg, *The Vietnam Trauma in American
Foreign Policy, 1945-75* (New Brunswick, N.J.: Transaction
Books, 1980), pp. 324-25. See also Robert L. Galucci, *Neither
Peace nor Honor: The Politics of American Military Policy in
Viet-Nam* (Baltimore: Johns Hopkins Press, 1975).

7. Lyndon Baines Johnson, *The Vantage Point: Perspectives of the Presidency, 1963-1969* (New York: Holt, Rinehart
and Winston, 1971).

8. David Halberstam, *The Best and the Brightest* (New York: Random House, 1972), and Leslie Gelb with Richard K. Betts, *The Irony of Vietnam: The System Worked* (Washington, D.C.: Brookings Institution, 1979).

9. Sir Robert Thompson, *Defeating Communist Insurgency: The Lessons of Malaya and Vietnam* (New York: Praeger, 1966), p. 19.

10. Neil Sheehan, Hedrick Smith, E. W. Kenworthy, and Fox Butterfield, *The Pentagon Papers* (New York: Bantam Books, 1971). A number of researchers and authorities do not accept this version of the Pentagon Papers, pointing out that there are many omissions, inaccuracies, and one-sided political interpretations. The *Senator Gravel Edition* is more authoritative. See, for example, Russ Braley, *Bad News: The Foreign Policy of the New York Times* (Chicago: Regnery Gateway, 1984), pp. 378-427.

11. Summers.

12. Ibid., p. 2.

13. Ibid., p. 1.

14. See, for example, John Albright, John A. Cash, and Allan W. Sandstrum, *Seven Firefights in Vietnam* (Washington, D.C.: Government Printing Office, 1970); Michael Herr, *Dispatches* (New York: Avon Books, 1978); S. L. A. Marshall, *Vietnam: Three Battles* (New York: Da Capo Press, 1971); and Al Santoli, *Everything We Had* (New York: Ballantine Books, 1981).

15. Hugh Mulligan, *No Place to Die: The Agony of Vietnam* (New York: William Morrow, 1967), p. 317.

16. Ward Just, *Military Men* (New York: Alfred A. Knopf, 1970), p. 185.

17. Jonathan Schell, *The Military Half* (New York: Alfred A. Knopf, 1968), p. 42.

18. See, for example, Herr; Michael Maclear, *The Ten Thousand Day War—Vietnam: 1945-1975* (New York: Avon Books, 1981).

19. U. S. Army War College, *Study on Military Professionalism* (Carlisle Barracks, Penna.: Army War College, June 30, 1970). See also Sam C. Sarkesian, *Beyond the Battlefield: The New Military Professionalism* (New York: Pergamon Press, 1981).

20. War College Study, pp. 28-29.

21. William R. Peers, *The My Lai Inquiry* (New York: Norton, 1978). See also Joseph Goldstein, Burke Marshall, and

Jack Schwartz, *The My Lai Massacre and Its Cover-Up: Beyond the Reach of Law? The Peers Commission Report* (New York: Free Press, 1976).

22. Major Robert A. Doughty, *Leavenworth Papers: The Evolution of U.S. Army Tactical Doctrine, 1946-76* (Fort Leavenworth, Kans.: Army Command and General Staff College, August 1979), p. 40.

23. See Gerald Cannon Hickey, *Village in Vietnam* (New Haven: Yale University Press, 1968), and John T. McAlister, Jr., and Paul Mus, *The Vietnamese and Their Revolution* (New York: Harper and Row, 1970).

24. See Doughty. See also Bernard B. Fall, *The Two Viet-Nams: A Political and Military Analysis*, 2d rev. ed. (New York: Praeger, 1967), and Douglas Pike, *Viet Cong: The Organization and Techniques of the National Liberation Front of South Vietnam* (Cambridge, Mass.: MIT Press, 1967).

25. Fall, *The Two Viet-Nams*.

26. Thich Nhat Hanh, *Vietnam, Lotus in a Sea of Fire* (New York: Hill and Wang, 1967), pp. 63-64.

27. General Cao Van Vien, *The Final Collapse* (Washington, D.C.: Government Printing Office, 1982), pp. 5-6.

28. Nguyen Cao Ky, *How We Lost the Vietnam War* (New York: Stein and Day, 1984), p. 196.

29. Gloria Emerson, *Winners and Losers: Battles, Retreats, Gains, Losses, and Ruins from a Long War* (New York: Random House, 1976), and Frances Fitzgerald, *Fire in the Lake: The Vietnamese and the Americans in Vietnam* (Boston: Little, Brown, 1972).

30. See, for example, Truong Nhu Tang with David Chanoff and Doan Van Toai, *A Vietcong Memoir: An Inside Account of the Vietnam War and Its Aftermath* (New York: Harcourt Brace Jovanovich, 1985).

31. Gates.

32. See, for example, Schell; David Halberstam, *The Making of a Quagmire* (New York: Random House, 1965).

33. Maclear.

34. John G. Stoessinger, *Why Nations Go to War*, 3d ed. (New York: St. Martin's Press, 1982), p. 111.

35. See, for example, "Untold Story of the Road to War in Vietnam," *U.S. News and World Report*, October 10, 1983, pp. VN1-VN23, and "The 'Phantom Battle' That Led to War; Can It Happen Again?" *U.S. News and World Report*, July 23, 1984, pp. 56-57. See also George McTurnan Kahin and John

W. Lewis, *The United States in Vietnam: An Analysis in Depth of the History of America's Involvement in Vietnam*, rev. ed. (New York: Dell, 1969), pp. 157-59, 477-78.

36. Doughty, p. 30.

37. Peter Braestrup, *Big Story: How the American Press and Television Reported and Interpreted the Crisis of Tet 1968 in Vietnam and Washington* (Boulder, Colo.: Westview Press, 1977), 1: xxxi-xxxii.

38. Ibid., p. 705.

39. Maclear, p. 300.

40. See, for example, Cao Van Vien and Nguyen Cao Ky.

41. Cao Van Vien, p. 164.

42. "America's Secret Soldiers: The Buildup of U.S. Special Operations Forces," *Defense Monitor* 14, no. 2 (1985). See also P. J. Budahn, "Elite Force Buildup Seen Increasing War Threat," *Army Times,* May 6, 1985, p. 7, and *United States Military Posture for FY 1986* (Washington, D.C.: Organization of the Joint Chiefs of Staff, 1985), p. 68.

43. Ibid.

44. Jeff Gerth, "U.S. Military Creates Secret Units for Use in Sensitive Tasks Abroad," *New York Times,* June 8, 1984, p. 1.

45. Richard Halloran, "Military Chiefs Resist Improving Special Forces, Official Says," *New York Times,* May 27, 1984, p. 41.

46. Clinton H. Schemmer, "House Panel Formed to Oversee Special Operations Forces," *Armed Forces Journal International* (October 1984): 15.

47. Ibid.

48. *Defense Monitor;* Budahn.

49. Schemmer.

50. Benjamin F. Schemmer, "Commandant Directs Marines to Sharpen Their Inherent Special Ops Capability," *Armed Forces Journal International* (October 1985): 24.

6

The American Dilemma

Unconventional conflicts, more specifically special operations and low-intensity conflicts, have a number of characteristics that do not easily fit into American perceptions of war or into the American mind-set and world-view. If the military instrument reflects society, then one can understand the military problem of engaging in unconventional conflicts.

The continuing concern with strategic balance and deterrence requires considerable effort in force modernization, strategic weaponry, and research and development, items that absorb a great deal of defense dollars and manpower. Nuclear weaponry and strategy, arms control, and disarmament have been given considerable attention in academic circles, policy efforts, intellectual studies, and military analysis. Although more attention has recently been placed on unconventional conflicts, the critical thrust of effort remains on the big battle scenarios. Even when attention is given to the lessons of the past, such as Vietnam, the tendency is to view these in conventional terms.

The United States must continue its major effort in developing and modernizing strategic weaponry and general purpose forces and increase its capability in conventional conflicts in general. But the most likely conflicts are those whose characteristics differ considerably from the conventional and strategic dimensions of the big battle scenarios. This is at the root of the strategic and policy dilemma of the United States.

POLICY AND STRATEGY OVERVIEW

Policy, the goal of governments, is a never-ending process. Policy goals need to be continually assessed and reassessed, interpreted, and applied. What complicates the process and the study of policy is that the policy, in the larger sense, encompasses a variety of dimensions ranging from the pursuit of peace and human rights to developing favorable trade and military basing rights. At the same time, policy may also justify engaging in war, covert operations, and trade wars.

Policy includes crisis and noncrisis situations, as well as a variety of national security matters. It may also include a variety of subpolicies. Thus, the United States may have a particular policy with regard to Nigeria, a different policy toward the Soviet Union, and a still different policy for Western Europe. The long-range policy may be peaceful relationships, but this may include a particular policy with each individual state leading to several policies designed to achieve the long-range policy. Thus, even the simplest notions of policy can become complicated.

Strategy cannot be realistically studied without some attention to its relationship to policy. Many people use the terms *policy* and *strategy* synonymously; however, there are important distinctions between the two. *Strategy* refers to the means or methods used to achieve policy goals. Thus, it is conceivable that some states may resort to war in the short run in order to achieve peace in the long run. But strategy as a concept is a complicated subject and requires a closer look.

"Strategy," according to Clausewitz, "is the employment of the battle to gain the end of the War; it must therefore give an aim to the whole military action, which must be in accordance with the object of the war."[1]

General Bruce Palmer has written,

> The term "strategy," derived from the ancient Greek,
> originally pertained to the art of generalship or high
> command. In modern times, "grand strategy," has come
> into use to describe the overall defense plans of a nation
> or coalition of nations. Since the mid-twentieth century,
> "national strategy" has attained wide usage, meaning the
> coordinated employment of the total resources of a
> nation to achieve its national objective.[2]

But as Howard points out, "The term 'strategy' needs
continual definition. For most people, Clausewitz's for-
mulation . . . is clear enough. Strategy concerns the deployment and use of armed forces to attain a given political objective."[3] The utility of the modern state and conventional views regarding the relationship of war and
politics are essential parts of strategy. It is this kind of for-
mulation that guides the US military and is the basis of
much of US political wisdom.

In brief, in the modern context, military strategy in its
simplest definition retains as its centerpiece a Clausewitzian perspective in a modern genre of nuclear weapons and combat envisioned between major powers or
similarly postured powers. But some see the decreasing
utility of war as an instrument of US policy. Weigley
concludes,

> At no point on the spectrum of violence does the use of
> combat offer much promise for the United States
> today. . . . Because the record of nonnuclear limited war
> in obtaining acceptable decisions at tolerable cost is also
> scarcely heartening, the history of usable combat may at
> last be reaching its end.[4]

Many would disagree with this conclusion.

One school of thought within political-military circles
recognizes the challenge of unconventional conflicts.
This has led to the creation of the Special Operations
Command and to increasing resources and attention to
special operations forces. Not only has there been an in-

crease in military attention to special operations, but Congress has created a subcommittee to oversee such operations.   Yet in contrast to conventional and nuclear wars, the resources and efforts devoted to unconventional conflicts are miniscule.   Additionally, most US military forces are trained, educated, and organized around the big battle scenarios.

According to prevailing views, if special units whose missions are directly linked to unconventional conflicts are inadequate, then ground combat forces (those whose primary orientation and posture is conventional combat) may be committed.   It is in this context that we need to review the strategic principles separating conventional and unconventional conflicts.

Clausewitz and Sun Tzu

Clausewitz and Sun Tzu are particularly important in studying the distinctions between conventional and unconventional conflicts.[5]   It is useful for our study and understanding to become familiar with the general arguments and analysis of the classic treatise that each provides on the art of war, though Clausewitz and Sun Tzu are separated by centuries.

Clausewitz and Conventional War

Clausewitz argued that there must be a congruence among the government, the people, and the army.   This triad is the key to successful waging of war.   Clausewitz was speaking primarily of the kinds of wars that took place during his own lifetime (1780-1831).   Such wars involved national entities in a European setting and dominated most of Clausewitz's life from adolescence to adulthood; they encompassed the Napoleonic era and the war against Russia.   Wars were seen as a clash between armies arrayed against one another in highly traditional fashion. Thus, the concepts of mass, firepower, and maneuver across the landscape of Europe formed the context within which Clausewitz formulated his concept of war.   One authority writes,

The key to Clausewitz's thinking was the fact that it
grew out of a profound national crisis. . . . Clausewitz
neither glorified war nor sentimentalized its horrors.
He did not think of it as a tragedy to be avoided—a kind
of natural calamity—but as the only possible solution to
a genuinely desperate problem.[6]

Thus, the idea of the government, the people, and the
army mobilized and acting as one in national calamities
appeared to be the most effective way to wage war for a
successful political end: ensuring that the nation-state
survived.

Clausewitz was reacting against the eighteenth-century
concept of warfare, which aimed toward the rational and
scientific and a view that war had progressed to a more
ennobled encounter.   This led to complicated maneuvering, the avoidance of direct confrontation, and the occupation of strategic positions that would cause the adversary
to withdraw without battle.

Clausewitz objected to the view that war could be conducted under such mechanical rules, that war was something separate from the purpose of the state. He argued
that "war is an act of violence intended to compel our opponent to fulfill our will."[7] He went on to argue that "war
is an act of violence pushed to its utmost bounds."[8] In
sum, war is designed to carry out state policy.

Clausewitz insisted that the enemy's field forces were
the primary objective and battles the primary means of
warfare. This is the center of gravity of war. Although
there may be some disagreement as to Clausewitz's short-
term and long-term views on warfare and the relationships between the spirit of the army and the general
conduct of war, Clausewitz aimed primarily at the conduct
of war whose purpose was to "push to the utmost" in
defeating the enemy's armed forces.[9]

Clausewitzian notions of strategy are institutionalized
in US military thought and used as the criteria for effective strategy. Many of these principles have proved to be
appropriate and universal, but it would be imprudent to
presume that such principles generate doctrines always

applicable to unconventional warfare. To ignore the context in which Clausewitz lived, thought, and wrote is to ignore the principles that he developed. Indeed, one can argue that Clausewitz himself was reacting against the traditional military mind of his period. He closely linked war and politics, and yet many today ignore or overlook this fundamental Clausewitzian perspective.

Sun Tzu and Unconventional War

It is estimated that Sun Tzu's *Art of War* was completed during the fourth century B.C. Although there remains disagreement regarding the authorship and the dates of composition, there is no doubt that this series of essays had a profound impact on the conduct of war in China. It was written during the age of warring states in China, about a quarter of a century after the death of Confucius in 479 B.C.[10]

Sun Tzu became a general for the King of Wu, one of the eight states in China during this period. In this capacity and adhering to his view of the proper conduct of war, Sun Tzu defeated a rival state and was responsible for the State of Wu's dominating several other states.

The primary focus of Sun Tzu's essays was to provide a strategy of war based on rational planning and the conduct of military operations. "He believed that the skillful strategist should be able to subdue the enemy's army without engaging it, to take his cities without laying seige to them, and to overthrow his State without bloodying swords."[11]

Sun Tzu wrote,

> For to win one hundred victories in one hundred battles is not the acme of skill. To subdue the enemy without fighting is the acme of skill. . . . The nature of war is that it avoids heights and hastens to the lowlands. When a dam is broken, the water cascades with irresistible force. Now the shape of an army resembles water. Take advantage of the enemy's unpreparedness; attack him when he does not expect it; avoid his strength and strike his emptiness, and like water, none can oppose you.[12]

According to Sun Tzu, "All warfare is based on deception . . . [the] primary target is the mind of the opposing commander."[13]   The successful commander is one who can manipulate his opponent and, using psychological warfare and a variety of deceptive tactics, erode the enemy's will and effectiveness.   "The prudent commander bases his plans on the antagonists' 'shape.'   'Shape him', Sun Tzu says."[14]

Sun Tzu also introduced the idea of the unorthodox operation conducted by special elite units.   In conjunction with standard operations, these unorthodox operations were designed to distract the adversary so that a decisive blow could be aimed elsewhere.   Sun Tzu's view of the unorthodox was not limited to tactical operations but was intended to be part of the strategic plan.

Mao Tse-tung relied heavily on Sun Tzu for the conduct of the revolutionary war in China during the 1940s. Indeed, many of the peasant-oriented revolutions in the post-World War II period owe their doctrinal bases to Sun Tzu through Mao.

A Synthesis

The main thrust of Clausewitz and Sun Tzu differ. Not only did Clausewitz focus on the enemy's armed forces as the center of gravity of war, but his concern was on the "push to the utmost" in which the nation's policy is to defeat the enemy totally. To be sure, there is room in the Clausewitzian view for limited war, but the critical content of his writings seems to be on the totality of war.

Sun Tzu, long before Clausewitz, provided a critical analysis of war, brought on by the shift of armies from peasant levees to a professional group armed with modern weapons. His assessment emanated from the view that although war was of vital importance to the state and could lead to devastation, it could be fought wisely by a variety of actions aimed at the political-psychological center of the enemy. The center of gravity of war is the adversaries' will and resolve rather than on the actual battlefield.

It has been suggested that in the contemporary period, conflicts in the future are likely to be those adhering more closely to Sun Tzu's art of war rather than Clausewitzian strategy. This is not to suggest that Clausewitz is irrelevant. What it does suggest is that one should use Clausewitz's reaction against traditional military views as the starting point in interpreting his strategy and in applying Sun Tzu to the battlefields of the contemporary period.

Unconventional conflicts might more accurately be studied from a combination of Clausewitzian logic and Sun Tzu's views of war. Indeed, according to one authority, "Sun Tzu has clearer visions, more profound insight, and eternal freshness."[15]

US Policy and Strategy Perspectives

The United States is primarily postured toward wars of a global nature or conventional wars with an identifiable enemy, clear targets, and relatively cohesive and congruent political-military policy goals. In such circumstances, there is likely to be minimal domestic challenge to national will and political resolve. Also there is unlikely to be serious questions between the role of the military and its relationship to society. The problem is that the most likely conflicts probably will have questionable political objectives and will be enmeshed in strategic ambiguity.

It follows that US policy with respect to the Soviet Union, for example, may be relatively clear. The posture of the United States with respect to the possibility of conflict in Europe or nuclear exchange is also relatively clear. The policy is based on the defense of Europe and deterrence of nuclear conflict. Nuclear capability and military effectiveness is the fundamental basis for this policy. Strategy, in turn, is based on a conventional capability in Europe, backed by the possibility of the use of nuclear weapons, if necessary. Strategy for deterrence policy is based on the continuing effectiveness of the triad of air, sea, and land nuclear forces. Beyond Europe and deterrence, US policy and strategy are much less clear.

Thus, the United States seems reasonably well prepared for the least likely scenarios, the big battles in Europe, and least prepared for the most likely ones, unconventional conflicts in Third World areas. It is time for a redirection of US policy and strategy.

Western and US military thought rest primarily on Clausewitz. This is most appropriate for the kinds of wars envisioned in Europe and conventional conflicts in general. However, Sun Tzu is perhaps more appropriate as the basis for assessing unconventional conflicts. This is not to suggest that Clausewitz is wrong but that Clausewitzian logic must be placed in its proper context. Clausewitz must be tempered, if not totally subordinated, by Sun Tzu in dealing with unconventional conflicts.

What makes the strategic dilemma more profound is that Clausewitzian logic fits more easily into the general notions of war held by Americans. The military reflects society, and in this sense, society, the military, and many political leaders and decision makers are almost as one when it comes to profound national crisis.

Anything less than crisis creates problems of national will and political resolve and ultimately affects staying power. Committing forces beyond the clear notions of national crisis in effect places them in an extremely disadvantageous position with respect to their credibility within their own society. Why this is so is a result of the nature and character of democratic systems, or open systems, in general. And it is in the nature and character of open systems that we find some of the most compelling notions regarding conflict. The principles of democracy create conditions in open systems that place them at a distinct disadvantage in unconventional conflicts. The military of open systems are not positioned or mentally disposed to engage in unconventional conflicts. This problem is compounded by the fact that military systems reflect the system and society they are supposed to defend and are constrained and limited accordingly. In understanding these relationships, we need to examine in more detail US views of democracy and how these relate to the ability of open systems to engage in unconventional conflicts.

DEMOCRACY: AN AMERICAN PERSPECTIVE

Defining democracy is not easy. By its nature, democracy demands pluralism, variety, multiple centers of power, and a commitment to individual worth rather than that of the collectivity. Democracy is the only system in which government must share real power and legitimacy with a variety of nongovernment institutions and groups. Democracy as a system must share power and compete with other systems, including religious, economic, and social systems within the cultural boundaries of the nation-state. This leads to a number of important characteristics that are particularly relevant to the study of the American way of war. These characteristics provide important insights into the difficult American position with respect to its capability in unconventional conflicts and the strategic dilemma it faces.

Characteristics of Open Systems

The first, and perhaps most important, characteristic of open systems has to do with the individual. The focal point of democracy is the stress placed on the importance of the individual as a political entity. It follows that resolution of any conflict evolves from the engagement of rational, knowledgeable, and understanding individuals in political discourse. At a higher level, war is seen as a result of the breakdown of this political discourse.

Most Americans expect those in public office, government institutions, and other people in general to share this belief in the individual and behave in accordance with democratic principles. Such expectations also extend to those in the military. The problem is that interpretations of democratic principles vary, as one should expect in a democracy. At a general level, virtually all Americans are for freedom, justice, and fair play, for example. But when trying to design policy and programs based on these, a considerable amount of disagreement emerges, not over the principles but over their interpretation and implementation.

This is true with respect to security policy and strategy. Obviously the clearer and more threatening a crisis is, the more likely there will be agreement on strategic actions. But the kinds of conflicts characterizing the contemporary period are not those of a Pearl Harbor nature, nor are they likely to be viewed as crises.

In fact such conflicts rarely develop into large-scale battles, nor are they usually seen as clear threats to US security. The problem is that such conflicts can be threats over the long run and are best challenged at the outset. Given the nature of American democracy, however, it is difficult to develop the necessary governmental consensus, much less a consensus within the body politic, for the staying power needed to engage in such conflicts in a persistent and effective way. This can be traced directly to the nature of the American system—an open system—and the American view of war.

There are varieties of democracies, including such countries as England, Germany, France, Sweden, Canada, Japan, Italy, Norway, and the Netherlands, among others. Although these accept the general principles of democracy, they may differ in the interpretations and the way the government functions. For example, there is no Supreme Court in England that can overturn the decisions of the legislature. There the House of Commons is supreme. And although England is technically a monarchy, few would deny that it is a democracy.

In all of these various democracies, there is established and perpetuated a civic culture that accepts as fundamental and unchanging the responsibility of officials, accountability to the people, power to the people, and justice. This is nurtured by the right of the people to change officials peacefully and to engage in political organization, discourse, and action, even against the state. Thus, regardless of the variety of governments, the nature of open systems rests on these fundamental factors. Underpinning this basic commitment is the idea that morality and ethics are bound up in a higher law, requiring sensitivity, justice, and empathy to all human beings, even in time of war.

Open systems have several important characteristics. First is a commitment to the rule of law. The actions of officials and the political-military instruments must adhere to some standard of law that is widely recognized and accepted. Not only does such a condition create the basis for developing a comprehensive rule of law, but it creates a sense of predictability predicated on the idea that one need not fear the government. This implies that unacceptable action by officials or instruments of government can be challenged in a court of law, through other institutions, or by nonviolent political actions. The concepts of justice and individual worth are closely bound to the idea of rule by law.

Second, there must be a critical mass of officials, bureaucrats, police, and military leaders who are committed to the principles of an open system. Thus, the responsibility of those in power is never separated from accountability to the people.

Third, there must be a general sense and commitment on the part of the populace that the system is legitimate, that change can be brought about peacefully, and that there is a stake in the system as it now exists in principle.

Fourth, instruments of policy, domestic and foreign, must operate in accordance with basic rules of law, principles of democracy, and the proper notions of morality and ethics. Although these may be interpreted broadly, giving more latitude to police and military instruments, for example, in time of crisis or war, they still apply, particularly in terms of accountability. It follows that the populace must have a sense of confidence in the government's ability to control its policy instruments.

Finally, with particular respect to the United States, there must be a total commitment to a pluralistic system. This does not necessarily mean ethnic or racial pluralism to the detriment of national cohesiveness. Rather, it means a commitment to political pluralism and the creation of an environment that invites the rise of political groups and the broadening of political participation. All of this must be done in accord with the accepted rules of the game.

Democracy is more complex than this, which is why it is so difficult to define clearly and precisely. This difficulty is particularly evident when trying to compare democracy and communism. Not only is there no single source of democratic legitimacy or ideology, but there is no single all-powerful institution that subsumes all others. This is in contrast to communism, where in the Soviet Union, for example, there is a preoccupation with ideology and a single source that legitimizes Marxism-Leninism.

Obviously no system, regardless of how open it may be, is perfect. The essential point is the degree of commitment of leaders, elite, major political actors, and the rest of the American people to these principles in general. Few would deny that the US political system has institutionalized these principles and has constantly moved in the direction of trying to perfect them, even though at times this is done imperfectly and ineffectively.

American Way of War

Although the United States has had a great deal of experience in unconventional conflicts, the modern way of war and military mind-sets are shaped by the big battles of World War I and World War II. Early in US history, the battles of the Revolution and the War of 1812 formed the backdrop for American views of conflict. Equally important, the British and later the French and German models of military organization and doctrine guided US military professionalism and organization.

Americans viewed conflict in terms of clashes of armies or navies. Even unconventional wars were seen through conventional lenses by military and civilians alike. This should be expected. Until the post-World War II period, US involvement in conflicts revolved around great issues of the period and were determined by the military of the nation mobilized for war. The Civil War, World War I, and World War II are critical and enduring events in history. Even the Spanish-American War, viewed as the "splendid little war," was seen as a milestone in US history.

All of these wars were marked by identifiable adversaries and clear purposes and were driven by conventional military strategy and doctrines. Whether all Americans agreed on policy in these conflicts is not the issue here. The point is that the move from peace to war was relatively clear; there was a clear demarcation from one to the other. The position of the adversary was generally clear to most Americans, and what needed to be done was also accepted by most. Moreover, the military was postured conventionally and expanded in the same way. This is not to say that the military was adequately prepared for any of the conflicts.

Once engaged in conflict, it was generally expected that the military would behave according to an accepted code of conduct reflected in "Duty, Honor, Country." This code was perceived and interpreted as a direct link to fundamental democratic principles. Proper conduct on the battlefield was expected of the military. To be sure, there was a greater degree of latitude since the pressures of combat demanded it. But Americans expected honorable behavior even in times of war. In mundane terms, Americans expected their military to be at a higher moral plane than that of the enemy; the military was struggling against the forces of evil. Morally and ethically, such perceptions and beliefs justified conflict; US involvement was viewed as just and necessary. Although some today castigate the United States for this seemingly self-righteous posture, the fact is that many Americans sincerely believed this position. Equally important and contrary to many other countries and people, Americans invariably engaged in critical self-analysis of what they were doing and how they did it. Within the body politic there usually was a degree of doubt and discomfort with any position or involvement that stretched the notion of democratic morality.

Throughout most of US history, with the exceptions of short periods of time when the nation was involved in crisis, there has been a deeply ingrained attitude against standing armies. Not only was this evident in the American Revolution and in the debate over the American Constitution but in the Jacksonian antimilitarism of the 1800s, the isolation of the military in the post-Civil War era, and the return to isolationism in the years between World War I and World War II. This fear of standing armies, albeit in a modern guise, is an important consideration even in the current debates regarding nuclear strategy and weaponry.

One important result is that from the time of the American Revolution until the present, the concept of civilian control of the military has been accepted as a fundamental precept of the political system. It is also deeply institutionalized in the military profession.

THE UNITED STATES AS A SUPERPOWER

Although few Americans recognized it at the time, the United States emerged from World War II as the world's superpower, for a number of reasons. Not only was Europe devastated, but the United States had emerged from World War II with the most powerful military force in the world. The massive military machine was strengthened even further by the atomic bomb. Moreover, the United States had developed an extraordinary economic system able not only to produce war materiel but also a wide variety of consumer goods, even during the height of the war.

Although the Soviet Union had developed a massive military machine, its economy was in ruins, and it had suffered millions of casualties. At the end of World War II, it was no match for the United States. China was in the same condition, and Japan lay exposed to further atomic devastation had it not surrendered.

Americans longed to return quickly to peaceful pursuits. Presuming that the world would return to the tranquil period before the rise of Hitler's Germany, Americans turned immediately to the good life that they expected in their own country now that the war had ended.

Almost overnight, most of the military machine was disbanded, deactivated, and put into mothballs. Selective service was ended, and the United States offered to give up its atomic monopoly to the newly formed United Nations. Indeed, it was thought that the United Nations would solve the problem of war.[16]

At the same time, the Soviet Union not only maintained its wartime military force, it used this to consolidate its hold on Eastern Europe. The Yalta conference seemed to have opened the way for the Soviet Union to create its sphere of influence over all of Eastern Europe.

A communist government was installed in Poland and other Eastern European countries. The coup in Czechoslovakia by communists and the death of its leader Jan Masaryk signaled the beginning of the Cold War. Churchill's now-famous "iron curtain" speech marked the transition from a period of struggle against the Third Reich to the opening of the cold war between the West and the Soviet Union.

These events, among others, revealed the nature of Stalinism and the communist system. What Americans saw was disturbing and frightening: a former ally using its military power and totalitarian structure to suppress free-dom in Eastern Europe. Under the guise of revenge against Germany, Stalin's troops subdued and then destroyed democratic systems. And for the first time, the world saw the marriage between Marxist-Leninist ideology and a powerful and expansionist totalitarian state, as the Soviet Union also gained superpower status. It had demonstrated its capability to control Eastern Europe. Later it developed its own atomic weaponry. Following the victory of the Chinese communists and their conquest of mainland China, it appeared to many that the tide was running against the West. The collapse of Europe, the weakened position of England and France, and the rise of powerful Marxist-Leninist states left little choice for the United States but to become the mainspring in defense of Europe and democracy. Americans were thrust onto the main stage of world politics.

The Soviet Union emerged as a superpower committed to the expansion of Marxism-Leninism, threatening what many Americans felt was the very heart of democracy and the purpose for which World War II was fought. With its military power and its newfound status as a superpower, the Soviet Union appeared to be pursuing a goal of creating a Stalinist empire under the guise of "power to the proletariat." It was not hesitant to threaten the use of military power to achieve its goals. It became the foremost adversary to the United States and the rest of the West. It is no wonder that the United States focused its political-military posture on defense against the Soviet Union.

The Truman Doctrine was the first major post-World War II shift in US policy in an effort to forestall further Soviet gains in the European area. In a 1947 address to both houses of Congress, President Harry S. Truman pledged the United States to support free peoples resisting attempted subjugation by armed minorities or by outside pressures. Although aimed specifically at US support of Greece and Turkey, the Truman Doctrine took on global dimensions. It was strongly supported by both major American political parties and set a new course that is reflected today in US security policy.

This was followed by the Marshall Plan which provided the basis for the rebuilding of Europe. The North Atlantic Treaty Organization (NATO) was the framework around which the defense of Europe was developed. There was

much more—from the establishment of a series of treaties
following a containment policy to the creation of nuclear
weapons, eventually leading to a deterrence policy in
which both superpowers were able to balance one another
by nuclear weapons.[17]

The United States became involved in Korea in 1950,
Vietnam in 1960, and Central America in 1980 in response
to perceived communist challenges. US involvement in
these areas in one form or another goes on. This is not to
mention other engagements such as Greece, the Philippines, Lebanon, Santo Domingo, Cuba, and Grenada, all
within a short span of four decades.

Over the past decades, the United States and the rest of
the West have faced a variety of conflicts, many of which
were communist inspired and supported by external communist forces. The basic problem is that the United States
has not been able to respond effectively enough to nationalist aspirations and the social and economic grievances
within many Third World noncommunist states. Even
when conflicts have been nationalist and noncommunist
inspired, communist parties and groups have been able to
grasp the reins of leadership and shape the nationalist
revolution to their own purposes. Vietnam, Cuba, and
Nicaragua are cases in point. These political-military
events have had their parallel in the evolution of US
strategy.

Evolution of US Strategy

US strategy has been focused on the Soviet Union. This
has taken a specific form in terms of the defense of Europe, where US involvement in NATO and the creation of
a worldwide command structure is linked to the main adversary, the Soviet Union. This is not to ignore the fact
that the United States has been faced with a variety of
challenges outside the European area. Even in such cases,
however, the political-military instruments have not
strayed very far from the character of the European battlefield.

US strategy has gone through a number of major changes since the end of World War II. Nuclear superiority of the 1950s prompted the Eisenhower administration to adopt a nuclear-dominant strategy, considered the most economical and effective way to prevent war and to achieve policy goals. This "bigger bang for the buck" posture relegated conventional military forces to little more than home guard and follow-on forces after a nuclear engagement. The air force and navy became the mainstay of US strategy, with their capability to deliver nuclear weapons on any target. One result was the reorganization of the army around "pentomic" structures based primarily on the use of nuclear weapons. The "pentomic" army divisions consisted of five relatively self-contained battle groups. Each battle group contained five rifle companies. Many of the support elements as well as armor units were also organized with five integral units.

Conflicts in Southeast Asia and challenges in other parts of the world soon revealed the inappropriateness and ineffectiveness of the nuclear-dominant policy. Could the United States threaten the use of nuclear weapons against even the smallest nation that defied the United States? Was it not more realistic to assume that nuclear weapons would be used only in the most severe and direct challenge to the homeland? The nuclear-dominant strategy soon lost its credibility.

John F. Kennedy's flexible response, the next strategy, envisioned a graduated and proportional response to aggression by a military capable of undertaking a variety of contingencies from nuclear war to limited military operations. The intent was to fashion a response appropriate to the character of the aggression or threat. US involvement in Vietnam epitomized this strategy; it also revealed its basic weakness. Incrementalism in political-military strategy was shown to be ineffective in that it allowed the adversary time to adjust and adapt and raise the ante, as the North Vietnamese did in South Vietnam. Some argue that such a strategy was contrary to the principles of war, which include mass, firepower, and overwhelming force at the point of the adversary's weakness.[18]

The military refashioned its posture, with ground forces taking on a more important role. The pentomic structure was abolished, and the US Army evolved into a more traditional organization oriented toward conventional combat, particularly aimed at Europe; however, Special Forces became particularly prominent during this period as President Kennedy stressed counterinsurgency in response to the situation in Southeast Asia.

Even with US involvement in Southeast Asia, the role of the Soviet Union remained the main concern of US policy and overall strategy. Indeed there was an underlying fear that the Soviet Union would take advantage of the US engagement in Southeast Asia to move elsewhere, particularly in Europe.

In the aftermath of Vietnam, US strategy seemed to return to a modern version of flexible response in which the focus was on Europe, but more attention was given to conventional capability and extended deterrence. There also developed new initiatives in nuclear strategy, sophisticated battlefield weapons, and the electronic battlefield. The army put into place light divisions on the premise that their rapid mobility could serve as an effective response to challenges outside the European area.[19] Similarly, attention was also given to special operations forces designed for unconventional warfare.

Throughout all of these strategic adjustments, the main adversary in the eyes of political-military policy makers has been and remains the Soviet Union, either directly or indirectly. The battle in Europe and the big battle scenarios dominate US military thinking and organization. Many Americans, including those on Capitol Hill, see little serious challenge to US interests outside of the Soviet-European framework. Furthermore, the major defense budget expenditures rest primarily on weaponry and efforts aimed at Soviet military capability. As such, there is a clear technological and operational effort on European-type battlefields.

To be sure, general purpose forces have been strengthened, as has air and sea mobility. But the critical thrust of
all of the services remains on traditional missions, control
of the air, strategic bombing, interdiction, control of the
sea-lanes, amphibious assault, and conventional ground
combat. All of this is viewed in the context of a deterrence
strategy, based on a political posture and policy that retains the Soviet threat as its centerpiece.

There is a continuing need to understand the Soviet
threat and a need to develop appropriate strategies and
effective political-military instruments to implement
them, but there must be recognition that threats to the
United States emanate from a number of other quarters.
What makes this recognition difficult is the fact that in a
number of instances, the Soviet Union has exploited
situations through surrogates or proxies. In the name of
human rights and justice, Marxist-Leninist ideology and
political structures have been established in a number of
areas in which the Soviet Union has avoided direct confrontation, where it has appeared that the United States is
weak, or where there is a power vacuum, as in Ethiopia,
Angola, and Mozambique. In such cases, the threats still
emanate from the Soviet Union through its proxies and
surrogates and its ability to project power.

Many of these threats and challenges are less well
understood by the American people and many of its representatives. What makes the problem even more challenging and frustrating is that the American way of war
seems to accept more easily the European context and the
big battle scenarios. In other words, the American people
and their political-military instrument are more com-
fortable facing an adversary such as the Soviet Union than
even the minor state of Nicaragua.

The strategic dilemma is clear. Much of the effort of the
United States is designed to deter the Soviet Union. This
effort is mainly in the form of strategic weaponry and
ground, sea, and air forces, largely organized around conventional military principles. Deterrence is based on the
proposition that billions of dollars must be spent on the

military instrument for the very purpose of not using it. This money is invested in a military posture, however, that is not well positioned or disposed to engage in unconventional conflicts—conflicts that are the major characteristic of the contemporary period.

It is characteristic of the American mind-set that war and peace are distinctly separate spheres: there is a clear demarcation from peace to war. Thus, although the Clausewitzian view of battle and principles of war seem to be well established in political and military circles, the notion that war and politics are closely interconnected seems to have been misinterpreted. For Americans, therefore, there still seems to be a belief that there are separate instruments of peace: politics and diplomacy versus the instruments of war. This fits in well with the idea of the Pearl Harbor concept of war. Thus it is difficult for most Americans to adapt to the idea that in unconventional conflicts there is rarely a clear line between war and peace. Nor is it easy to accept the view that a number of states engage in unconventional conflicts as an almost normal course of action in international politics. This is particularly the case in the projection of Marxist-Leninist ideology, Soviet power, and the involvement of Soviet surrogates and proxies.

It seems clear that a new strategy must be designed, based on clear policy guidelines. This new strategy does not necessarily mean lessening the importance of the Soviet-European environment. At the minimum, however, it means a strategy encompassing unconventional conflicts and a political-military posture capable of effective response to such conflicts.

New Strategic Dimensions

To change or shift the basis of strategic thought is not easy. In the main, existing strategic orientation evolves from philosophical bases and mind-sets nurtured by the political-military posture and values of American society. Therefore strategic change, and even a reassessment, is

indirectly a challenge to the thought patterns and philosophical basis of the larger society. Nonetheless, without
some attention to reexamining prevailing strategic views
as well as political-military policy, it is difficult to see how
the United States can adequately prepare for Third World
conflicts.[20]

In a particularly perceptive study, Howard challenges
the Western concept of strategy:

> To make a nuclear threat an effective instrument either
> of offensive or defensive coercion, the engagement of
> conventional forces is a prior necessity. . . . The more
> remote a crisis or a country from the territory of a nu-
> clear power, the more necessary it will be for that power
> to deploy conventional forces if he wishes to demon-
> strate the intensity of his interest in that area, and the
> less will be the significance of its bare nuclear strength.[21]

To take this a step further, to be effective in Third
World areas, particularly those that are at a distance from
the United States, not only must there be a conventional
capability, but, more important, there must be a capability
to engage effectively in conflicts that are characteristic of
the Third World. Following Howard's logic, this in itself
would develop some element of deterrence; however, it is
likely that such capability would have to be demonstrated
not only to maintain the perception of effectiveness but
also to engage in conflicts that are a long-range threat to
US security interests.

Howard has specified four dimensions of strategy:
operational, logistical, social, and the *technological*.[22] Although all of these do not have the same importance or
impact in every war, "under different circumstances, one
or another of these dimensions might dominate."[23]

Although his concern was primarily on nuclear strategy, it is equally appropriate for unconventional conflicts.
For example, US capacity in Vietnam may have been
effective in logistical and technological dimensions. In
operational terms, it may have been effective in the conduct of conventional or set-piece battles but questionable

in unconventional situations.   But the most important
dimension may have been the social, and it is this dimension that dominated the conflict over the long run.
In brief, the degree of social cohesion of the protagonists
was critical in the Vietnam conflict.   This is important in
every type of conflict, but in unconventional conflicts
characterized by political ambiguities, protractedness,
asymmetry, and unconventional tactics, social cohesion in
democracies tends to be fragile at best.

The social dimension is not only important in assessing
strategy with respect to the immediate combatants (US
forces, South Vietnam, the Vietcong and the North
Vietnamese) but also with respect to the social condition
in the domestic political arena.   Thus, the political environment had much to do with the outcome of the Vietnamese conflict.   On the one hand, the North Vietnamese
appeared to be totally committed politically, militarily,
and psychologically to final victory.   On the other hand,
US staying power (national will and political resolve)
eroded rapidly following the Tet offensive in 1968.   Although US forces were usually decisive on the batttlefield,
the outcome of the war was dictated by the degree of
staying power of the United States (and that of South
Vietnam) as compared to that of the Vietcong and North
Vietnam.

Equally important, a conflict undertaken in conventional terms aimed at the adversary's armed elements
may be incidental to the real nature of unconventional
war.   That is, the political cadre, the revolutionary leadership, and the political system are the center of gravity of
the conflict.   That is where the major effort should be
concentrated.   This is the social dimension of strategy that
is critical and dominant in unconventional conflicts.

In the broader range of conflicts, the US military has
been historically oriented toward a professional ethos
deeply rooted in success in battle.   This, in turn, is seen in
military terms.   Success in battle means coming to grips

with enemy armed forces, bringing to bear effective firepower and forces, and destroying or capturing enemy forces. There is little room to consider the social dimension, much less concern with the political-social posture of the enemy.

Firepower, maneuver, effective use of conventionally organized forces, adequate forces, and effective military leadership as envisioned in Clausewitzian notions underpin US military professionalism. Indeed this is the basis for modern military forces in general. There is a distinct separation between the military and political spheres of the conflict, at least in the minds of many US political and military leaders and indeed Americans in general. In most Western political systems, the military is often seen as separate from the political structure. Civil-military relations are analyzed in accordance with that premise. In brief, civilian control of the military is a sine qua non of democracy. It follows that military men have no business dabbling in political matters, either on the battlefield or at home.

Carried to its extreme, which many tend to do, this means that military men should limit their concern to defeating the enemy of the battlefield—and this means in accord with the notions of war that dominate the US political system. Thus, involvement in unconventional conflicts not only places the US political system at a disadvantage, it also places the military at a disadvantage in the conflict area and with respect to its credibility within its own system. This is made worse by the fact that the adversary knows this and, having access to the open environment in the United States, can undertake a political-psychological campaign that can be more effective than any military victory. It is no wonder that a member of the Vietnamese Politburo, Le Duc Tho, at the tenth anniversary of the fall of Saigon and the defeat of South Vietnam publicly thanked the American people on television for helping the North in their victory.

SUMMARY AND CONCLUSIONS

Clear policy must be the first order of business. It is from policy that strategy evolves. In this respect, democracies cannot afford the luxury of presuming that people will inherently seek freedom and justice and that political systems will develop in the Third World that are pointed toward democracy. Most systems in the Thirld World are fragile. Although many desire to become democratic, the process of modernization and change exposes them to internal and external forces whose ideology and system are diametrically opposed to democracy. Moreover, there may be many systems, even those that are perceived to be nondemocratic, whose susceptibility to democratic forces is much greater than any established Marxist-Leninist system. Indeed, left-wing fascist revolutions are, in the long run, more dangerous to democracy than existing nondemocratic and even authoritarian (non-Marxist-Leninist) systems. Over the past several decades, no Marxist-Leninist system has been overthrown through internal efforts, Chile's Allende notwithstanding, yet many nondemocratic, non-Marxist-Leninist systems have been overthrown.

Once a Marxist-Leninist system is installed, its political structure, ideology, elite power, system of control, and linkage with other Marxist-Leninist systems make it extremely difficult to challenge and change. Equally important, the nature of democracies makes them hesitant and most times opposed to undertaking operations to overthrow antidemocratic systems. Implicitly, then, Marxist-Leninist systems installed in the Third World tend to be accepted as legitimate by many democracies. At the same time, non-Marxist-Leninist but nondemocratic systems tend to be perceived as illegitimate by the same democracies: "What we end up with in what is conventionally called Western society is a topsy-turvy situation in which those seeking to destroy democracy appear to be fighting for legitimate aims, while its defenders are pictured as repressive reactionaries."[24]

Democracies must not only seek to protect their political system and values, they must seek ways to support like-minded systems—that is, open systems attempting to move toward political democracy. Even nondemocratic systems that are non-Marxist-Leninist should be examined to find ways to move them toward political democracy. In the long run, such systems may be less threatening to democracy than left-wing fascist revolutionary systems. Indeed, non-Marxist-Leninist, nondemocratic systems may be vulnerable to change by the efforts of democratic forces, in contrast to Marxist-Leninist systems in the Third World.

A new policy dimension needs to be created based on the view that certain systems are critical to the maintenance and perpetuation of democracy, even if such systems are not democratic. These systems may deserve the serious support and assistance of the United States for long-run security interests and also as a means of expanding the notion of democratic systems. This shifts a reactive policy (which seems to characterize US policy in most of the Third World), based on "anti-"posture, to one of initiative and positive orientation—that is, to a policy of democratic nation building. Once systems develop reasonably well-functioning democracies, they would be in the best position to resist left-wing revolutionary challenges, as well as challenges from right-wing groups.

Strategy developed from a policy of democratic nation building includes measures ranging from diplomacy to military assistance to involvement in unconventional conflict. Indeed, one can also argue that such a policy opens the way for support of revolutions against Marxist-Leninist systems. Policy and strategy, however, cannot be based on the assumption that all systems must be aided by the United States. Policy cannot be based on policing the entire Third World. In a number of cases, existing systems are capable of maintaining internal order and reasonably effective government. Moreover, there has developed a certain sense of regionalism in areas of the world, such as Central America, that may be enough to create an internal support base between states within regions without serious external involvement. Further, situations such as the Middle East may preclude large-scale direct intervention by either superpower. Finally, there may be instances where US involvement may worsen the situation.

But in certain areas of the world, unconventional conflicts persist and are likely to persist. In a number of such areas, the United States has long-term security interests, such as Central America and the Horn of Africa. In such cases, US public pronouncements and economic aid may not be adequate to support and maintain the existing system. Further, US credibility and trust can be major issues, leading to questions of staying power. Support and assistance may require wide-ranging political and military efforts. It may be reasonable to ask, therefore, whether the United States should be willing to support systems that can be moved toward democracy or those that are fragile open systems. According to one authority,

> A democracy which genuinely aspires to civilized values will of course promote adherence to the law and due process whenever possible.... And yet, the good society cannot be summed up once and for all in a particular legal corde or set of moral values. Beyond all good laws and rules may be discerned the transcendent purpose of civilization.... Morality may require of the defenders of civilization something other than strict adherence to law and due process.... In order to uphold the principle of respect for law, even in situations involving war, espionage, etc., a society may try to anticipate and define circumstances in which some laws can be legally set aside. Even so, the needs of morality cannot be captured in advance in a network of rules.[25]

In brief, democracies may need to engage in certain policies and employ strategy that may stretch the notion of democracy and may even contradict some democratic principles, albeit temporarily. This may be done for the sake of a higher moral order and to protect the system, but this does not allow resort to any means, since the ends-means relationship in an open system is critical. The means used must be within acceptable moral bounds and propriety. Further, such policy and strategy need not be limited to protection and survival of the homeland. Such a narrow view of democratic morality may in itself be contrary to the notions of democratic principles. Additionally, waiting until such a threat to the homeland occurs may mean it is too late for that democracy. The demands of a higher law may require that democracies support and maintain other democracies and create conditions for the development of democracy. If this is the case, it demands something more than a passive policy and strategy—something that goes beyond traditional diplomacy and state-to-state relationships.

But when an appeal to a higher morality is made for the sake of going beyond prevailing rules, it cannot be based on a set of rules determined beforehand. Rather, such actions must be assessed in each case and appeal to a higher moral law painstakingly and prudently examined to ensure that there is no doubt that the higher moral law prevails. In the long run, democracy must adhere to moral laws and moral accountability. Yet it may be that the highest morality is the protection and survival of democracy and its value system.

This complex matter was addressed by one authority with respect to wars and US society. According to the author, in the post-World War II period,

> It was time for free, decent societies to continue to control their military forces, but to quit demanding from them impossible acquiescence in the liberal view of life. A "modern" infantry may ride sky vehicles into combat, fire and sense its weapons through instrumentation, employ devices of frightening lethality in the future— but it must also be old-fashioned enough to be iron-hard, poised for instant obedience, and prepared to die in the mud. . . . If liberal, decent societies cannot discipline themselves to do all of these things, they may have nothing to offer the world. They may not last long enough.[26]

Although applying specifically to the US military and society, the principle applies equally well with respect to the support and maintenance of democratic systems.

Translated into contemporary US posture, these issues may be best addressed by a series of questions. Can and should the United States support nationalist and democratically directed revolutions against existing systems? Should the United States support counterrevolutions against left-wing fascist revolutionary groups? Is there anything in democratic principles that prevents a democracy from fighting for its own soul? Is it not legitimate for democracies to support aggressively the creation of other democracies? Given the nature of contemporary conflicts and the deep difference between democratic (open) and nondemocratic (closed) systems, these issues go beyond short-term geopolitical maneuvering.

These are the philosophical and ideological issues that shape the political-psychological environment of international politics. In order to develop understanding and awareness, it is necessary for Americans to take a critical look at the contemporary international situation and the nature of their own system, not in a spasm of panic or anticommunist mania but on the basis that democracies are worth supporting. Systems that are susceptible to democratic forces and those that can be moved in the direction of open systems may be worth supporting in the short run, regardless of the type of system currently installed, on the expectations of achieving long-range goals. It is hoped that such systems can be transformed into open systems eventually.

It is difficult for democracies to reconcile long-run goals with short-run strategy—that is, reconciliation of the needs for stretching notions of democracy and in some cases setting aside strict adherence to law temporarily to a higher morality in order to advance democracy in the long run. This is not an easy matter. Not only does it challenge popular notions of democracy, but it exposes open systems to even more external forces intent on creating disorder. As de Tocqueville wrote,

It is especially in the conduct of foreign relations that democracies appear to be decidedly inferior to other governments. . . . A democracy can only with great difficulty regulate the details of an important undertaking, persevere in a fixed design, and work out its execution in spite of serious obstacles. It cannot combine its measures with secrecy or await their consequences with patience.[27]

Nowhere is this truer than in the challenges posed to the United States and other democracies by unconventional conflicts.

NOTES

1. Carl von Clausewitz, *On War*, ed. Anatol Rapoport (Baltimore, Md.: Penguin Books, 1971), p. 241.

2. Bruce Palmer, Jr., "Strategic Guidelines for the United States in the 1980s," in Bruce Palmer, Jr., ed., *Grand Strategy for the 1980s* (Washington, D.C.: American Enterprise Institute, 1978), p. 73.

3. Michael Howard, *The Causes of War and Other Essays*, 2d ed., enlarged (Cambridge: Harvard University Press, 1984), p. 112.

4. Russell F. Weigley, *The American Way of War: A History of United States Military Strategy and Policy* (Bloomington: Indiana University Press, 1977), p. 477.

5. Western military thought also includes attention to Jomini. Serious study of strategy should include both Clausewitz and Jomini, among others. For the purposes here, the distinctions between Clausewitz and Sun Tzu are clear and illustrate the thrust of Western military thought in contrast to the needs of unconventional conflicts. For a useful discussion of strategists and theorists, see Edward Mead Earle, *Makers of Modern Strategy: Military Thought from Machiavelli to Hitler* (New York: Atheneum, 1969).

6. Thomas Powers, *Thinking about the Next War* (New York: Alfred A. Knopf, 1982), p. 95.

7. Rapoport, *On War*, p. 101.

8. Ibid., p. 103.

9. This equates to the idea of battlefield victory and the systematic application of massive military power to overwhelm enemy armed forces.

10. Sun Tzu, *The Art of War*, trans. and with an introduction by Samuel B. Griffith (New York: Oxford University Press, 1971), p. 20.

11. Ibid., p. x.

12. Ibid., pp. 77-78.

13. Ibid., pp. 42-43.

14. Ibid., p. 42.

15. Ibid., Foreword.

16. See, for example, James Schlesinger, "The Eagle and the Bear," *Foreign Affairs* (Summer 1985): 938.

17. There is little need to recount all of these major events over the past three decades. Much of this has been well covered in a variety of excellent publications. See, for example, Lawrence Freedman, *The Evolution of Nuclear Strategy* (New York: St. Martin's Press, 1981); Frederick H. Hartmann and Robert L. Wendzel, *To Preserve the Republic: United States Foreign Policy* (New York: Macmillan, 1985); and John Spanier, *American Foreign Policy since World War II*, 9th ed. (New York: Holt, Rinehart and Winston, 1983).

18. See, for example, Harry G. Summers, Jr., *On Strategy: The Vietnam War in Context* (Carlisle Barracks, Penna.: Army War College, 1981).

19. The creation of light infantry divisions in the US Army is based on the view that highly mobile, immediately deployable forces are necessary for various contingencies in Third World areas. Light infantry divisions are supposed to have slightly more than 10,000 personnel (about 3,000 to 5,000 fewer than standard divisions), be air mobile, and be armed with weapons capable of being taken anywhere. Plans are underway to activate five such divisions without increasing the total troop strength in the army. See William J. Olson, "The Light Force Initiative, " *Military Review* 65, no. 6 (June 1985): 2-17, and John D. May, Jr., "Heavy versus Light Forces: A Question of Balance," in Asa A. Clark IV, Peter W. Chiarelli, Jeffrey S. McKitrick, and James W. Reed, eds., *The Defense Reform Debate; Issues and Analysis* (Baltimore, Md.: Johns Hopkins University Press, 1984), pp. 166-78.

20. In this respect, one of the most recent biting criticisms of US strategy and the art of war is Edward N. Luttwak, *The Pentagon and the Art of War: The Question of Military*

Reform (New York: Simon and Schuster, 1984).   See also Clark et al.

21. Howard, p. 97.

22. Ibid., pp. 104-6.

23. Ibid., p. 105.

24. Jean-François Revel, *How Democracies Perish* (Garden City, N.Y.: Doubleday, 1983), pp. 4-5.

25. Claes G. Ryn, "The Ethical Problem of Democratic Statecraft," in James P. O'Leary, Jeffrey Salmon, and Richard Shultz, eds., *Power, Principles and Interests: A Reader in World Politics* (Lexington, Mass.:   Ginn Press, 1985), p. 119.

26. T. R. Fehrenbach, *This Kind of War: A Study in Unpreparedness* (New York: Simon and Schuster, 1963), p. 706. Reference is made to this quotation in James H. Toner, "American Society and the American Way of War: Korea and Beyond," *Parameters* 11, no. 1 (March 1981): 89.

27. Alexis de Tocqueville, *Democracy in America*, trans. George Lawrence and ed. J. P. Mayer (Garden City, N.Y.: Anchor Books, 1969), pp. 228-29.

7

Challenge and Response

President Calvin Coolidge appointed Henry L. Stimson as his personal representative in 1927 to mediate the Nicaraguan civil war and establish the basis for fair elections there in 1928. Coolidge's policy in Nicaragua was under heavy attack in Congress and by a number of other political actors. In response to his own mission and to the critics of US policy in Nicaragua, Stimson stated,

> No one asks that our government should be free from criticism in its foreign relations. But our government has a right to ask that the criticism leveled against it by its own citizens in respect to those foreign relations shall be responsible and based upon a reasonable amount of investigation of the facts. That has not been the case in the past in respect to the criticism leveled at our Nicaraguan policy.[1]

These words could be just as well spoken today with the same relevance and urgency. The issue of US involvement in Nicaragua in 1985 evoked responses similar to those in 1927. In 1985, however, US policy in Nicaragua was part of the larger problem of US involvement in the Third World.

A recent study of US policy in Central America concluded that getting the United States more deeply involved in the region would surely drive Americans further apart.[2]   This conclusion was based partly on US historical experience in the Southern Hemisphere, partly on the domestic political climate in the 1980s, and partly on the experience of the Vietnam War.   Thus, it would seem that American attitudes in the late 1980s precluded serious US involvement anywhere in the Third World except in humanitarian and economic terms.

There is also a growing feeling within US military circles that the military should not be committed unless there is strong public support for such a policy.   In agreement with this view, Secretary of Defense Caspar Weinberger outlined the criteria for commitment of US forces.[3]   A strict application of such criteria would seem to preclude commitment of US forces except in clear crises, supported by the American people, and then only as a last resort.

However, President Reagan's foreign and security policy in the 1980s seems to be based on a strong possibility of the use of military force, which disturbs some Americans. Indeed, the Grenada operation in 1983 is still condemned by some, although the operation uncovered a storehouse full of documents demonstrating Soviet-Cuban involvement in Grenada and its potential for becoming another Cuba.[4]   Similarly, administration support for the freedom fighters (contras) in Nicaragua and for the Duarte regime in El Salvador has many critics in the United States as well as in Europe and Latin America.

Nonetheless, attempts to reassert a more positive US leadership role and the dramatic change in political-military posture brought on by the Reagan presidency created a new political posture in the United States.   But opinion has not evolved into a consensus on foreign policy, nor has it provided the basis for credible staying power in the Third World.   This is particularly the case with respect to US capability in unconventional conflicts.

It is ironic that at the very time when the United States is trying to shake off its Vietnam complex and is divided on policy and strategy in the Third World, the Soviet Union seems to have developed an even greater capacity to influence Third World states.   One authority has pointed out,

> Between 1945 and 1980, well over 100 separate wars took place around the globe, the vast majority of them in or between developing countries.   The Soviet Union was involved as a major arms supplier and diplomatic actor in some 20 of these conflicts.   Although these figures suggest that the USSR steered clear of local wars far more often than not, involvement in 20 conflicts nevertheless represents an extraordinarily high level of foreign commitment for a country that prior to World War II only rarely had acted as a major supplier of arms, or even as a principal diplomatic actor, in conflicts outside Europe.[5]

What is also important is that in some of the most recent conflicts, the Soviet Union has committed military advisers, commanders, and *Spetsnatz* forces.[6] These changes in Soviet policy and strategy were followed in 1985 by the ascension to power of Mikhail Gorbachev. Many experts see this as the beginning of a long tenure of leadership for Gorbachev as he consolidates his hold in the Politburo and on the other instruments of Soviet government.[7] This new, younger, more forceful leadership brings with it a more potent political and military leadership. For the West, this promises a long period in which the leadership of the United States and the rest of the West will be challenged to a degree and in a manner not seen over the past generation. It also may bring a more forceful posture and an expanding Soviet presence in the Third World, even with increasing internal Soviet problems.

Soviet power projection is not solely or even primarily dependent on actual commitment of military forces. Rather, power projection is seen as the ability of the Soviet state to use a variety of instruments, ranging from military aid and arms sales to diplomacy and covert operations, to affect Third World states (see Appendix). The Soviet Union seems to have developed a growing capacity to exploit unconventional conflicts to its own advantage. Soviet involvement in Afghanistan also shows that it is prepared to use direct military force, at least in contiguous areas.

But the problem of US policy toward Third World conflicts goes beyond East-West relations. It has more to do with the character of the challenge emanating directly from Third World states. Although many of these are immediate, the long-range problems promise to be more serious because they have to do with ideology and the nature of the political systems that are evolving in Third World states.

THE CHALLENGE

The importance of the Third World to the United States may be overlooked because the dangers do not appear to be immediate or challenging to US national security. How often does one hear, for example, that a small island like Cuba is surely not a serious security challenge to the United States or that a Marxist-Leninist system in Nicaragua could not possibly be a serious challenge to the United States?

These questions can be partially answered by showing how a number of states in Central America and in the Caribbean sit astride critical US sea-lanes that would be required in order to support Western allies and US forces in Europe should a war occur. Although states such as Nicaragua may not pose a critical security challenge on their own, they can be used as conduits for stronger external forces to jeopardize US security.

The real danger, however, lies in the possibility that increasing numbers of Third World states may be driven into adopting closed systems not only through the urging of the Soviets and Marxist-Leninist ideology but also by the challenges of modernity and the drive to consolidate the power of governing elites. Of particular importance is the inherent fear that such systems and elites have of open systems. Closed systems foster a conflict mentality in regard to their relationships with open systems and the way they perceive the world. At the heart of the problem is that closed systems in general are placed in jeopardy if they allow the values and political style of open systems to coexist peacefully. It is feared that under such conditions, the open qualities will invariably find their way into closed systems, undermining their legitimacy.

This long-range conflict is rarely recognized by open systems. What adds a critical dimension is that many Third World states have adopted important features of closed systems and seem to follow a pattern established by Marxist-Leninist states. According to one report,

> The new Third World regimes have striking similarities. Among them are a steady centralization of power, suppression of political pluralism, close alignment with and support for the Soviet Union and other Marxist states, military cooperation with the Soviet Union, and internal weakness and lack of popular legitimacy.[8]

In some instances, such systems follow deliberate policies and strategies leading to conflict and confrontation. One can see such patterns in Central America.

In brief, US and other Western interests in Third World areas are both immediate and long term. They range from geopolitical importance and energy sources to political-psychological interests. Linked closely to all of these is the East-West adversarial relationship. But US policy problems and challenges stem as much from the nature of the Third World environment as the nature and policy of the Soviet system.

Third World Instability

Third World states tend to be unstable and governed by fragile political institutions. Those in power seek to maintain that power at almost any cost. This is not to suggest that all Third World states are governed by power-hungry elites, but in much of the Third World, politics and power is everything. From politics flows economic and social power, status, and money. There are few areas outside of politics in which these goals can be achieved. To lose power is tantamount to losing everything. For those not in power, the most compelling desire is to gain political power.

Much of this results from the problems of modernity: economic development and political change. Changing political institutions and the bases of political power, combined with attempts at moving from a subsistence to an industrial economy, create revolutionary conditions and expose existing institutions and the governing elite to a variety of internal challenges.

Policies and strategies adopted by existing systems to maintain some cohesion and control must therefore address a spectrum of interconnected problems, ranging from security to import-export issues and foreign aid, to training, education, and economic productivity. The demands and the pressures this creates are beyond the capabilities and resources of many Third World states. As a result, most Third World states require and seek a great deal of external aid and assistance.

At the same time, revolutionary groups may form to overthrow the existing system. Leadership for such groups does not usually come from the downtrodden peasantry. On the contrary, leaders come from the upwardly mobile and more educated elements; Mao, Ho Chi Minh, Guevara, Castro, and Ortega are examples. Typically revolutionary rhetoric appeals to the liberal-Lockean tendencies of US society and the West in general.[9]

An example of these complex problems, the confusion, the mixing of myth and reality and historical distortions, can be found in US public attitudes and policy regarding Central America. The revolution in El Salvador and the establishment of a Marxist-Leninist regime in Nicaragua seemed to reawaken American fears of another Vietnam. By the mid-1980s, the lines were drawn in the United States. Some stood against any US intervention. Indeed, some of these same people were also opposed to the Duarte administration in El Salvador, although the Duarte government in 1985 promised the best opportunity for a reasonably effective non-Marxist system. Much of this was based on the historical patterns of US intervention in Latin America and the prevailing distrust of US intentions.

Another group of Americans feared another Cuba and the threat of expanded Soviet penetration of Central and Latin America. They demanded firm response, including military force if necessary, perhaps similar to the Grenada operation. Still another group could not make up their minds. They feared Soviet and Cuban expansion and the threat this posed to the United States. Yet they also feared another Vietnam and defeat. Thus they advocated some kind of aid, but primarily humanitarian and economic. This last group seemed to be in the majority.

Nature of the Challenge

According to a recent study of Central America and US policy,

> Two broad conclusions can be drawn from these case studies. The first is that each time the United States has attempted to intervene militarily in Central America after 1920 it has, in the long run, worsened the situation it meant to correct. . . . No major U.S. aid plan can sufficiently improve economic conditions and deal with the structural political problems until governments attain power that have no interest in maintaining the status quo.[10]

If this is the case, it follows that a revolution must occur before a US aid plan can have any hope of success. Given historical experience and the impact of Marxist-Leninist systems, waiting until a revolution occurs may be too late for an effective response.

Thus, the United States is faced with a policy and strategy dilemma. Strong forces within the United States oppose major involvement in Third World systems, particularly systems ripe for revolution. At the same time, the Soviet Union has increased its capability to project its power into Third World areas through various strategies —from the use of proxies and surrogates to direct military involvement. Yet it is also becoming clear that a number of Third World states are important to US national security through geopolitical, economic, or political-psychological considerations.

These problems are compounded by the fact that many Third World states are not democratic according to US standards, revealing a lack of US understanding of the cultural and nationalistic character of these systems. Further, internal problems make many Third World states susceptible to unconventional conflicts. Finally, some Third World states engage in or support terrorism to further their policy goals, much of the time rationalized as a response to US foreign policy. To say that the Third World is complex is surely an understatement. There are few clear issues. It is no wonder then that US policy and strategy in Third World areas are open to much criticism. They are so harried by political rhetoric, distortions, domestic partisanship, visions of Vietnam, and misinformation that they are at best unclear and at worst ineffective and hesitant, lacking credible staying power. To cut through the verbiage and misinformation, we need to understand the basis of US policy.

BASIS OF POLICY

There are four important elements to developing a realistic basis for US policy in Third World areas: US national interests, the Soviet role, the historical relationship of the West to the Third World, and the problem of modernity in the Third World.

US National Interests

The concept of national interests is not easily defined or interpreted, leading to hazy and varied notions. Some interpret it in different ways on the basis of ideological posturing, political partisanship, or at times honest disagreement over its meaning. One scholar writes,

> The term *national interests* has long been used by statesmen and scholars to describe the foreign policy goals of nation-states. Although the concept is not new there is ambiguity about its meaning, and most scholars have chosen to use their own descriptions rather than follow the formulations of others.[11]

National interest is seen as "the well-being of American citizens and enterprise operating *outside* the United States and thus beyond the administrative jurisdiction of the U.S. Government."[12] The author identifies four basic interests: "Defense of the Homeland; Economic Well-being; Favorable World Order; and Promotion of Values (Ideology)."[13] Accordingly, it is the intensity of interest regarding specific issues relating to these four long-term interests that is the basis for commitment of resources and determination of policy and strategy—survival, vital, major, and peripheral. It is in this context that US interests and policy toward the Third World can be assessed and designed.

Although most Third World forces may not threaten survival or even vital US interests in the immediate period, they may do so over the long run. What is occurring today may be the basis for threatening vital US interests in the future. The shape of the Third World with respect to ideology and political systems is indeed vital to the United States over the long run. As such, it is essential to develop the requisite policies and strategy now to minimize later threats.

There is nothing inherently evil about the attempt of the United States to influence Third World states (as seen through the four elements of national interest). Indeed foreign policy in general attempts to protect US interests and influence other states into accepting US interests as valid and legitimate. US policy toward Third World states is no exception.

There must be concern for the US political system and its values. These must be interpreted in realistic terms with respect to Third World systems. For example, it may be that in the short run, Americans must deal with non-democratic systems in the hope that in the long run, the systems can be altered without resort to massive violence.

Many of the unconventional conflicts that are characteristic of the Third World are based on the serious political, economic, and social transformations these systems are experiencing. Most are not initiated by Moscow, but it must be recognized that Soviet policy and strategy are aimed at exploiting such conflicts. Soviet political and military leaders seem to realize the importance of such conflicts with respect to their own power and that of the West. Marxist-Leninist ideology does not hamper the flexibility of the Soviet political and military leadership in dealing with situations where the US position is weak or where there is a power vacuum.

The Soviet Union and the Third World

Although the Soviet Union's main concern is Europe, the Third World has become an important focus. As Trotsky stated, "The road to Paris and London lies through the towns of Afghanistan, the Punjab, and Bengal."[14] He could just as well have added that the road to Washington lies through the towns of Central America and Mexico.

American scholars disagree as to the successes or failures of the Soviet Union in the Third World. Some argue that Soviet interests in the Third World are as legitimate as those of the United States and that Soviet success is

mixed and poses as many dangers to the Soviets as opportunities. According to one authority,

> If Moscow's opportunities are greater than before, the
> complexity of the situations are also greater. To argue
> because of the absence of Soviet casualties that Moscow
> has followed a course of maximum benefits with little
> costs is to miss the complexity of the problem. With
> benefits come costs, and the Kremlin will—if it has not
> already done so—learn this as did the United States and
> all the world's other imperial powers of the past.[15]

But others see Soviet effectiveness somewhat different-
ly. For example, after analyzing five cases of Soviet
involvement in Third World conflicts, one researcher
concluded, "Soviet leaders seem to view conflict as the
fundamental feature of world politics and, as a result,
identify incipient conflicts and respond to them at an
earlier point of time."[16] The author goes on:

> Regardless of what gains or setbacks the USSR has ex-
> perienced in various countries and regions, the simple
> fact of its involvement in the Third World has con-
> tributed to the weakening of Western influence there.
> ... Soviet-backed military victories have contributed to a
> growing perception among Third World leaders that the
> future lies with the East rather than the West and that it
> is, in any event, imprudent not to maintain a good rela-
> tionship with Moscow.[17]

A recent report from the Rand Corporation concludes
that with respect to new Marxist-Leninist regimes in the
Third World, "On balance ... the new regimes have
clearly benefited the Soviet Union by providing a starting
point for increased Soviet influence in the third world."[18]
Even analyses that conclude that the Soviet Union's
record in the Third World has not been particularly successful or at best mixed admit to the seriousness of the
Soviet challenge. For example, although there is evidence
to the contrary, some authors claim that "there is no
Soviet drive for Africa in progress and no imminent

Soviet threat."[19] But even in these cases, the seriousness of the Soviet involvement in the Third World is acknowledged. With respect to Africa, for example, one scholar concludes,

> The West can therefore expect continual challenges as the USSR attempts to extend its political and military influence in a manner consonant with its role as a global power. Future setbacks and success will result from not only Soviet actions and Western response, but also from the dynamics of African regional and local politics.[20]

Some tend to analyze Soviet policy, strategy, and intentions using criteria based on US values. Thus, they conclude that the Soviet Union's policies and strategies are those of any other imperialist power, the assumption being that the United States also behaves like an imperialist power. Even the Soviet leadership is likely to say, for example, that US involvement in Central America is like Soviet involvement in Afghanistan. These simplistic and erroneous views have advocates in the United States, and more often than not, they find their way into the mass media.

The Soviet Union cannot be assessed logically except in terms of the values, attitudes, and structure of its own political system. To equate a closed with an open system is incorrect and misleading. To presume that the Soviet system, with its control structure and lack of serious political counteracting forces, is the same as the United States is grossly misleading.

Open systems pose a permanent threat to closed systems not because of any war-making capacity but because of their values, their political pluralism, and the limits placed on the governing system and ruling groups. One authority with years of experience in negotiating with the Soviets has stated, "Totalitarians are insecure. Whenever a small group of people governs large masses without the legitimacy or stability that comes from consent, they are afraid. They fear their neighbors, they fear strangers, they fear one another."[21]

Closed systems, then, deeply fear open systems, and this fear is translated into institutionalized conflict against open systems. This can be seen in the ideology of Marxism-Leninism in its various forms and the policy and strategy adopted by such systems. The United States stands as an epitome of open systems and as such is seen as the greatest threat to closed systems, particularly those professing a Marxist-Leninist ideology. This does not mean that closed systems will wage visible war against the United States. Rather, a variety of means, including unconventional conflicts, are used, depending on the circumstances and the relative strength or weakness of the United States in any particular area.[22] For many closed systems, conflict is accepted as a normal state of affairs; peace and war become almost indistinguishable, short of major conflicts, with the added complexity of terrorism.

The Soviet System: A Brief Overview

To guard against unwarranted views regarding US capability in the Third World and against distorted expectations regarding US-Soviet relationships, there must be a realistic assessment of the Soviet political system and its value structure. At the same time, it must also be recognized that as much as Americans do not understand the Soviets, the Soviets do not fully understand Americans. To presume that Soviet policy and strategy parallel US efforts is therefore dangerous.

To begin to understand the Soviet system and its political-military posture requires serious reading of the literature, some knowledge of Russian history, and familiarity with the nature and character of the Marxist-Leninist revolution of 1917. But a sense of the Soviet system and its values can be developed by looking at recent events and reading of some of the more popular books on the Soviet system. These may not provide the in-depth understanding required of policy makers, but they will cause most thoughtful Americans to pause and rethink the real nature of the Soviet system.

In a recently acclaimed book on the Soviet system, one author concludes, in part,

> But the idea of democracy never gained much favor, even in the quiet of personal attitudes. Few Russians comprehended the principle of a free press, free elections, open debate, and individual liberties; few could grasp the curious American notion that government was to be distrusted and contained and kept out of private lives. And those who understood often found the ideas distasteful, productive only of disorder. Black-marketeering was much more popular than political dissent, though just as dangerous: Many more Soviet citizens were willing to risk imprisonment for buying and selling jeans than for advocating free speech.[23]

There is some confusion in trying to understand and identify Soviet policies and intentions regarding the United States, just as there are Soviet misperceptions and ignorance regarding the essence of American politics and culture. At one level, the desires of individual Russians may parallel those of individual Americans. These have to do with aspirations associated with jobs, careers, and family. At another level however, there is deep divergence. This has to do with the role of leaders and the responsibility of those in power to the people. This includes matters such as how people view their role in the political system, accountability of those who govern, and the mind sets regarding their own system and the external world. In other words, there is a fundamental difference between the Soviet Union as a closed system and the United States as an open system.

Many Americans will find that the Soviet system and its values are in direct contrast to those of the United States and not likely to change in the foreseeable future. Thoughtful Americans are also likely to find that the Soviet value system has a built-in threat factor: the threat of open systems. Translated into foreign policy, this leads the Soviet Union to support expansionist Third World closed systems that accept Marxist-Leninist views—those that are outright Marxist-Leninist systems or those that seek a rationale for perpetuating an elite rule dedicated to control of the system. In this respect, one scholar concludes,

> The Soviet Union and the Soviet system constitute the last of the major nineteenth-century empires. . . . The Soviet overseas empire in 1980 was more extensive than it had been in 1970. . . . In the 1980s the development of the Soviet empire is likely to pose two major challenges to global peace and Western security. . . . That empire's impetus to expand [and] the processes within the empire toward disintegration. . . . Soviet leaders are more likely to use extreme forms of military force to maintain their empire than to expand it.[24]

There is a certain amount of truth in the proposition that Marxist-Leninist ideology is viewed by many in the Soviet Union as irrelevant. Nonetheless, the Soviet leadership and party bureaucracy remain committed to Marxist-Leninist ideology as the basis for legitimizing their power. They are prisoners of their ideology. Even the new leadership under Mikhail Gorbachev appears to rationalize the problems of the Soviet Union in terms of improper working of the system rather than any fault with the ideology and the nature of the Soviet system. Moreover, Gorbachev appears to be stressing the need for strong leadership in order to ensure that the Marxist-Leninist ideology is properly implemented.

It is unlikely, therefore, that there will be a significant change in Soviet policy and intentions, even with the change in Soviet leadership in 1985 and the attempt to ease relationships as a result of the 1985 Geneva Summit. It is more likely that the Soviets will consolidate their presence in the Third World, reassert the validity of Marxist-Leninist ideology to developing states, and support established Marxist-Leninist Third World states in a new version of the Brezhnev Doctrine; established Marxist-Leninist states must be preserved.

A policy and strategy of minimum risk and highest benefit from the Soviet perspective is associated with the Third World. It is in the Third World that the US and the West appear most vulnerable and where Marxist-Leninist ideologies can be revitalized. It appears that Soviet leadership may be convinced that persistent Soviet efforts in the Third World using a number of Communist states, such as Cuba, East Germany, Czechoslovakia, and Bulgaria, as conduits for Soviet policy, combined with major efforts at solving domestic problems may shift the correlation of forces in favor of the Soviet Union.

An understanding of the Soviet system and its policy cannot be limited to the postrevolutionary period (after 1917). A great deal of Soviet policy and strategy is a continuation from the Czarist period of Russia. Part of Soviet policy is based on seeking a role as a superpower. Yet the drive for a warm water seaport, deep involvement in Afghanistan, and an inbred fear of Western powers emanates from the historical relationships and policies of Czarist Russia. The clearest example of this is the Soviet concern (fear) of China traced back to the Mongol invasions of old Russia.

Finally, throughout Russian and Soviet history, two contradictory forces have been at play: anarchy and centralization. Briefly, the fear of invasions and the perceived threats from both East and West convinced the Russians that only a strong central government could ensure protection of Russia. The invasion of the Soviet Union by Germany and the millions of Russian casualties in World War II reinforced this view of history in Russian eyes.

This is probably at the core of the centralized position of the Czars, as both secular and religious leaders; however, the inability of some groups to have their grievances heard combined with democratic impulses penetrating Russia from the West drove some people to react against the Russian system by organizing secret resistance groups and engaging in terrorist activity relevant to the times. Such activity was justified in the eyes of some Russians as the only outlet available for expressing grievances and in opposing the Czarist system and its secret police.

The modern Soviet system is a mix of Russian historical continuities, the centralized Soviet system, and Marxist-Leninist ideology. In the aftermath of World War II, this system was bolstered by a huge military machine. The synthesis of the system with military power is at the heart of the USSR's present superpower status. This has led to a dangerous confrontation with the United States and between two ideologies and value systems: communism and democracy. Such confrontations are not limited to Europe or to specific US-USSR relationships. They have taken on a global dimension, with the Third World playing an increasingly important role.

The Third World and Marxism-Leninism

Third World systems that have adopted Marxist-Leninist political styles are unlikely to vary significantly from communist values. Even given the cultural and political differences between and within Third World systems and Marxist-Leninist concepts, the power of the controlling elite in most Third World states rests to no small degree on an ideology and control system that perpetuates the elite's power and places them philosophically in opposition to the concepts of pluralism and open systems. This philosophical commitment arises out of the revolutionary struggle, which is seen as an anticolonial and anti-imperialistic struggle shaped in Marxist-Leninist terms, to the detriment of national democratic forces. Revolution becomes the basis for legitimizing the system and as such determines the shape of the system that will evolve out of it.

Such a commitment does not necessarily mean that the Soviet or the Chinese model will be adopted in their totality by other states. It does mean that the basic principles of anticapitalism, anticolonialism, and the supremacy of the collectivity will prevail. Rule by a closed elite for the good of others is the cardinal principle.

Marxist-Leninist rhetoric provides all of the arguments for such rule, even if the system does not adhere specifically to the Soviet notions of Marxism-Leninism. The danger to the West is that as such elites perpetuate their rule, they will increasingly justify it in terms of Marxism-Leninism and will develop mind-sets intent on consolidating their rule and the system along the lines of the Soviet model. This tendency is reinforced by the historical relationship of the West to Third World systems.

The West and the Third World

The relationship of the West to most Third World systems was primarily that of colonialism. Only in the immediate post-World War II period did colonialism start to unravel. The colonialists were white, European, Christian states. This remains part of the Third World experience, one that the Soviet Union and China do not hesitate to exploit.

Although the United States was not a colonial power, many Latin Americans see it as the giant to the north that has intervened on numerous occasions in the affairs of the Southern Hemisphere. This suspicion of US intentions remains part of the policy problems faced by the United States in dealing with Latin America.

Although such problems do not exist on a similar scale in other Third World areas, the United States is seen as the leader of the West, with all of the perceptual baggage this carries with respect to the historical Western experience in Third World areas. Moreover, the perception that US and Western staying power is fragile in the Third World gives little comfort to US friends and allies. Vast expenditures on military hardware do not affect such perceptions.

The Third World view is complicated by the North-South alignment. The South (Third World) is arrayed against the North (First and Second Worlds, consisting of the developed Western and developed socialist worlds) over economic power, with the South demanding a better

share of the world's economic benefits. Here again the
primary target of the South is the United States, which for
them seems to epitomize the materialistic and economic
power of the North, which they view as exploitive.

Economic Development and Political Change

The basis for US policy must rest on an understanding
of the problems of modernity. Unconventional conflicts
—revolution and counterrevolution—flow out of the
serious problems posed by modernity. Volumes on theories and models of underdevelopment and modernity
have been written from virtually every disciplinary and
policy perspective.[25] Despite this, there is still serious
disagreement as to the meaning of modernity, how to
cope with the problems it poses, and the processes involved. Equally confusing is the debate over US policy
toward modernity. Many of the studies about modernity
and US policy overlook or misinterpret the cultural differences and nationalistic aspirations characteristic of most
Third World states, particularly with respect to US policy
toward Latin America. The Third World policy and
strategy of the United States have not come to grips with
the linkage among conflict, development, and change.

One authority argues, "The political and social changes
required for economic development are apt to be revolutionary in nature." And there is no assurance that the
efforts to achieve modernity will be successful. Finally,
"the price of development is apt to be political and economic authoritarianism."[26]

The tendency toward conflict and revolutionary dynamics can usually be traced to the desire of modernizing
elites to break out of the traditional style of government
and politics, which affords them little opportunity. But
traditional elites are unlikely to give up their power
peacefully. As a result of such political challenges, as well
as the host of social and economic changes that are
necessary, conflict usually determines the outcome.

Prospects for Democracy

Given such circumstances, it is extremely difficult for Third World states to develop Western-type democracies at the outset. It is even more difficult when such systems are faced with revolution. But successful revolutions have been shaped by Marxist-Leninist systems and represent, in many instances, Soviet power projections. In short, the condition of Third World states and the problems to which they must respond do not bode well for parliamentary democracy. Even when governing elites are philosophically committed to some form of democracy, the problems posed by modernization are not easily resolved through democratic procedures. This is particularly true when such states are faced with unconventional conflicts. Yet such systems may deserve US support. Marshall points out,

> For some people, it is hard to affirm commitment to a military cause on a premise of unequivocal good arrayed against unmitigated evil. In combined efforts, this notion requires postulating an immaculate ally. The trouble is that immaculate allies are fabled rather than real.[27]

Revolutions rarely breed moderation. It is extremely difficult to develop and maintain a moderate, centrist position when faced by revolutionaries. Revolution reflects a mind-set and leadership committed to the overthrow of the existing system and demands nothing less than total war. It is a matter of survival, a position inherently devoid of moderation. The same holds true for the counterrevolution once the seriousness of the revolutionary challenge is recognized.

For the United States, the hope is that those who are nationalist and democratic and engaged in revolution will accept the fact that revolution is only a means to bring to power an elite who will quickly establish the prerequisites of an open system. Unfortunately, those of a democratic and nationalistic orientation are at a great disadvantage not only in their struggle against an authoritarian system but in the internal power struggle over control of the revolution. It is interesting to note that no Marxist-Leninist system has been overthrown by other revolutions. The reason is that the populace is quickly organized and mobilized by the elite through control of the military and militia, control of information channels, and the relative cohesiveness of the elite. In sum, most important features of closed systems are quickly established. In the process, non-Marxist elements are exterminated or reduced to political impotence. This process was followed in China, Vietnam, Cuba, and Nicaragua, among others.

Liberation Theology

In the search for a meaningful ideology to rationalize aggressive action and violence against existing systems, a number of Latin American clergy, as well as revolutionary elites, have adopted what is now called liberation theology. Marked by controversy, this ideological posture attempts to combine elements of Marxism with Christianity. Indeed, some advocates have claimed that one can be both a Marxist and a Christian.[28]

In the United States, liberation theology has been supported by the Maryknoll Order not only in their actions but in publications by Orbis Books.[29] The main concern of the Maryknolls is the view that the problems and issues of Third World politics and economics necessitate a new intellectual focus:

> Total development will demand the restructuring of oppressive political and social orders wherever they exist, in Calcutta or Chicago, New York, or Recife. For this reason, the word *development* should be replaced by *liberation*.[30]

In his analysis of liberation theology, this author notes, however, that "it is quite remarkable that the list of cities requiring liberation did not include Cracow or Leningrad, Havana or Peking, Hanoi or Prague."[31]

These observations indicate the deep divisions that liberation theology has created not only within Latin America, since such an approach is primarily a product of the Spanish-speaking world, but also within the Catholic church.[32]

Liberation theology conceives of colonization, liberation, and organization in Marxist terms. Accordingly, the class struggle is a fundamental fact in Latin America, and, the argument goes, religion cannot stay neutral in such a conflict. Thus, the marriage of theology, ideology, and action, labeled "praxis," is an absolute necessity to uplift the masses. It follows that the church must be visible in fighting for the poor and the oppressed. Indeed, the argument goes, Christ's mission on earth was to do just that: liberate the masses. This stance is supported by reference to a variety of passages in the Bible. The theology of liberation is "a critical reflection on Christian praxis in light of the Word." This latter definition is a formula continually repeated in the writings of the theologians of liberation.[33] In sum, the theology of liberation is based on the Marxist concepts that "knowledge comes through revolutionary action."[34] One author writes,

> Latin American economists and political thinkers rejected the categories of development tied to the perpetuation of a "liberal" economy and worked out their own. . . . The theology of liberation developed from this reflection, directly challenging the "theological ideologies" of the status quo. . . . When the theologians of liberation use such concepts as "praxis", "reality" or their equivalents, they mean the social, economic and political situation as this is analysed by means of Marxist or neo-Marxist sociological tools. It is this interpretation of the Latin American situation which *is most influenced* by the origin and development of the theology of liberation.[35]

The theology of liberation strongly condemns the capitalistic system and liberal society, which stresses property rights and promotes the rights of a privileged few. Concepts such as international monopolies, imperialism, and the international economic system are castigated because these, among other things, are against the public good. Liberation theology

> makes a strong appeal for a new just social order in which man, particularly the popular classes, fully participating in the processes of government, may be the subject of his history and not the arbitrary object of speculation and "profit without end," of grass-roots organizations which would fight for their rights.[36]

Such views came out of the Second General Conference of the Latin American bishops at Medellín in 1968.[37] Many analysts believe that this conference was a watershed for the development of liberation theology.

One of the most important works on liberation theology is by Segundo. This work is the basis for the rationalization and motivation of some American theologians who support liberation theology. For example, in a sympathetic analysis of Segundo's work, an American Jesuit writes,

> My partiality is to that majority of the human race, in my own nation and abroad, that are not only poor but are daily victims of massive human suffering. The assembled bishops of my own church referred to this situation in 1965 as "the scandal of humanity," and I wholeheartedly concur. The theology that best responds to such a scandal at the present time is, in my judgement, liberation theology.[38]

Although there is evidence that contradicts many of the author's conclusions regarding the scope of suffering humanity, particularly in the United States, his views are typical of those held by many in the Maryknoll order, as well as others who support liberation theology.[39]

Regardless of the attempts by theologians in Latin America, the United States, as well as in Canada and Europe, to influence the Catholic church to a position supportive of liberation theology, the stand of the church is clear. According to Vatican II,

> The role and competence of the Church being what it is, she must in no way be confused with the political community, nor bound to any political system. . . . Solutions proposed by one side or another may be easily confused by many people with the Gospel message. Hence it is necessary for people to remember that no one is allowed in the aforementioned situations to appropriate the Church's authority for his opinion.[40]

The church and Pope John Paul II have stated in a variety of messages that the church rejects any materialistic interpretation or position and any historical view based on materialistic concepts. The church's mission on earth is the human spiritual condition. Although the church understands and recognizes the existence of many unjust social systems, its role evolves primarily out of its spiritual dimension.[41]

The solutions to such problems in the construct of Christianity do not lie in the materialistic realm of the class struggle, nor do they evolve from class conflict. Rather, such solutions must be rooted in the spiritual and in the concept of the whole person. The church must use its spiritual power not only to influence existing systems but also to provide the inner strength for people to take control of their own lives. Through the teaching of Christ and the Gospel spiritual power is to change the human condition and bring about a future as envisioned by Christianity. To distort the meaning of Christ and the Gospel message for the sake of an expedient and atheistic ideology on the premise that it will uplift the masses now is to deny the essence of Christianity, in the view of many churchmen.

These views were reaffirmed emphatically by Pope John Paul's message in Salvador, Brazil, in 1980. In stressing the church's position of peaceful reform as opposed to violent revolution, the Pope said,

Every society ought to establish a just social order unless it wishes to be destroyed from within. This appeal is not a justification of the class struggle—for the class struggle is destined to sterility and destruction—but it is an appeal to a noble struggle for the sake of social justice throughout society. . . . The Church is convinced that it is its right and its duty to promote a social pastorate, that is, to exert an influence, through the means proper to it, so that society may become more just, thanks to joint, decided, but always peaceful action on the part of all citizens.[42]

Yet liberation theologists continue to insist that Vatican II opened the way for their path to salvation. At both Medellín and Puebla, the Latin American Bishops Conference, according to this view, provided the proper interpretation. One source reports,

The bringing together of the concerns of Vatican II and a fresh socio-political and economic analysis of Latin America in the documents of the Medellín (1968) became a significant catalyst for the "theology of liberation."[43]

There is little question that the issues raised by liberation theology will continue to characterize the Latin American scene. As a doctrine, it still seems to be in the process of evolving. Nonetheless, as long as liberation theology links Christianity to a Marxist or neo-Marxist concept of politics and society, it is likely to trigger strong reaction from many other Christians.

The idea that an atheistic ideology such as Marxism can be reconciled with the deep spiritual dimensions of Christians and of the meaning of Christ is repugnant to many Christians and seems to violate the very essence of Christianity. This, however, does not lessen the influence of liberation theology as the basis for church activism in Latin America. For some, liberation theology is the basis for revolution. Given their view of the political and economic conditions of Latin America, liberation theology provides a Christian connotation to revolutionary struggle, particularly appealing to certain segments of the population in Latin America and to theologians seeking immediate solutions to what they see as otherwise insoluble problems even though most liberation theologians completely neglect any commentary or critical analysis of the historical realities of Marxism in the Soviet Union and in Eastern Europe.

Summary

US policy with respect to the Third World is faced with a number of challenges, both short and long range, and a number of dilemmas. The Soviet Union's ability to influence Third World states and its capacity for power projection have changed its earlier political-military posture. At the same time, Third World states have fallen behind in attempts at modernization and are facing increasingly serious internal problems. Most Third World states must seek external aid and assistance from the developed states and as a result are extremely vulnerable to external influences.

The United States and the West have a number of security interests in Third World areas. Many of these evolve from strategic and geopolitical issues, such as energy sources and access to sea routes. There is also a vital interest in minimizing conflict and inducing peaceful resolution and development. Beyond these important issues is a recognition that the majority of the world's population is in the Third World and that there is a long-range interest in peaceful and effective economic development. The values of open systems make it difficult to ignore the plight of many Third World states, compelling the adoption of policies that reflect democratic morality and purposes.

The relations between the United States and USSR, although focused on Europe and strategic conflicts, are increasingly turning a number of Third World states into important areas. The conflicts that seem to be endemic to the Third World compound their problems, making many of them less susceptible to peaceful solutions and shifting the advantage to the Soviet Union and other closed systems.

Finally, the evolution of non-Western ideologies such as liberation theology, creates a more complex challenge to the liberal-Lockean position. Not only does such an ideology seem to rationalize and justify violence against existing systems, but it bases its analysis on historical evidence and sociological tools supplied through Marxian logic. Thus, the greatest challenge in the long run may not be in terms of economic development but in the realm of ideas and ideology.

US POLICY AND STRATEGY

There is little consensus within the United States on Third World policy. The more aggressive policy of the Reagan administration toward certain areas, such as Central America, combined with a more low-key approach in other areas (Afghanistan and black Africa), has confused some and triggered criticism by others. In the Carter administration, the human rights policy followed in the last half of the 1970s was applied unevenly and was seen by some as a poor substitute for serious application of power. During this period a number of gains were made by the Soviet Union and other closed systems in Ethiopia, Angola, Mozambique, and Central America.

Earlier, President Kennedy's Alliance for Progress and the Johnson administration's focus on Vietnam, both of which were seen as failures, or, at best, ineffective policy, seemed to reflect the inconsistencies and inadequacies of US Third World policy. In the main, black Africa has remained secondary in US policy, usually based on arms-length relationships, cautious and low key, with the former colonial countries taking the lead. Although there have been exceptions over the past three decades, US policy in the Third World has been largely episodic and uneven. There have been times of high visibility in response to certain threats, followed by a rapid decline in interest. What made these policy stops and starts more confusing is that up to the Vietnam War, some policy initiatives in Latin and Central America were reminiscent of the 1920s interventionist posture and based on a modern version of the Monroe Doctrine that justified intervention.

The Vietnam War was a clear watershed in US policy toward the Third World. Inability to resolve the conflict in accord with American purposes left a bitter legacy not only within the body politic but also in policy-making circles. One result was a peculiarly American sensitivity to involvement in Third World areas that for some bordered on timidity and vacillation, particularly in responding to Third World conflicts.

In this light, what should be US policy in the Third World? What can and should the United States do about unconventional conflicts?

US Policy and Third World Conflicts

Foreign policy and *national security policy* are used synonymously by many writers since they are so closely related, yet there are some distinctions. Foreign policy is more encompassing than national security policy because it deals with virtually all relationships among foreign states, as well as between foreign states and nonstate international actors such as the United Nations. National security policy tends to focus heavily on the probable use of the military instrument and specifically with the protection and survival of the state.

"While American foreign policy is thus primarily concerned with assuring a nation's security, we refer to the more specific policies which seek to do this as security policies."[44] In turn, national security policies often are categorized into crisis and noncrisis policies, or manpower policy, arms control policies, strategic policy, and so forth. National security policy can also be studied from three perspectives: short term, middle range, and long term.

For simplicity, *foreign* and *national security policy* are used interchangeably here, keeping in mind that national security policy may overshadow foreign policy when it is clear that military force must be used. National security policy tends to focus more on the capabilities of the military instrument than on the more traditional aspects of foreign policy such as diplomacy and economic instruments. Foreign policy, on the other hand, refers primarily to the end goals of the United States, which are interpreted primarily in political and moral terms. Specifically, what are the goals of US policy in the Third World? What is US policy regarding unconventional conflicts?

Policy Goals

Policy identifies the goals or ends of the state's purpose and strategy as the plan of action (means) to reach those goals. Thus, a policy may have a number of strategic options or mixes. For example, peace as a policy goal may be pursued through economic aid and assistance, diplomacy, and even war, or a combination of all of these. Similarly peace may be sought by some states through the conquest of their neighbors or the creation of a Leviathan.[45]

The basic purpose of US policy is the protection and survival of the US political system and its values: in brief, the protection of US national interests (See Chapter 7). It is unfortunate that some critics substitute semantics for the substance of such statements. National interests, in such cases, tend to be defined as selfish self-interest and disregard for the moral and ethical components of democratic values. Nothing is further from the truth. Indeed the fundamental component of US interests is the protection of democratic values and open systems. It follows that the perpetuation of such values and systems and their growth is essential to US interests. A number of policy goals evolve from this fundamental proposition.

First, applied to the Third World, US policy needs to support and protect leaders and governing elites who are committed to open systems, those who are likely to develop the basis for open systems, or who are still trying to determine directions and ideological posture for their systems. This requires the existence of local leaders who are self-reliant and self-confident. At the minimum, such a policy needs to be based on the possibility that such leadership can evolve. This is especially important in responding to unconventional conflicts.

Second, US policy in the Third World must be based on sovereignty, self-determination, and openness. Recognizing that these concepts can rarely, if ever, be applied absolutely given the interdependence of states and the nature of international security issues, the United States nevertheless needs to stress these principles as policy goals. This would tend to blunt, if not preclude, the tendency of expansionist closed systems (Marxist-Leninist systems) to try to legitimize the concept of international revolutionary movements and external support of internal conflicts. At the least, such a policy will provide a moral basis for accepting political change—but only if such change is stimulated by internal factors and free from outside interference.

Third, US policy must make clear its commitment to the development of open systems. That is, the policy need not accept closed systems as final but should see their existence as part of the real world and recognize their nature and character. At the same time, US policy must seek to influence and reshape such systems toward openness. Socialist systems are likely to characterize a number of Third World states. The problems faced by such states virtually preclude the early establishment of Western-type democracies. There is a need, then, for understanding, patience, and a recognition that socialist systems in the Third World may be transitory. US policy should seek to assist transition to more open systems. This is also the case with non-Marxist closed systems, keeping in mind that most Third World states have not as yet developed effective enough instruments to institutionalize a particular type of regime. There are exceptions, of course, and these are primarily, but not exclusively, Marxist-Leninist systems.[46]

Fourth, US policy must be flexible enough to develop policies to account for the differences in the various states with which it must deal. Thus, there may be one policy with respect to a Third World state that is moving toward openness and another policy with respect to a state that remains closed but is vulnerable to external influences.

Fifth, any policy toward the Third World must have as its goal economic aid and development assistance to aid such states to modernize. At the same time such policy must recognize that conflict is a residue of political change and economic development. US policy must also be directed toward accepting the inherent instability and conflict potential in Third World areas. It follows that there must be a policy designed for unconventional conflicts. It should not be a policy goal in itself but specifically designed with other policy goals in mind. That is, involvement in unconventional conflicts should not be an end in itself but one supportive of US national interests. At the same time, the policy must consider noninvolvement as an option that may in the long run achieve other policy goals. At a minimum, the United States must adopt policies that raise the costs for any adversaries that may be intent on engaging in unconventional conflicts as a means to achieve long-range political goals.

Sixth, Americans should also understand that too enthusiastic an endorsement and embrace of leaders or governing elites in any particular Third World state may cause many people in the Third World to interpret such an endorsement as US attempts to control the indigenous leadership and to establish neocolonialist relationships. Too close a relationship with the United States may tarnish the nationalistic image of leaders and limit their own independence and flexibility in political matters. For example, there is a great deal of distrust in Latin America regarding US policy because of a heritage of interventionist policies during the 1920s. Subsequently, non-Marxist Latin American leaders must be careful in their relationships with the United States, if for no other reason than to preclude being tarnished by distrust of the United States. US policy must be cognizant of this distrust and follow a course designed to foster the self-determination and legitimacy of non-Marxist leadership without Americanizing the effort.

Seventh, policy must aim at developing regional and multinational efforts in Third World areas, whether for goals of modernity or in response to instability and conflict. Obviously this is easier said than done since directions and goals of policy may be contradictory to those of various states within Third World areas. Nonetheless, there are points of commonality and agreement from which regional and multinational efforts can be developed—for example, the need for economic development, peaceful change, and sovereignty and self-determination.

Finally, US policy must be based on developing initiatives of its own and not be solely reactive. Even without Soviet involvement, US policy must account for Third World issues. Policy must be based on US interests as they relate directly to Third World interests and issues and not simply a policy of East-West confrontation.

These Third World policy and strategy considerations must be placed in the broader context of international security issues and weighed with respect to the Soviet political-military posture and efforts in the Third World. In the light of the historical evidence, it is unlikely that the Soviet Union will radically change its efforts at influencing Third World areas.[47] Indeed, it is likely that the Soviet Union will devote considerable time and energy to consolidate its position in the Third World.

Strategic Options

The basic components of any strategy built on these policy goals must be nonmilitary instruments. Combinations of diplomacy, psychological warfare, and political-economic and intelligence instruments, for example, remain critical instruments for carrying out strategy. Although these may be traditional strategic tools, they need to be more effectively balanced and employed than in the past.

Nonmilitary Options

The basic needs of most Third World states are for aid and assistance to modernize. From the perspective of United States policy and strategy, this requires a whole range of strategic options that are directly linked to economic aid, such as grants, loans, technology transfers and skilled advisers. (See the Appendix for a summary of US aid and assistance.) It is also important for the United States to create opportunities for US investments and trade. Much of this is already being done, although there is a great deal of debate regarding its effectiveness, the proper mixes, and the degree of effort. One of the major problems is linking strategy to policy goals: should such economic aid be given only to those states likely to benefit US policy?

US friends and allies need to be supported, but economic aid and assistance can also be used to influence states even though they may not be leaning toward the United States. Economic aid and assistance should be provided for basic moral reasons, regardless of the importance of a particular Third World state. An example is famine relief to the Marxist regime in Ethiopia. Lest the United States fall into the aid and assistance abyss, however, economic strategies must be listed in priority, with the first and major efforts to the states most likely to benefit US policy. Otherwise this quagmire of economic aid can lead to a strategy of supporting everyone with minimal and essentially inadequate economic support, depleting resources and benefiting few, if anyone, including the United States.

Long-run nonmilitary strategy has to do with political and psychological issues. The essence of the Third World drive is political control. Economic development is important and directly related to this issue, but as the late

Kwame Nkrumah of Ghana recognized, political control and power are the essence of Third World dynamics.

US strategic options must therefore integrate political and psychological programs and link these to economic development. Such strategies should be designed to preclude or forestall internal conflicts within the Third World and to develop the most favorable climate for the evolution of open systems. Part of these strategies must include effective intelligence about the Third World state. The United States must engage in an effective information and data-gathering effort with skilled analysts who can identify political trends, issues, problems, basis of dissidence, and a variety of other important political characteristics. Only through such efforts can effective political and psychological strategies be carried out.

The psychological effort must include the use of the mass media to tell the American story. This effort must go beyond the straight news programming of the Voice of America. An advocacy approach must be adopted in publicizing the benefits of an open system and the values, practices, and attitudes nurtured in such systems. The start of Radio Marti in 1985 aimed at Castro's Cuba is a case in point. That the United States hesitates to use all of its instrumentalities to advocate its system and to sell the democratic idea and its economic system throughout the world must surely amaze and please US adversaries. The war of ideas is a crucial part of unconventional conflicts and is inseparable from any strategic option.[48]

Security Issues and Options

Although the primary strategic option needs to be based on the use of nonmilitary instruments, security issues within the Third World, particularly those directly linked to US security interests, must be given priority attention. A strategic option must consider the possibility of involvement in unconventional conflicts. In the light of experience over the past decade, such an option is highly probable. It must be clear, however, that such a strategy must have a direct and distinct connection to policy goals.

Instruments designed for unconventional conflicts should be composed of civilian-military mixes, joint political-military structures, and interservice integration. This stops short of committing standard US military forces (such as light divisions). Rather, such an option should be based on the use of Special Forces for purposes of supporting the indigenous system and its leaders. This strategy must not be based on the use of Special Forces alone. The very concept of Special Forces requires attention to political, social, and economic factors. The commitment of Special Forces must be in conjunction with a comprehensive strategy designed to support a whole range of political and economic programs in the indigenous system.

Special Forces are not primarily designed for ground combat operations. Rather, they are primarily for support of indigenous forces and in assisting in the training, organization, coordination, and planning of indigenous forces and operations. Not Americanizing the conflict is essential for the success of such a strategy. This can be done by a variety of means, the most important being the quality and capability of the personnel committed to the area. (This presumes that there is a significant US interest in involvement.) Most important, the strategy must be designed and implemented so as to ensure that the indigenous government and forces are seen to be in control of the counterrevolutionary effort.

Another component of any strategic response to unconventional conflict is covert operations. Covert operations are not limited to secret military operations; they cover a wide range of activities from secret negotiations and preemptive counterintelligence operations to secret military operations. In the main, covert refers to those operations in which the United States is involved but does not wish to be identified as the source because of the possibility of compromising the larger national security issues. For example, in dealing with terrorists, the United States may adopt covert strategy intended to identify and penetrate terrorist groups or potential terrorist groups. The publication of specifics about such activity not only could compromise the operation but could endanger Americans not directly involved in the operation (for instance, tourists and businesses).

Covert operations may also include the use of a variety of instruments to support leaders and groups engaged in revolutions against Marxist-Leninist systems. For example, US assistance to the contras in Nicaragua, although hardly covert, may involve assistance beyond humanitarian aid. Similarly, assistance to the Afghan revolutionaries arrayed against the Kabul government and its Soviet supporters may involve covert operations. The same may be true with the forces of Jonas Savimbi and UNITA in 1985 fighting against the Marxist-Leninist regime in Angola.

US covert operations may include involvement of the CIA as well as Special Forces. Here again success is contingent upon not visibly Americanizing the involvement.[49]

It is clear that a number of anti-Marxist revolutions are in progress in Afghanistan, Angola, Ethiopia, Kampuchea, Mozambique, and Nicaragua. The outcomes of these revolutions are not clear. The fact is that a number of Marxist-Leninist systems are being hard pressed by revolutionaries. The Soviet Union is having difficulty subduing Afghan revolutionaries, though it began its campaign in 1979.

The United States is still searching for a coherent policy and effective strategies to respond to revolutions that appear favorable to US interests. The hesitancy and extreme caution in the position of the United States with respect to its response in dealing with such revolutions reflects most of the same problems facing open systems in responding as counterrevolutionaries. Support of revolutions must be included in US strategic options and implemented if it is directly in support of policy. It must be in accord with democratic oversight and open system necessities as discussed earlier (see Chapter 6).

Last-Resort Strategy

Another strategic option is the commitment of ground forces in support of an existing counterrevolutionary system. This is a two-part strategy. The first part is the commitment of US light division units.[50] Such a strategy should be adopted only after it is clear that the protection and survival of the existing system are vital to US national security.

Clearly this represents a major change from low visibility and non-Americanization to a higher level of commitment, making it increasingly difficult to withdraw without serious political and military costs. The first part of ground troop commitment, in the form of light divisions, should not necessitate the vast logistical and administrative structures that were created in Vietnam. In theory, light division forces are intended to be highly mobile, with minimum heavy weaponry, and easily adaptable to unconventional conflict, minimizing the kinds of problems encountered in Vietnam. Although this strategy represents a higher level of commitment, it should not necessarily mean going beyond the use of elements of a light division or paralleling a Vietnam-type operation. Such a strategy presumes that the existing system cannot be effectively maintained by the Special Forces phase of US support.

This strategy is based on the presumption that light divisions are adequately trained and are manned by high-quality personnel who can integrate, if necessary, into the forces of the indigenous counterrevolutionary system. The primary purpose of such a commitment is to shore up the indigenous force structure and provide a force multiplier and strong point around which indigenous forces can develop more effective strategies and which can be used as a support base. The success of such a strategy is largely dependent on doctrine.

The second part of this strategy is the commitment of standard military forces if the light division commitment is inadequate. This may mean the Americanization of the war, following a path similar to the Vietnam experience. This can be avoided through the prudent development of joint command arrangements, ensuring the prominence and visibility of indigenous leaders and ensuring that there is a core of indigenous leaders prepared to make the decisions and provide the necessary leadership to develop effective counterrevolutionary programs. Clearly this type of strategy must have a specific political and psychological component. Even so, it can lead to perceptions of the United States as an occupying power, with all of the anti-American and nationalistic response this could trigger, unless the situation follows the Grenada pattern—in quickly and withdraw quickly.

In the long run, such a strategy must have or develop the support of major political actors in the United States, including Congress, and the majority of Americans. Moreover, such a strategy must be aimed at a specific and clearly articulated policy and be conducted in such a way that a reasonable and acceptable outcome is a distinct possibility, albeit not necessarily an assured one. This is a last-resort strategy based on the view that the existing system must survive under any circumstances because it is vital to US national interests.

US Intelligence System

For most Americans, it is self-evident that knowledge of the enemy is necessary before effective measures can be designed and implemented. It follows that most Americans accept the idea that an effective intelligence system is necessary in open systems. Beyond this broad view, however, the issue of intelligence in open systems becomes complicated and complex. Although most citizens accept passive intelligence measures (such as gathering information about the enemy), active measures (such as penetration of revolutionary groups and preemptive operations against its leadership) create a dilemma.

Most active measures and, indeed some passive ones, may appear to some to violate or threaten the notion of democratic morality and ethics. For example, collecting information on possible terrorist groups may require close scrutiny of a variety of groups, some of whom may, in the long run, not be involved in terrorism. Yet the fact of information collection and penetration of such groups by intelligence agencies may be seen as counter to democratic norms and the rule of law.

Unless there is a full understanding of the nature and character of unconventional conflicts, strategies involving intelligence efforts can be so interpreted and constrained as to make them useless. Without some agreement within governing circles and some understanding and acceptance by major political actors of the dimensions of unconventional conflicts and the options and costs of one strategy over another, it is unlikely that an effective intelligence system can be developed. Without such a system, it is unlikely that reasonably effective responses can be made to unconventional conflicts.

The importance of the intelligence function, particularly counterintelligence and covert operations, must be understood in the context of democratic survival. To this end, the public must be provided with realistic information on unconventional conflicts, understand the special needs of a democracy to respond to such threats, and appreciate the importance of intelligence to the capability and effectiveness of political-military policy and strategy. In addressing these matters, it must also be recognized that a checks-and-balance system is essential for maintaining the credibility as well as legitimacy of intelligence operations. No institution in democracy can be allowed to have unfettered autonomy in designing its own purposes and implementing them with little attention to the means employed or to the nature of the system the institution is supposed to serve.

Conclusions

Policy must drive strategy and not vice-versa. Strategic options should not be adopted for strategies' sake; they must be directly and specifically aimed at achieving particular policy goals. Without clear policy goals, strategy can drive policy and determine its own goals. This is a quick road to disaster.

The adoption of one strategy does not preclude the use of a combination of strategies. Thus, although there may be a commitment of US ground forces, for example, the nonmilitary as well as Special Forces options may also be in place and continued. In sum, involvement in unconventional conflicts in Third World areas usually demands a combination of strategic options once it is clear that the issue is one of survival or vital to US security. But these must be driven by policy goals so that involvement in unconventional conflict has realistic and attainable goals.

Finally, the use of any strategic option must constantly be linked to withdrawal options. That is, before moving into a higher phase or a more Americanized option, careful consideration must be given to withdrawing entirely or moving into a lower-visibility strategy, keeping in mind long-range policy goals. The possibility always exists that the commitment of standard ground forces, for example, may totally destroy the legitimacy of the indigenous system, even if such forces are able to control and defeat revolutionary systems.

DOCTRINE

A great deal of the strategic success of the United States in dealing with Third World conflicts rests in doctrine. Doctrine refers primarily to the way strategy and tactics are implemented. But doctrine, as is the case with strategy, has a number of interpretations.[51] A useful definition is that doctrine guides conduct in the carrying out of military missions. It describes how the military intends to fight. "Doctrine provides a mental framework for promoting a common approach to solving military problems; it provides a common reference from which military professionals can think."[52]

Success in unconventional conflicts requires that doctrine differ from doctrines designed for conventional and nuclear conflicts. Many of these differences were part of earlier discussions on low-intensity conflicts and special operations and characteristics of revolution and counter-revolution. Nonetheless, at this point it is important to focus specifically on doctrine. The purpose here is not to provide a detailed outline of US military doctrine in Third World conflicts. This is better done by military specialists and those charged with the doctrinal issues— those who are charged, for example, with developing and publishing the army field manual, *FM 100-20, Low Intensity Conflict*.[53] Rather, the intent here is to touch the high points of doctrine and connect them with strategy and policy. It is especially important to point out the different thrust of unconventional as contrasted to conventional doctrines.

Special Forces Doctrine

Doctrine for the operations of Special Forces should be grounded in the concept of training and cadre for indigenous political-military forces. This needs to stress the ability to operate in a foreign environment as teachers, role models, and patient and understanding friends. Moreover, the doctrine must stress language skills and a mentality that empathizes with indigenous culture and motivations in a highly political context. Further, Special Forces must learn to function effectively with a variety of civilian agencies, both American and indigenous.

Special Forces personnel can be incorporated into indigenous units and serve as commanders, leaders, and trainers in a variety of operational units. For example, between 1927 and 1933, US Marine officers and noncommissioned officers served as officers and commanders in the Nicaraguan National Guard.

Often Special Forces teams can provide strong points around which indigenous forces can pin their own operations. At other times, Special Forces personnel and teams become role models for taking the fight to the adversary. Such purposes serve not only the counterrevolutionary effort but can also be a pivotal point in support of revolutions.[54]

Doctrine must also be designed to guide Special Forces as supporters of revolutionary efforts. Such a doctrine requires the development of a revolutionary mentality in the context of indigenous systems.

Special Forces training for low-intensity conflict (revolution and counterrevolution) is particularly appropriate when the strategic option of involvement in unconventional conflict is adopted. Such doctrines must also include guidance to Special Forces personnel should they be committed prior to the outbreak of unconventional conflicts. Part of the aid and assistance provided for modernity includes attention to security efforts within the indigenous area.

Unconventional Doctrine for Conventional Units

Commitment of US forces beyond the Special Forces phases must also include unconventional warfare doctrine. And this is where the military appears to be at its weakest: the inability to adopt standard forces to the unconventional environment.

Unconventional doctrines must direct military operations to function closely with indigenous forces and stress combined civilian-military operations and tactical behavior appropriate for revolutionary and counterrevolutionary conflicts. Doctrine must guide the intermix of US and indigenous forces specifically at the operational level and aim at carrying out operations with a minimum of heavy weapons and air and logistical support. Doctrine must provide for an intermix of US and indigenous forces while allowing a large degree of autonomy and visibility to indigenous forces.

For example, US ground force involvement in counter-revolutionary conflicts (similar to Vietnam) may require a doctrine that stresses long-range patrols and individualized combat operations (small unit operations) rather than the use of large units for broad sweep operations. This is not to suggest that the large unit doctrine should not be considered. When faced with large concentrations of revolutionary armed forces, for example, large units and massive firepower may be the answer. Yet it is also clear that if large units must be used in a counterrevolutionary role, the revolutionaries have already reached a major milestone in their efforts. They would have progressed to a point where they were able to field relatively large armed forces with enough weapons and logistics to challenge seriously the existing system almost in a conventional fashion. This is what Mao Tse-tung called phase two revolutionary progress, as was the case in South Vietnam in 1965. At this point, even the commitment of large US units will not necessarily defeat the revolutionaries, although it may forestall and even preclude the ability of the revolutionaries to progress to a higher phase of revolutionary war.

In the study of US involvement in Nicaragua between 1927 and 1933, one authority concludes, "Ideally, combat operations against guerrillas should be exclusively by native troops. Their proper employment in the earlier stages of a guerrilla conflict can prevent a situation in which foreign forces must be called in to shore up a crumbling regime."[55] And in focusing on doctrine, he observes,

> Wars against guerrillas are won by de-escalating them into wars of patrol actions. Instead of deploying a division to "clear" an area of a regiment of guerrillas, a regiment of soldiers should be sent in to hunt down and destroy the guerrillas. Each component unit of the anti-guerrilla regiment, down to the squad level, should be capable of sustained independent patrol action.[56]

The ability to do this presumes that the existing system has an effective intelligence system and capable leadership at all operational levels. The author also notes,

> This kind of warfare is not popular with conservative American military men, because it denies the classic infantry role of seizing and holding terrain. . . . The American soldier realizes that his job is to close with and destroy the enemy, but he is made to believe that, even in guerrilla war, this is done by moving great masses of men and machines across a stretch of land.[57]

US political-military doctrines responding to these kinds of situations require a high degree of skill and leadership ability among junior officers and noncommissioned officers. Also, members of light division forces must be trained to function in an unconventional environment in small units capable of long periods of almost independent operation with minimum central support.

Doctrine must stress the need to be sensitive to the desires and needs of the civilian populace. Thus the concept of civic action is a critical part of such doctrines. This also means that special attention must be given to operating in populated areas for purposes of population control, physical security, and intelligence gathering. In brief, US forces in light divisions must be skilled in semipolice and paramilitary operations and must carry them out in such a way as to minimize the Americanization of the war while attempting to establish reasonably good relations with the populace. This cannot be done by Americans operating as Americans in an alien population area. Rather, this is best achieved by integrated US-indigenous units, where the visibility of the indigenous unit is high.

SUMMARY

The Third World poses a serious and, in certain instances, a vital challenge to US interests. These include challenges not only in terms of the kinds of political systems that are evolving but in the character of the forces determining the shape of such systems. Many Third World states, faced with problems of modernity and political change, are inherently unstable, a situation that creates the roots for unconventional warfare, particularly revolution and counterrevolution. The vulnerability of many Third World states to external forces provides ample opportunity for the Soviet Union, for example, to project its power through surrogates and proxies or directly.

While many people in the United States and the West focus primarily on the European scenario and relationships with the USSR, the battleground in the Third World is given only passing interest. Although there are signs of an increasing concern, there have not yet developed policies and strategies to deal effectively with serious Third World issues, specifically unconventional conflicts.

Policy, strategy, and doctrine must be based on a recognition of the complex nature of the Third World and unconventional conflicts associated with it. This may require a rethinking of the way Americans view conflicts and their role in the Third World. Moreover, an effective political-military posture requires a variety of mixes based on military and nonmilitary options with the use of ground forces as a last-resort strategy. Special Forces commitment in a combined civilian-military strategy is an important first option.

Finally, neither policy, strategy, nor doctrine can be effective if leadership and commitment are lacking among the governing body of the existing system. Americans alone cannot substitute for indigenous leadership. Americans cannot develop legitimacy for the existing system or its leadership. Unless there is a core of such indigenous leaders, it is futile for the United States to become involved unless it is prepared to take over the entire system and function as an occupying power.

NOTES

1. Henry L. Stimson, *American Policy in Nicaragua* (New York: Arno Press, 1970), p. 127. There are a number of accounts of US policy in Central America in the current period. Many of these draw on history in support of one or the other position. There are also a number of unbalanced and biased accounts. See, for example, Martin Dishkin, ed., *Trouble in Our Backyard: Central America and the United States in the Eighties* (New York: Pantheon Books, 1983). In the introduction, for example, the editor sets the tone for the volume, writing, "The United States can, and probably will, rain death on innocent people in Central America, as it did in Southeast Asia some years ago, but the impulses that Guatemalan Indians, Salvadoran peasants, and Nicaraguan workers are now expressing through their lives and deaths are meaningful" (p. xxxiii). To ensure that readers do not forget the focus of the book, Günter Grass in the Epilogue goes so far as to compare Nicaraguan Sandinistas with the Polish trade union movement Solidarity. See also *Revolution in Central America*, edited by Stanford Central America Action Network (Boulder, Colo.: Westview Press, 1983). In my view, these are typical of the polemic and distortions of US policy in Central America and Nicaragua that Henry L. Stimson probably stood against in his 1927 message.

2. Walter Lafeber, "The Burdens of the Past," in Robert S. Leiken, ed., *Central American: Anatomy of Conflict* (New York: Pergamon Press, 1984), p. 64.

3. See, for example, Walter Andrews, "U.S. Lists 6 Criteria for Using Troops," *Washington Times*, November 30, 1984, p. 1.

4. See, for example, Departments of State and Defense, "The Soviet-Cuban Connection in Central America and the Caribbean," (Washington, D.C.: Government Printing Office, March 1985), and Roger Fontaine, "Captured Records Reveal Communist Strategy, Tactics," *Washington Times*, April 25, 1985, p. 1. See also Paul Seabury and Walter A. McDougall, eds., *The Grenada Papers* (San Francisco: ICS Press, 1985).

5. Bruce D. Porter, *The USSR in Third World Conflicts: Soviet Arms and Diplomacy in Local Wars, 1945-1980* (Cambridge: Cambridge University Press, 1984), p. 5.

6. For a discussion of Soviet *Spetsnatz* forces, see Viktor Suvorov, "Spetsnatz, the Soviet Union's Special Forces," *International Defense Review* 16, no. 9 (1983).

7. See, for example, Jerry F. Hough, "Gorbachev's Strategy," *Foreign Affairs* 64, no. 1 (Fall 1985):33-55. See also Gerrit W. Gong, Angela E. Stent, and Rebecca V. Strode, "Conclusions," in Gong, Stent, and Strode, *Areas of Challenge for Soviet Foreign Policy in the 1980s* (Bloomington: Indiana University Press, 1984). The authors write, "The importance to the Kremlin of Third World developments will lie primarily in their impact on Soviet policy toward Western Europe, the United States, and the People's Republic of China." (p. 131).

8. Tom Cockrell, ed., "The New Marxist-Leninist States in the Third World, by Francis Fukuyama, September 1984," *RAND Checklist*, no. 333 (May 1985):10.

9. *Liberal-Lockean tendencies* refers to the notions of equality, justice, liberty, and freedom that are an inherent part of the American heritage.

10. LaFeber, pp. 64-65.

11. Donald E. Nuechterlein, *America Overcommitted, United States National Interests in the 1980s* (Lexington: University Press of Kentucky, 1985), p. 1.

12. Ibid., p. 6.

13. Ibid., p. 12. The intensity of interest is categorized into four: survival, vital, major, and peripheral (minor). Each of these require a certain type of response. Survival is essentially one of protecting the homeland to ensure its survival. The rest are in lesser degrees of intensity (pp. 9-18).

14. As quoted in the *Armed Forces Journal International* (March 1985).

15. Keith A. Dunn, "Soviet Involvement in the Third World: Implications of US Policy Assumptions," in Robert H. Donaldson, ed., *The Soviet Union in the Third World: Success and Failures* (Boulder, Colo.: Westview Press, 1981), p. 429.

16. Porter, p. 234.

17. Ibid., p. 239.

18. Cockrell.

19. R. Craig Nation, "Soviet Engagement in Africa: Motives, Means, and Prospects," in R. Craig Nation and Mark V. Kauppi, eds., *The Soviet Impact in Africa* (Lexington, Mass.: Lexington Books, 1984), p. 49.

20. Porter, p. 234. A useful analysis of Soviet views of the Third World is Daniel S. Papp, *Soviet Perceptions of the Developing World in the 1980s: The Ideological Basis* (Lexington, Mass.: Lexington Books, 1985). The author analyzes the Soviet view of the socialist path to development and identifies three categories—national revolutionary states, revolutionary democratic states, and Marxist-Leninist states—each with different characteristics and purposes and each necessitating differing levels of Soviet support (pp. 61-76).

21. Max Kampelman, in "Beyond Containment? The Future of U.S.-Soviet Relations," *Policy Review*, no. 31 (Winter 1985):39.

22. The difficulties of the United States in trying to respond to terrorists were clearly demonstrated in the hostage taking of Americans on TWA flight 847 by Shiite Moslems in June 1985.

23. David K. Shipler, *Russia: Broken Idols, Solemn Dreams* (New York: Penguin Books, 1984), p. 348. See also Kevin Klose, *Russia and the Russians: Inside the Closed Society* (New York: W. W. Norton, 1984), for an excellent insight into Soviet society. An excellent analysis of the domestic and foreign problems facing the new Soviet leadership under Mikhail Gorbachev is Seweryn Bialer and Joan Afferica, "The Genesis of Gorbachev's World," *Foreign Affairs, America and the World, 1985*, 64, no. 3 (1986):605-44.

24. Samuel P. Huntington, "The Renewal of Strategy," in Samuel P. Huntington, ed., *The Strategic Imperative: New Policies for American Security* (Cambridge, Mass.: Ballinger Publishing Co., 1982), pp. 4-5.

25. See, for example, Monte Palmer, *Dilemmas of Political Development*, 2d ed. (Itasca, Ill.: Peacock, 1980), and Scott W. Thompson, *The Third World: Premises of U.S. Policy*, rev. ed. (San Francisco: Institute for Contemporary Studies, 1983).

26. Robert L. Heilbroner, *The Great Ascent: The Struggle for Economic Development in Our Time* (New York: Harper & Row, 1963), pp. 17-18, 20-21.

27. Charles Burton Marshall, "Morality and National Liberation Wars," *Southeast Asian Perspectives*, no. 4 (December 1971).

28. Adam Wolfson, "The Good, the Bad, and the Ugly; Who's Who in Nicaragua," *Policy Review*, no. 3 (Summer 1985):64. Ernesto Cardenal is quoted as saying, "Not only can a Christian be a Marxist, but that in order for him to be authentically Christian, he must be a Marxist."

29. Quentin L. Quade, ed., *The Pope and Revolution: John Paul II Confronts Liberation Theology* (Washington, D.C.: Ethics and Policy Center, 1982), p. 77.

30. Ibid.

31. Ibid.

32. Liberation theology has been addressed in a variety of works, Gustavo Gutierrez, *A Theology of Liberation* (Maryknoll, N.Y.: Orbis Books, 1976); Alfred T. Hennelly, *Theologies in Conflict: The Challenge of Juan Luis Segundo* (Maryknoll, N.Y.: Orbis Books 1979); J. Andrew Kirk, *Liberation Theology: An Evangelical View from the Third World* (Atlanta: John Knox Press, 1979); Juan Luis Segundo, *The Liberation of Theology* (Maryknoll, N.Y.: Orbis Books, 1976); and Quade. These and other books are required reading to develop an understanding that goes be-yond the rhetoric and polemics that have characterized the debate over this issue. For our study, we can only touch on some key points of liberation theology and its relationship to revolution.

33. Kirk, p. 23.

34. Ibid., p. 162.

35. Ibid., pp. 25-26. See also Peadar Kirby, *Lessons in Liberation: The Church in Latin America* (Dublin, Ireland: Dominican Publications, 1981).

36. Ibid., p. 28.

37. Quade, pp. 141-56. See also the assessment of the Latin American bishops' conference in Puebla, Mexico, 1979, and references to Medellín in Kirby, pp. 97-108. Kirby provides a highly sympathetic view and interpretations that avoid references to Marxist-Leninist assessments.

38. Hennelly, pp. xxi-xxii.

39. Data for the United States show that over the period 1965-1985, for example, major improvements were made in the quality of life, and these continue. Other data show that in the world as a whole, people are living longer and are healthier, the environment has improved, and there is less disease. For example, life expectancy in the poorer nations in the world increased from 42 years in 1960 to 59 years in 1982. These improvements were made under a liberal-capitalistic international economic system with linkages to the Third World. This is not to suggest that there do not exist serious human problems; the drought in Africa and starving children are examples. Nor is this to suggest that the liberal-capitalistic route is the best answer for some states. But to presume that

liberation theology is the only answer disregards the historical evidence, particularly in terms of the Marxist-Leninist record. For detailed data on these and other elements, see Office of Management and Budget, *The United States Budget in Brief, FY 1985* (Washington, D.C.: Government Printing Office, 1984), p. 69. The data show, for example, that in current and constant (fiscal year 1972) prices, nondefense outlays jumped from $67.8 billion in 1965 to over $653 billion in 1985. At the same time, payments to individuals jumped from $33.7 billion in 1960 to over $440 billion in 1985. See also Ben J. Wattenberg, *The Good News Is the Bad News Is Wrong* (New York: Simon & Schuster, 1984), esp. chap. 7.

40. Quade, p. 4.

41. See Michael Novak, "Liberation Theology and the Pope," in ibid., pp. 75-76.

42. John Paul II, "Peaceful Reform vs. Violent Revolution," address in Salvador, Brazil, July 6, 1980, in Quade, pp. 134-35. See also "Evangelization, Liberation, and Human Promotion," in Quade, pp. 159-60.

43. Kirk, p. 16.

44. John Spanier and Eric M. Uslaner, *American Foreign Policy Making and the Democratic Dilemmas*, 4th ed. (New York: Holt, Rinehart and Winston, 1985), p. 12.

45. See, for example, W. T. Jones, *Masters of Political Thought, Vol. 2: Machiavelli to Bentham* (Boston: Houghton Mifflin, 1968), chap. 4. See also George H. Sabine, *A History of Political Theory*, 4th ed. rev. (Hinsdale, Ill.: Dryden Press, 1973), chap. 4.

46. See Porter, p. 234 and Papp, pp. 61-76.

47. Ibid.

48. See, for example, Stanley Kober, "Why There Is a War of Ideas," and Richard E. Bissell, "The War of Ideas," in James P. O'Leary, Jeffrey Salmon, and Richard Shultz, eds., *Power, Principles and Interests: A Reader in World Politics* (Lexington, Mass.: Ginn Press, 1985), pp. 245-60.

49. For useful insights into such operations, see Theodore Shackley, *The Third Option: An American View of Counterinsurgency Operations* (New York: Reader's Digest Press, 1981).

50. Light divisions have been established in the US Army, and some are in the planning stage. These divisions are to be composed of about 10,000 personnel, lightly armed and highly

mobile. The purpose is to provide a quick action force that can be inserted rapidly in a number of Third World areas.

51. For a useful review of operational doctrine, see Major Wayne M. Hall, "A Critique of the Doctrine-Training Fit," *Military Review* 65, no. 6 (June 1985):30-44.

52. Ibid., pp. 32-33.

53. Department of the Army, *FM 100-20, Low Intensity Conflict* (Washington, D.C.: Department of the Army, January 1981). This field manual is being revised.

54. Neill Macaulay, *The Sandino Affair* (Chicago: Quadrangle Books, 1967), p. 270.

55. For example, the French used GCMA's (Groupement de Commandos Mextes Aeroportes) in North Vietnam against the Vietminh. See Robert J. O'Neill, *General Giap: Politician and Strategist* (New York: Praeger, 1969). The author writes, "During 1952 the French began to employ considerable numbers of troops to strike at Giap's rear areas and force him into the same over-commitment which the French faced. . . . The GCMAs set up a number of base areas in the most remote parts of the Tonkin mountains. . . . Giap was never able to rid himself of these irregular groups and by 1954 at least ten Vietminh battalions were tied down in routine security duties" (pp. 115-17).

56. Macaulay, p. 269.

57. Ibid., p. 270.

8

The New Realism

The United States, and other open systems in general, are extremely vulnerable to unconventional conflicts and are at a serious disadvantage in developing the capacity to respond effectively. Some Americans will argue the opposite. They believe that the Third World is no threat to the United States; that the United States needs to keep its relationships on moral high ground; that the Soviet Union is a nonthreatening state whose system is becoming more open; and that the United States should have learned its lesson in Vietnam (to stay out of Third World conflicts and the Third World in general). Others, on both the Right and the Left, have ideological and political views that cannot be changed regardless of the information or evidence to the contrary. And still others are troubled enough to wonder what the United States should and can do. The search for answers to these questions requires examining and understanding the issues addressed and questions raised here and reviewing how Americans look at the world, particularly the Third World, and how they should look at the world. This is the basis for the new realism.

The new realism is concerned with developing a broader perspective and a realistic view of the nature of the Third World and unconventional conflicts. The new realism seeks a more practical application of democratic principles based on the national interests of the United States, which remain the protection and perpetuation of democracy and open systems. Also, the new realism recognizes that conflicts are a fact of international life; that they are dirty, deadly, and demanding; and that some states use conflicts to further their own goals—many times to ensure the establishment and perpetuation of closed systems or to establish their own brand of ideology. Finally, new realism is based on the recognition that unconventional conflicts—especially revolutions shaped by Marxist-Leninist groups—are long-range threats to the existence and growth of open systems. They are a serious challenge to the vital interests and the survival of the United States. The new realism recognizes the need to respond to the new battlefield of unconventional conflicts.

In order to grasp this new battlefield, one must first reexamine the general character of unconventional conflicts and US historical experience in such conflicts. Attention must be given to the nature and character of the values, norms, and expectations that place the United States in a disadvantageous position in trying to deal with these Third World conflicts.

DIMENSIONS OF NEW REALISM

Several years ago, the Carnegie Foundation for the Advancement of Teaching published a report on curricula and teaching in US colleges and universities. One of the major conclusions was that there was a growing "illiteracy about public issues." Calling this "civic illiteracy," the report went on to state,

> Today, public-policy circuits appear to be dangerously overloaded. In frustration, many Americans now seek simple solutions to complex problems. They turn to repressive censorship, align themselves with narrowly focused special-interest groups, retreat into nostalgia for a world that never was, succumb to the blandishments

of glib electronic soothsayers, or—worst of all—simply withdraw completely, convinced that nothing can be done.[1]

Directed at college and university teachers, students, and curriculum, the charge of civic illiteracy applies equally well to most Americans, including those who represent the political system. In this respect, many people tend to adopt simple-minded policy positions on complex issues. Many ignore or do not understand that painful choices must be made, and these choices must be made among a variety of less than ideal policy options.[2] Rarely does the policy maker face clear choices between good and evil. Rather, he or she usually has to choose among a variety of bad policies. Unfortunately, there are too few Americans who understand the complexities of such problems, and of those who do understand, some use these issues for their own political advantage. This is especially true with respect to the view of many Americans regarding unconventional conflicts. Compounding the problem are the characteristics of the US political system and the mind-sets it creates. According to some scholars, "The American political system is poorly suited to conduct a limited war; and the American people are lacking in two important requisites for a sound foreign policy—patience, and an understanding of the role that power plays in world affairs."[3]

Complicating these matters, the mass media perpetuate simplistic notions. Television programming rarely provides in-depth, serious, and balanced analysis of complex policy issues. Moreover, the tendency for some members of the media to incorporate their own political biases in reporting can distort a number of public issues. Combined with the power of the media in establishing and publicizing its own agenda of what is important, it makes it extremely difficult for many Americans to get a fair and balanced assessment of critical public issues.

The nature and character of democracy is the most important factor in studying the American perspective on policy issues. Committed to the idea of an open system and open access, the US political system, as is the case in any other democracy, is placed in a position where it gives maximum opportunity to even its most dangerous adversaries to gain access to democratic instruments. Thus, the way is open to disinformation, manipulation, and open dissidence—all in the name of democracy.

Civic illiteracy, the role of the mass media in the United States, and the nature and character of democracy are critical factors in the problem of making public policy in the United States. These factors are especially important in understanding US views and policy regarding unconventional conflicts.

Democracy and Civic Illiteracy

In a particularly caustic criticism of democracy, Jean-François Revel contends:

> Democracy tends to ignore, even deny, threats to its existence because it loathes doing what is needed to counter them. It awakens only when the danger becomes deadly, imminent, evident. By then, either there is too little time left for it to save itself, or the price of survival has become crushingly high.[4]

Although focusing primarily on the communist challenge to democracies, Revel has also captured the essence of the challenge posed by unconventional conflicts. Revolutions and counterrevolutions that are inspired or captured by Marxist-Leninist groups threaten the long-run existence of democratic systems. Many such threats are not immediately evident or do not seem compelling enough at the time to arouse democracies. These are not threats that emanate from public declarations of war or Pearl Harbor-type attacks, rather they evolve from protracted, low-visibility conflicts whose nature is misunderstood by democracies. Combined with an effective disinformation campaign over a period of time, adversaries of the United States use many of democracy's most sacred principles to advance their own cause through the use of unconventional conflicts and access to open systems.

A case in point was the US-Nicaraguan confrontation in 1985. A public relations firm in the United States was paid over $300,000 annually by Managua to lobby for Nicaragua. One newspaper reported, "From all outside appearances the firm has ably represented its clients. An accounting of the lobbyists' appointments with legislators and staff reads like a Who's Who Among Senate and House liberals."[5] The Managua regime was presented as a nationalistic regime designed to bring a better life to the Nicaraguans. The Nicaraguan leaders were presented as committed to justice, fair play, and political pluralism—in direct contrast to the so-called imperialistic policy of the Reagan administration. Little was said about statements from exiled opposition leaders or the bishop of Managua regarding the repressiveness of the Nicaraguan regime.[6] The issue here is not the contending positions but rather an adversary's access to the instrumentalities of an open system.

Adversaries not only have access to the vast and independent information systems within the United States from which disinformation can be disseminated and psychological warfare conducted, but they also have access to sympathetic groups whose opposition to government policies is part of the groups' purposes, either ideologically, politically, or both. Compounding the problem for the United States is that it is denied access to the adversaries' political system by the very nature of that system. Again as Revel points out,

> Any society of any type in the world today can accede to democracy, with a single exception: communist society, which cannot go democratic without destroying itself. Understandably, then, totalitarian strategists try to reverse or block this tendency in the still malleable world around them. What is less easy to understand is that they can recruit some of their most assiduous disciples from among democracy's guides and thinkers.[7]

These characteristics of the American system, and other open systems in general, place the United States at a distinct disadvantage in meeting external challenges of the kind posed in Vietnam and since. The Shiite Moslem hijacking of TWA flight 847 dramatically showed this disadvantage and its vulnerability. The terrorists used the US media to make demands, announce their political platform, and play on the emotions of families and the hostages, as well as the American public, in a form of psychological warfare designed to force acquiescence. The terrorists had access to many instruments of an open system; the United States had little access to the terrorist community and its supporters.

Over the long run, these characteristics are also the strength of the American system, but this strength rests on the premise that Americans are knowledgeable about the world in broad terms and understand that democracy demands much from individuals that goes beyond voting, joining political parties, and paying taxes. Democracy cannot flourish without constant attention by those who profess to be democratic—a difficult task since the nature of democracy tends to focus attention not on political confrontation or threats but on peaceful pursuits, quality of life, and all of those other things associated with human rights and justice. These are not pursuits that position individuals or the system in the most effective way to meet current challenges. This is particularly true with respect to US foreign and national security policy, especially in trying to deal with Third World conflicts.

US Foreign Policy and Contemporary Conflicts

Foreign policy and national security policy are so closely interwoven that they have become virtually the same in the contemporary world. There is some distinction, however. Foreign policy includes all activities that encompass government-to-government relationships; national security policy focuses on issues that are seen as significant threats to US security. National security, then, hinges on the capability, effectiveness, and use of the military instrument.

US foreign policy and national security policy have historically been driven by three forces: isolationism, morality, and pragmatism. Rather than a balance of these three forces in any given period, usually first one and then another of these forces dominated. This resulted in vacillation in foreign policy, as first one and then the other force reflected the national mood. A similar pattern can be seen in national security policy. Spanier concludes that

> on the whole, American foreign policy has tended to swing from an isolationist position in which the country served as an example of democratic brotherhood and social justice on earth to a posture of massive and violent intervention once provoked. Level-headed, consistent participation in the international system has been difficult; all-or-nothing swings have been the more common pattern.[8]

US response to wars and national security issues has also been determined by these forces. Americans have viewed "peace and war as two mutually exclusive states of affairs. ... War was a purely military instrument whose sole aim was the destruction of the enemy's forces and of his despotic regime so that the people could be democratized."[9]

Foreign and national security policy thus evolved from domestic sources resting on democratic principles. These were based on the presumption that conflict was an abnormal state of affairs, separate from the peaceful pursuits and purposes of government. This democratic mind-set also affected the relationships between the military and society; the military became important only when there was a sense of national crisis.

The onset of the Cold War and the continuing confrontation between the United States and the USSR has modified the perceptions of the military to the point where most Americans now accept the need for a strong military force to counter the Soviet Union. Beyond that, however, issues of national security become blurred. Because much of US foreign policy is now synonymous with national security policy, ambiguity becomes the rule rather than the exception. This creates a situation in which Americans in 1985 could ask, for example, "Why do we trade with the Soviet Union yet support the Afghanistan revolution against the Soviet occupation?" Similarly, questions were raised regarding US policy that supports the Nicaraguan freedom fighters operating out of Honduras (the contras) and also maintains diplomatic relations with Managua.

Since the decolonization of the world and the rise of Third World states and since the shift in the power base at the United Nations from a Western to a Third World orientation, issues of foreign policy and national security policy have become more complex, ambiguous, and challenging. Policy issues beyond the need to contain the Soviet Union have become particularly difficult to understand and unravel. Even with respect to the Soviet Union, the United States at times displays ambivalent policies swinging from one position to another (isolationism, pragmatism, and morality). Similarly, beyond the European continent, US policy and strategy to deal with the Soviet Union and its surrogates appear even more ambiguous and vacillating. Although some of this is caused by the increasing capability of the Soviet Union in the international field, much of it has to do with the US style in foreign policy and its democratic mind-set.

Rethinking National Security Policy

Over the past three decades US national security has evolved primarily out of the perceived threat of the Soviet Union. Containment and deterrence are cornerstones of national security policy. Multilateral alliances such as NATO and nuclear forces remain critical to US security. General purpose forces and conventional capability have taken on an increasingly important role as Soviet conventional capability in Europe has increased.

Extended deterrence has become part of the US nuclear posture, suggesting the use of nuclear weapons in Europe if conventional forces are deemed inadequate. In responding to the contemporary challenge, however, a new dimension must be added to national security, a dimension deserving more than mere lip-service or superficial policy and strategy attention. Unconventional conflicts form the new battlefield.

In the light of the changed international security situation, there must be a serious reassessment of US policy and strategy. According to one scholar, "As far as American strategy and national security policy are concerned, however, the most important change of the 1970s was the relative decline in American military power compared to that of the Soviet Union."[10] The author goes on to say, "The reconstitution of American military power, however, has to be directed to the needs of the 1980s and shaped by ideas relevant to this decade."[11] Although much of this reconstitution and rethinking must focus on strategy and military posture with respect to the Soviet Union, an important, indeed, crucial part must be on unconventional warfare.

Non-European Conflict Arena

The conflicts most likely to be faced by the United States in this and the coming decade are not necessarily in Europe but in Third World areas. This is not meant to suggest that Europe or the Soviet Union are unimportant. The fact is that Soviet power projections and increased political-military capability have extended the conflict potential well beyond the European boundaries into Third World areas. One authority has concluded,

> The dominant motive force of Soviet political and military action is dialectical: the compelling "push to the utmost" derived from Clausewitz is moderated by the restraining Leninist caveat regarding the avoidance of "adventurism." There is little doubt that the Soviets are committed to gradual, non-provocative but sustained exploration of vulnerable regions of the Third World as

targets of opportunity. They are building the requisite forces, weapons, and technologies to project Soviet influ-ence and power into these regions during this decade. Their doctrines and operational and tactical guidelines and their training programs are congruent with these objectives.[12]

Soviet power projection seeks to avoid direct confronta-tion with the United States; however, in areas in which the Soviets perceive US weakness or where a power vacuum exists, they have and will continue to push. Proxy forces and surrogates of the Soviets play important roles in this power projection; examples are Cuba and Nicaragua. In other cases, some states such as Vietnam and Ethiopia following Soviet policy provide bridges for Soviet power and influence into various regions.

Often the opportunity for Soviet power projection is through surrogates and proxies which take advantage of the instability created by the problems of economic development and political change. The move to mod-ernity requires a number of drastic political, social, and economic changes, which usually lead directly to insta-bility within Third World states, making them vulnerable to external forces. Moreover, the need for external aid and assistance compounds the vulnerability of many Third World states.

An aggressive, expansionist state whose ideology is dia-metrically opposed to that of open systems poses a long-range threat to US interests and in some instances also a short-range or immediate threat. A brief review of the nature of communist systems shows their antagonistic posture toward open systems. Communist systems pre-clude open dissidence, denigrate the importance of the individual as a political entity, give homage to the collec-tivity above all else, and perpetuate rule by a closed elite. The spread of such systems based primarily on relative free choice of the people and based on a nationalistic, nonexpansionist posture is one thing. But the expansion of such systems through conflict, unconventional or otherwise, and by threats and use of surrogates is another.

Many closed systems tend to institutionalize expansionism. They generally accept as a basic truth the need to engage in protracted conflict in order to spread their ideology and expand their power base. There are, of course, exceptions to this, primarily some Eastern European states whose economy tends to adopt a variety of capitalistic characteristics leading to some looseness in their political control over these sectors. Closed systems' fear of democracy, however, reflects an inherent weakness in the character of nondemocratic systems. Their greatest fear is the openness of democracy and what this can do to undermine the basis of closed systems. The policy and strategy of protracted conflict provide closed systems a great advantage over the United States. It is in unconventional conflicts that US national security policy is particularly lacking.

Summary

Since the end of World War II, the United States has devoted much of its defense expenditures and strategic thought and posturing to counter the Soviet Union in the European area. The US public has been conditioned to accept the Soviet Union and Europe as the main focus of US national security and nuclear weaponry as the critical equation of military strength. After years of debate and discussion on these issues, the major problems appear relatively clear, as seen through conventional lenses and democratic mind-sets. Shifting attention to non-European areas and unconventional conflicts has not only created a muddled landscape but has generated civic illiteracy on these issues. The mass media have done little to overcome this civic illiteracy.

MASS MEDIA AND THE POLICY PROCESS

The First Amendment to the US Constitution makes it clear that free expression is an inherent part of open systems and that the press is one instrument of free expression. One of the most important instruments of closed systems is control of the media and other information systems; flow of information from outside is also controlled.

The role of the media in the United States has recently come under attack from a variety of sources: ideological, political, and pragmatic. The criticism has primarily centered around fairness and balance in the presentation of events. It is now becoming recognized that there is an information elite in the United States, a group of individuals in the media who control access to media instruments and who determine what should be aired. This elite has a great deal of power according to some observers.[13] Their power comes not only from controlling the instruments for dispensing information but also because commentary and editorials reflecting a certain point of view can be transmitted in type and over radio and television. The power base of the information elite is strengthened by the ability to report the news in such a way as to slant the story according to certain biases while still maintaining the facade of factual reporting. This power is increased by the ability of the elite to deny access to information systems or at least make gaining access extremely difficult.

There is ample evidence of incomplete and slanted reporting in the media. One of the most flagrant violations of fairness and balanced reporting took place during the Vietnam War. In 1968, the North Vietnamese and Vietcong conducted the Tet offensive. At the time of Tet (the Buddhist New Year), a major military offensive was undertaken by the North Vietnamese and the Vietcong that was intended to trigger a massive urban uprising against the South Vietnamese government and the United States. Not only were major provincial and district centers attacked, but Saigon itself was a target. The Vietcong managed to enter the US embassy and hold it for an extended period of time. Vietcong and North Vietnamese units challenged South Vietnamese and US units across all of South Vietnam, making a particularly successful bid in taking and holding Hue, the imperial capital of Vietnam. As a result, many of the South's Revolutionary Development Teams and military units had to be withdrawn from the countryside to protect major population centers. Similarly, some US units had to focus on battling the revolutionaries in Hue and Saigon, among other places.

The result, however, was not a massive uprising but a significant North Vietnamese and Vietcong military defeat. The South Vietnamese army fought well, and in the main, little was lost by the South Vietnamese government. The reporting of the event by US television and news reporters, however, was so inaccurate that the American people received news accounts claiming a great US and South Vietnamese defeat. Indeed, from television accounts, Americans got the impression that there was widespread panic in the South, and US units were running helter-skelter trying to defeat the enemy.

The true events were well documented and expressed by Peter Braestrup:

> What began as hasty initial reporting of disaster in Vietnam became conventional wisdom when magnified in media commentary and recycled on the hustings in New Hampshire, in campus protest, and in the discussions on Capitol Hill. The press "rebroadcast" it all uncritically, even enthusiastically, although many in the news media should have known better.[14]

In an even more damning observation, Braestrup concluded,

> The generalized effect of the news media's contemporary coverage of Tet in February-March 1968 was a distortion of reality—through sins of omission and commission—on a scale that helped spur major repercussions in U.S. domestic politics, if not in foreign policy.[15]

In domestic politics, there are examples of equally distorted news reporting. For example, the coverage of Chicago's mayoral election of 1983 reflected deep political and racial divisions. In her study of the press coverage of that campaign, Graber gathered evidence that showed a decided imbalance in coverage favoring Harold Washington. She concluded that "the obvious message is that choices made by journalists, rather than the nature of available news, made the difference. If journalists had desired more balanced coverage, they could have attained it."[16]

The message that came across the media was that the mayoral primary of Jane Byrne, Richard Daley, and Harold Washington was in reality a "contest between 'Bad Jane,' 'Good Richie,' and 'Simon-Pure Harold.'"[17] During the campaign between Democrat Harold Washington and Republican Bernie Epton, similar news distortions were evident. Graber concludes that "since it is customary for Chicago's media to view Republican candidacies as doomed, they treated 1983 as no exception. In the tradition of follow-the-leader pack journalism, few reporters strayed from the fold."[18]

One can argue that as long as there are many news sources, balance and fairness can be achieved by reading and listening to a variety of them. But this is difficult to do unless the individual is aware of the nature of the media process and the controlling interests. As Bagdikian points out, a relatively small group of large corporations owns most media sources. They not only control television stations but newspapers and radio stations.[19] Moreover, editorial policy is established throughout the corporate structure, and the information instruments reflect that point of view.

The issue is particularly sensitive because ideological biases may be reflected in much of the media. One of the few studies made of values and mind-sets of major media personalities suggests a decided left-leaning bias in outlooks. According to the Lichter and Rothman study, "The influence of the press is based not on money or political power but on information and ideas they transmit to other social leaders, as well as to the general public."[20] In their study, these researchers conducted "hour-long interviews with 240 journalists and broadcasters at the most influential media outlets." This included the *New York Times*, the *Washington Post*, the *Wall Street Journal*, *Newsweek*, *Time*, and *U.S. News and World Report*. Additionally they interviewed individuals at CBS, NBC, ABC, and PBS, among others. The researchers found that most of the media elite were in the upper socioeconomic levels with the following characteristics: 95 percent were white, 79 percent were male, 68 percent were from northeast or north central states, 54 percent claimed that they were politically liberal, and 50 percent claimed no religion. The vast majority of those interviewed strongly supported the candidates of the Democratic party for president. In 1964, 94 percent supported Johnson against Goldwater; in 1968, 87 percent supported Humphrey against Nixon; in 1972, 81 percent supported McGovern against Nixon; and in 1976, 81 percent supported Carter against Ford.

On foreign policy, there were also some particularly strong attitudes. For example, 56 percent felt that the "U.S. exploits [the] Third World, causes poverty." In the response to the statement that the "West has helped [the] Third World," 75 percent disagreed.

In another report, however, the researcher concluded that in the two weeks in September 1984 following Labor Day, equal time was given to both Democratic and Republican presidential campaigns.[21] "The networks had taken pains to provide quotations on both sides of political issues in the campaign." This report, though, focuses on only one narrow time period and does not include content analysis or the way the news was interpreted and presented. The researcher noted that during the Republican convention in 1984, there was a considerable amount of news commentary and discussion about the far Right and ultra Right but hardly any focus on the Left. He concluded "I do believe that networks brought a vocabulary to this campaign that reflects their notion of the political spectrum, a world in which Lowell Weicker is a 'moderate' and the Republican Party is the 'conservative' or 'ultra-conservative' party."

Care must be taken not to presume that these attitudes necessarily affect news reporting. Such a linkage has not been thoroughly researched, and conclusions are at best tenuous. Nonetheless, the Lichter and Rothman study, among others, shows there is cause for concern about fairness and balance, particularly in dealing with complex and politically sensitive issues. There is a lingering suspicion among some Americans that members of the media are swayed largely by their ideology and biases and that there may be some cases in which the media will inject their own views and interpret events according to their own value systems and predispositions.

The need for independent media is fundamental to democratic systems. That the media are imperfect and in a number of instances biased must be accepted along with the need for free expression. The important point is that the American people must understand the character of the media and their biases and how these may distort news reporting. Moreover, the system must provide the means to ensure that the information elite—the media elite—remain open and abide by professional ethics that demand fairness and balance and that this fairness and balance should not be left solely to the judgment of the elite.

Alternate points of view and alternate interpretations of news events should be a top priority for the information elite. From all indications, it is not.

What does this have to do with unconventional conflicts and the ability of the United States to respond to protracted conflict? In the light of the Vietnam experience, it may be that the media have developed a subtle (at times not so subtle) bias against US involvement in any conflict outside of the well-established European defense system. The media are also affected by the nature of democratic systems and the tendency to favor open systems heavily. There is an underlying fear about US support of nondemocratic systems, which tend to characterize much of the Third World.

Worse, it is conceivable that political mind-sets of the information elite as reflected in the Lichter and Rothman study may be stronger than admitted in assessing foreign news. For example, revolutions against nondemocratic systems may be viewed favorably in comparison to counterrevolutionary systems, most of which are nondemocratic.[22]

Last, one of the most important characteristics of the information elite is an adversarial relationship with the government, particularly when the government's ideology and policy are contradictory to the information elite's views of the world. Thus, foreign and national security policy that may stray from the traditional and conventional view regarding peaceful relationships is generally attacked and interpreted by members of the information elite as misguided and antidemocratic. It is difficult, for example, for many in the media to support aggressive US intelligence activities or news blackouts in the name of national security.

These attitudes are reflected in the news reported and tend to support preconceived notions of simplistic policy choices, reinforcing civic illiteracy. Policy is seen as a clear choice between good and evil, reflecting civic illiteracy.

Rarely is there critical analysis of various policy options, nor are there serious attempts to assess the costs and consequences associated with various degrees of foreign involvement or noninvolvement. Finally, the news media rarely give serious attention to the long-range threats emanating from ideological and expansionist systems in the Third World. There are exceptions to these generalizations, but the criticism holds regardless of whether one is dealing with political and ideological attitudes on the Right or the Left.

The information elite has little patience for outside criticism. In the main, they tend to shelter themselves behind the notion that they are professionals and therefore objective, that they serve the American people, and that they are capable of controlling their own. The information elite tend to stress their own integrity, and although admitting some mistakes, tend to discount them quickly, even though there have been notable and major news distortions, such as the Janet Cooke affair, the Tet offensive, the handling of the 1983 Chicago mayoral campaign, and the reporting of the terrorist skyjacking and hostage taking of TWA flight 847 in 1985, among others.

The solution for corrective action is not to create a body to oversee proper news reporting. Neither is self-analysis and self-regulation by the information elite more than, at best, a partial answer. What is needed is awareness and understanding on the part of the American people of how the information elite operate, their characteristics and attitudes, and the fact that information by the mass media can be biased, politically motivated, and inaccurate.

In addition to a more balanced presentation and fair interpretation of the news, the media must become more critical of their methods and news selection. One noted media professional has stated,

> I think there is, frankly, scorn for fairness in some journalistic quarters. . . . There is an attitude common in the media that any good journalist can apply common sense and quickly fathom what is right and what is wrong in any complicated issue. . . . Coupled with this attitude is one in which a reporter or a camera crew acts as though their presence, their action in covering a story, is more important than the event they are covering.[23]

The commentator went on to note that "unless our profession redefines fairness and its importance to us, others will increasingly try to define it for us—and perhaps succeed."[24]

Further, for a more balanced and fair accounting, one must read and listen to a variety of views on major news events from which one can then draw one's own conclusions. For example, reading the *Washington Post* for information on what is going on in the nation's capital should be balanced by reading the *Washington Times* and the *Washington Enquirer* to provide different perspectives and interpretations. Reading the *Chicago Sun-Times* is only partly the answer to understanding the issues in Chicago. It is also necessary to read the *Chicago Tribune* and the *Chicago Defender*. Similar balancing needs to be done for all major information outlets. Unfortunately this kind of balancing and attention to news sources is a difficult and time-consuming task. As a result, it is more likely that most Americans read one newspaper and follow one newscaster or television station, with all of the dangers that this creates for accepting unbalanced and politically motivated news reporting.

What does all of this have to do with responding to unconventional conflicts? The answer seems reasonably clear. Most information on such conflicts and foreign and security policy in general, comes from television and newspapers. Vietnam was a prime example, being the first television war. Foreign policy is particularly susceptible to various interpretations. Yet the views of a member of the information elite may shape the presentation of the news and may shape interpretations for most other information sources. For example, foreign news as reported and interpreted by the *New York Times* and the *Washington Post* is usually the basis of foreign news accounts in many local papers throughout the country.

Fundamental to understanding the information system elite is their ability to set the agenda for national debate. By presenting and focusing on only certain news events, the media can make them matters of the highest priority in the eyes of the public. By doing so and by directing attention to policy makers and officials, the media elite become part of the policy-making process.

In one study, the researchers conclude,

> To control what people will see and hear means to control the public's view of political reality. By covering certain news events, by simply giving them space, the media signals the importance of these events to the citizenry. By not reporting other activities, the media hides portions of reality from everyone but the few people directly affected. . . . Events and problems placed

on the national agenda by the media excite public interest and become objects of government action.[25]

This is an extremely powerful position for any person or group in a democracy. Adding to their power is the fact that the information elite is just that: an elite. It is difficult for the average American to have much influence on such an elite. Indeed, one of the prime characteristics of an elite is the creation of barriers to outside interference. This is not likely to change in the near future. According to some, the advent of new technology and the role of the computer in the information industry is likely to make the information elite even more powerful:

> The future is murky. Essentially the same people who own and manage newspapers and television now control the new technologies. They are guided by the same elite-sanctioned values, the same desire for profit. New journalistic and entertainment practices and effects will flourish, but technological innovations are unlikely significantly to disrupt the structure of power or undermine its legitimacy.[26]

The concern with the immediate and the tendency to report most news items quickly (sometimes in a matter of a few seconds) while seeking clear insights concentrates the attention of the media on presenting even the most complex issues simplistically.[27] Or in the case of terrorist dramas, for example, the media become so much involved in the event that they tend to become part of the event rather than an objective and neutral instrument. Rarely can such approaches capture the subtleties, nuances, and complex relationships among options, costs, and consequences, much less the deep-seated political and cultural values and interplay in unconventional conflicts and Third World issues.

There is a tendency to interpret events so as to make them appear as a zero-sum game; someone wins and someone loses. This parallels and supports the notion that US policy options are clear choices between good and evil. Inadvertently or otherwise, the information elite thus perpetuate the civic illiteracy of the American people. To be sure, there are exceptions in which the media have sought to provide in-depth analysis with clear identification of the various policy options. But even these attempts evoke charges of unfair and unbalanced presentations. If history is any guide, the power and role of the information elite in American society are likely to continue, although there are signs that Americans are becoming highly skeptical of the media's claim to fairness and professionalism.[28]

The best position for any American is to accept the need for an independent information system. This must be balanced, however, by an understanding of the characteristics of the information elite and the role they play in dispensing the news and affecting the public agenda. This understanding can be strengthened by seeking a variety of sources for news and commentary. Only by such an effort can the average American go beyond political biases and ideological posturing, from either the left or right, that may affect information sources.

THE US SYSTEM AND POLICY ISSUES

Another major consideration in new realism is the working of the US political system and how this relates to the policy process. The legitimacy and credibility of governmental response to policy issues is partly a result of the traditions of the system and partly a reflection of the mood of the country. These must be considered in relation to civic illiteracy and the role of the information elite. In the US political system, not only are there certain fundamental principles that underpin foreign policy, but the way the political system functions also has an impact on foreign policy issues. Additionally, the mood of the country, or more specifically, the domestic political environment and public attitudes regarding war and the purposes and conduct of foreign policy, affect national will and political resolve to undertake any foreign involvement.

General Patterns of Foreign Policy

Throughout most of their history, Americans have been suspicious of involvement in the Old World. Not only was the American Revolution a struggle to create a new nation, it was also intended to separate the country from Great Britain and the rest of Europe physically and in terms of international relationships. Later, the Monroe Doctrine was intended to keep the Old World out of the Northern and Southern Hemispheres. Then the United States took it upon itself to police the Southern Hemisphere as a way of maintaining order and also in preventing intervention by Old World forces. From this historical basis there evolved the three components of US foreign policy: morality, isolationism, and pragmatism. However, a full understanding of US foreign policy must also include the commitment to Americanism, not an easy concept to define since parts of it overlap with the other three components. It can be understood in broad terms encompassing the view that the best type of governmental system derives from the American experience and that this system, although imperfect, provides the best opportunity for rule by the people and the best opportunity for individual achievement, both politically and economically. It follows that other systems are judged, implicitly or otherwise, according to this standard.

Americans have always viewed themselves from a moralistic point of view. That is, foreign policy and involvement in conflict have usually been seen as a moral crusade. The US experience in World War II epitomized the moral crusade. Earlier in history, the United States became involved in the Southern Hemisphere—many times because of the idea that it was bringing civilization to underdeveloped systems and other times in order to maintain law and order. Indeed, even the US response to the Plains Indians and the Seminoles in Florida in the nineteenth century was based partly on moral as well as pragmatic grounds.

Furthering the moralistic and pragmatic view was the conviction that the American system was best, bringing the most to individuals. Thus, any system that aimed toward an American type of system was to be applauded. Moreover, if US foreign policy and involvement in conflict were intended to further US aims, then this made policy and conflict involvement a furthering of what was good. Any US president involved in foreign ventures or considering US involvement in conflict had to place these policies in terms of the prevailing traditions of American experience and expectations.

The mood of the country has also been part of the equation determining the nature of US foreign policy and conflict involvement. Serious domestic problems obviously focused much of the energy and effort on internal matters. The depression of the 1930s left little energy and resources for external involvement; isolationism became the basis of foreign policy. Similarly, there is compelling evidence to show that the Watergate affair did much to undermine US efforts in Vietnam and in foreign policy in general.[29] Suspicions regarding presidential involvement in a third-rate burglary and the subsequent attempts by President Nixon to cover up the affair became the center of the information elite's concern, occupying much attention. Additionally congressional reaction, as well as the reaction of many other important political actors, to presidential behavior attracted a great deal of domestic political attention. It was difficult for the Nixon administration to carry on any serious foreign policy activities, much less conflict involvement, in these circumstances.

In the post-Vietnam period, there is much of the Vietnam and Watergate experience that still affects American attitudes toward the Third World in particular. Invariably, any involvement in Third World areas triggers fears of another Vietnam. In 1985 US relationships with Nicaragua and attempts to counteract the evolving Marxist-Leninist regime there ran into criticism brought on largely by the Vietnam heritage. Politically and ideologically oriented groups were quick to take advantage of anti-administration criticism. A political environment was created that held little hope for the development of a national consensus on US policy toward Nicaragua. This was also reflected in initial congressional reaction and partisanship in opposition to the administration's Nicaraguan policy, although in the summer of 1986 the Congress reversed itself and approved aid to the Nicaraguan freedom fighters.

Democracy and the Policy Process

For most Americans, the president stands at the center of the policy process. But a number of factors affect presidential power. In all but the clearest policy issues, Congress and the executive tend to develop adversarial relationships. Indeed, the concept of counterbalancing forces within the government—checks and balances and separation of powers—was intended to ensure that no one unit within government could gain absolute power over the other. Thus, although the president is the only legal representative of the United States in foreign relations and is commander in chief of the armed forces, it is Congress that must provide the money, and in many instances the consensual foundation, for conducting effective relationships and in providing funds for the armed forces. In times of crisis or where there is a generally accepted policy, there is usually a consensus in support of the president. When the president exercises positive leadership, even when taking unpopular positions, he has an advantage in trying to overcome congressional resistance because Americans tend to support strong presidential actions. In most instances, this is less difficult if the Senate and the House are controlled by the president's party.

There is a difference between the president's role in domestic policy and foreign policy (national security). In domestic policy, the president must reconcile a variety of interests because the process is based on broad participation. In foreign policy, however, what is generally sought is the best solution based on the expertise of a relatively small elite in the bureaucracy and in the presidential office.[30] This is a built-in dilemma in the system that creates difficult problems for the president in trying to reconcile democratic imperatives with firm and coherent leadership in foreign policy. This dilemma is difficult enough to resolve in foreign policy in general, and in unconventional conflicts, the resolution is even more difficult. Hans Morgenthau sums up the dilemma:

> A democratic government must accomplish two tasks: on the one hand, it must pursue policies which maximize the chances for success; on the other hand, it must secure the approval for these policies. . . . The conditions under which popular support can be obtained for a foreign policy are not necessarily identical with the conditions under which such a policy can be successfully pursued. A popular foreign policy is not necessarily a good one.[31]

Consensus and Policy

In a democracy, there will always be a problem in trying to reconcile the demands of democracy and those of successful foreign policy. This dilemma is to the disadvantage of the United States when dealing with unconventional conflicts.

From World War II until the Vietnam War, there was a national consensus on foreign policy according to most observers. That is, there was bipartisan support for US foreign policy on the premise that partisanship stopped at the "water's edge." But because of the Vietnam experience, among other things, there has been less reluctance for Congress to challenge the president on foreign policy issues. The politics within the Johnson administration over involvement in and conduct of the Vietnam conflict created deep political, ideological, and moral divisions within the nation. This set the stage for congressional reassertiveness and challenge to the executive in foreign affairs and national security. This now even extends to traditional relationships with Europe and NATO (some congresspersons advocate withdrawing US units from Europe).

This breakdown of national consensus on foreign policy was made worse by the Watergate affair. The credibility of the presidential office was considerably shaken by revelations of presidential misbehavior and the subsequent resignation of President Nixon. Thus, there is a deep fear of becoming entangled in another Vietnam, as well as skepticism about the effectiveness of government— probably reflecting a lingering reaction to Watergate, as well as a degree of disgust with the capability of Congress and behavior of certain congresspersons.[32]

While much of the skepticism and suspicion of the Oval Office has been blunted by the Reagan presidency, fears lie just below the surface and can be triggered by foreign involvement that may seem politically questionable. For example, the Grenada invasion in 1983 is still questioned by some, although massive evidence shows that Grenada was well on the way to becoming another Cuba.[33]

Open Systems and Access

The US political system invites open dissidence against the government. The right to resist and criticize government policies are fundamental principles of open systems. Therefore in many complex foreign and security policies, particularly those that deal with the Third World, a number of political groups can mobilize against the government, as can a number of congresspersons. The most complex policies—those that rarely provide a clear choice between good and evil—trigger the greatest counterreactions within the body politic. Not only is this a reflection of civic illiteracy and the role of the information elite, but it also reflects the nature and character of the US political system. This should not be construed as suggesting that all those who oppose government policies base their beliefs on civic illiteracy; a number of groups and individuals have thoughtfully analyzed the complex issues and dilemmas involved in trying to find solutions. Unfortunately, these are typically not groups or individuals who attract the attention of the media. Rather, a vocal minority is likely to gain the greatest access to the information elite. Such minorities usually shape their positions on the simplest and most understandable terms, which may in fact have little to do with the real policy choices.

Those in government seeking to develop a consensus or favorable response to government policies also try to gain access to the information channels and attempt to create the proper image of government policies; however, the inherent adversarial posture of most members of the information elite places such officials at a disadvantage in trying to deal with the elite.

In sum, the nature of the US political system creates a political environment that advocates criticism and resistance to the government as a fundamental right. Fostered by an adversarial information elite and the search for right answers, the American people tend to grasp at solutions that seem comprehensible and proper. In many instances, this convergence of adopting the most simplistic answers (civic illiteracy), the role of the media, and the nature of the US political system makes it almost impossible to disentangle myth from reality and equally difficult to develop an understanding of the problems of the Third World and the dangers posed by unconventional conflicts.

SEARCH FOR ANSWERS

The three dimensions for developing a new realism are civic illiteracy, the role of the media, and the nature of the American system. It seems clear that political style, the instruments of democracy, and the role of the individual create an openness as well as political dynamics and flexibility that are poorly postured to develop a cohesive and coherent policy and strategy to deal with the Third World and unconventional conflicts. The American value system and its expectations tend not to provide the kind of empathy or awareness needed to develop an understanding of foreign cultures, particularly those in the Third World, as a background for effective policy and strategy.

From a more individualistic perspective, an open system—democracy—demands much of the individual. It is not a passive system. Taking part in elections and abiding by the law are the most basic requirements of individual participation in the system. More important is the need for constant attention in holding officials accountable, developing the background to ensure serious assessment of policy issues, and understanding the working of the US political system. The key to rational political participation and policy choices is access to balanced and fair information sources. Information must be assessed with a healthy skepticism based on knowledge about the nature and power and role of the information elite.

It is within these circumstances that individuals must seek answers and understandable policy explanations. Unfortunately, the search usually borders on the simplistic and reflects the tendency toward civic illiteracy. Reinforcing this tendency toward civic illiteracy is the fact that there may be no right answer and that the problems may actually be insoluble. It may be that the problems are inherent in Third World characteristics and the United States must learn to live with them for the foreseeable future. The same may be true of unconventional conflicts, which are deeply enmeshed in the political-social milieu of Third World systems and do not lend themselves to simple military or economic solutions. They are problems of the political system, many of which evolve from economic development and political change. This means that the way government operates is changing, its ideology is usually being challenged, the economic structure is shifting from a subsistence agriculture base to industrialization, and social relationships are changing, among other things.

These changes create instability and make developing systems extremely vulnerable to revolution. Thus, answers do not lie in economic or military solutions alone but on a wide range of policies and strategies focusing on the system as a whole. These are primarily of a political nature. Making the matter even more difficult for most Americans, the values and cultures of most Third World systems are different from those in the United States. Cultural and value differences not only make it difficult for many Americans to understand Third World systems, but they make it difficult for many in the Third World to understand Americans and the American value system. This situation is particularly pronounced when the United States tries to deal with unconventional conflicts since such conflicts add an even more complex dimension to those already associated with political change and economic development.

Developing a sense of realism in dealing with unconventional conflicts is not an easy proposition for most Americans. Not only are issues in the Third World far distant from immediate problems, but the complexity of these issues has a chilling effect on serious attempts to study and understand them. This is reinforced by the factors discussed in this chapter that almost inundate the American people with information and political dialogue. No wonder, that for many, it is easier to adopt a civically illiterate posture.

It is easy to accept the proposition that all people long to be free and that all systems will eventually move toward democracy. It follows, then, that democracies should not interfere with the domestic affairs of other countries, particularly Third World countries; in the long run, people will decide their own fate, and this will be the best for American democracy. The principles of democracy demand fair play, justice, and self-determination. The answer, then, seems to lie in a modern version of morality and isolationism.

Jean-François Revel has identified the dangers in such a position.

> Not only do the democracies today blame themselves for sins they have not committed, but they have formed the habit of judging themselves by ideals so inaccessible that the defendants are automatically guilty. It follows that a

civilization that feels guilty for everything it is and does and thinks will lack the energy and conviction to defend itself when its existence is threatened. Drilling into civilization that it deserves defending only if it can incarnate absolute justice is tantamount to urging that it let itself die or be enslaved.[34]

This kind of democratic problem is crucial in unconventional conflicts. Such conflicts are not seen as a real threat, and criticizing everything that is less than absolute in terms of democratic ideals, Americans may tend to accept the notion that revolutionaries are fighting for democratic ideals, even after the revolutions are grasped by Marxist-Leninists, as many are. One authority observes,

> Major segments of the American establishment tend automatically to attribute legitimacy to revolutionary movements against Third World governments. They also tend almost automatically to attribute illegitimacy to any direct attack by one state on another across a recognized frontier. Consequently, there is likely to be a greater public willingness to help a friendly government respond to an external attack than to an internal attack.[35]

US adversaries understand this and resort to all types of unconventional conflicts while avoiding a direct and visible attack, except in the most obvious cases of US withdrawal or reluctance to respond. This is what took place in 1975 as the North Vietnamese overran the South.

In order to develop a new realism with respect to unconventional conflicts, it is necessary to understand that the nature of such conflicts precludes the notions of clear and present danger. The onset of revolutions usually indicates the existence of reasonably well-established groups already enmeshed within the political-social system of the conflict area. For democracies to wait until there is a clear and present danger may be too late. Even if it is not too late, waiting for a clear outbreak of conflict may place the United States in a disadvantageous position, considerably raising the costs of effective response.

This assumes that US national interests necessitate a response or require involvement in unconventional conflict in a given area to support a system against a Marxist-Leninist revolution. The same holds true with respect to the support of anti-Marxist revolutions.

The beginning of new realism is to understand the complex issues of unconventional conflicts and the Third World. This chapter has attempted to pinpoint a number of critical ones and has tried to identify sign posts that can lead to a better understanding of the Third World and unconventional conflicts. These may not necessarily lead to solutions, but they will provide a sound basis to weigh policy options and may provide the beginnings of civic literacy. It must also be recognized, though, that even the best policies and strategies may not lead to success. Given the imperfections of human beings and their institutions, there is no assurance that mistakes will not be made and effective policies adopted. Involvement in the foreign policy and security issues that have been addressed here is always a risk. But to assume that the United States should become involved only when success is ensured or when, in the words of Charles B. Marshall, the "ally is immaculate," is simply to wish away most of the problems of the Third World by adopting an air of self-righteous arrogance ensuring the demise of democracy.

The question that must now be addressed is how all of this can be accomplished. What programs, methods, and political-psychological changes are needed? What needs to be done to shape the American psyche and political system to be able to respond effectively to Third World conflicts?

NOTES

1. Malcolm G. Scully, "Colleges Urged to Combat 'Civic' Illiteracy." *Chronicle of Higher Education*, November 25, 1981, pp. 1, 8.
2. Ibid., p. 8.

3. Ole R. Holsti and James N. Rosenau, *American Leadership in World Affairs: Vietnam and the Breakdown of Consensus* (Boston: Allen and Unwin, 1984), p. 70.

4. Jean-François Revel, *How Democracies Perish* (Garden City, N.Y.: Doubleday, 1983), p. 4.

5. Jim Denton, "Contra Atrocities, or a Covert Propaganda War? A Lobbying Drive Began in Managua," *Wall Street Journal*, April 23, 1985.

6. See, for example, Georgie Anne Geyer, "To Fathom Nicaragua, Look beyond the Labels," *Chicago Sun-Times*, June 2, 1985, p. 60; Ricardo Lizano, "A Revolution of Disillusion; Nicaragua's Repression by Another Name," *World Press Review* (June 1983):37-38; and "In Nicaragua, a Revolution Gone Sour," *U.S. News and World Report*, October 18, 1982, pp. 41, 44. See also Ike Skelton, "Central America: A Whole New Set of U.S. Concerns," *Army* 35, no. 5 (May 1985):41-45, esp. p. 43.

7. Revel, p. 345.

8. John Spanier, *American Foreign Policy since World War II*, 9th ed. (New York: Holt, Rinehart and Winston, 1983), p. 11.

9. Ibid., p. 10.

10. Samuel P. Huntington, "The Renewal of Strategy," in Samuel P. Huntington, ed., *The Strategic Imperative: New Policies for American Security* (Cambridge, Mass.: Ballinger Publishing Co., 1982), p. 1. See also Edward N. Luttwak, *The Pentagon and the Art of War: The Question of Military Reform* (New York: Simon & Schuster, 1984), pp. 93-129.

11. Huntington, p. 49.

12. Roman Kolkowicz, "Military Strategy and Political Interests: The Soviet Union and the United States," ACIS Working Paper no. 30 (Los Angeles: Center for International and Strategic Affairs, University of California, Los Angeles, January 1981), pp. 34-35.

13. See, for example, Ben H. Bagdikian, *The Media Monopoly* (Boston: Beacon Press, 1983), and S. Robert Lichter and Stanley Rothman, "Media and Business Elites," *Public Opinion* (October-November 1981):42-46, 59-60.

14. Peter Braestrup, *Big Story: How the American Press and Television Reported and Interpreted the Crisis of Tet 1968 in Vietnam and Washington* (Boulder, Colo.: Westview Press, 1977), 1:xxxiii.

15. Ibid., p. 184.

16. Doris Graber, "Media Magic: Fashioning Characters for the 1983 Mayoral Race," in Melvin G. Holli and Paul M. Green, eds., *The Making of the Mayor, Chicago, 1983* (Grand Rapids, Mich.: William B. Eerdmans Publishing Co., 1984), p. 67.

17. Ibid.

18. Ibid., p. 68.

19. See, for example, Bagdikian.

20. Lichter and Rothman, p. 42. The material presented in the following paragraphs is quoted from this report. Although some attempt has been made by some members of the media to discredit the report, the Lichter and Rothman study remains a credible basis for assessing the attitudes of the media elite. In a later survey conducted by the *Los Angeles Times* in August, 1985, much of the Lichter and Rothman study was confirmed. According to the *Los Angeles Times* survey of 3,165 newspaper editors and reporters around the country, the attitudes of those surveyed were very similar to those of the media elite as reported by Lichter and Rothman. Interestingly, the *Los Angeles Times* also surveyed 3,000 members of the public and found that their attitudes on controversial issues were in striking contrast to those of newspaper editors and reporters. See David Shaw, "The Public and the Press—Two Viewpoints," *Los Angeles Times*, August 11, 1985, p. 1. See also Reed Irvine, "Media Liberalism Not Limited to the Elite," *Washington Times*, September 6, 1985, p. 5.

21. This summary and quotes are taken from "1984 Campaign Coverage," *AIM Report* (October-B 1984):XIII-20. This report has extensive coverage and assessment of the study completed by Michael Robinson. The study was sponsored by the American Enterprise Institute and George Washington University.

22. See, for example, Jim Watson, "Report on Nicaragua," *Washington Times*, August 30, 1985, p. 7B.

23. Robert MacNeil, "Why Do They Hate Us?" *Columbia Magazine* (June 1985):17.

24. Ibid.

25. Thomas E. Patterson and Robert D. McClure, *The Unseeing Eye: The Myth of Television Power in National Elections* (New York: G. P. Putnam's Sons, 1976), p. 75.

26. David L. Paletz and Robert M. Entman, *Media Power Politics* (New York: Free Press, 1981), pp. 253-54.

27. An excellent presentation of this problem is Michael J. Arlen, *Living Room War* (New York: Penguin Books, 1982), pp. 80-85, 103-22. See also Doris A. Graber, ed., *Media Power in Politics* (Washington, D.C.: CQ Press, 1984).

28. See, for example, Thomas B. Rosentiel, "Journalist Poll Finds Doubt on Papers' Esteem," *Los Angeles Times*, October 30, 1985, part 1, p. 3. See also MacNeil, p. 17.

29. See, for example, Henry Kissinger, *White House Years* (Boston: Little, Brown and Co., 1979), p. 986 in which the author writes, "The one circumstance we could not foresee was the debacle of Watergate. It was that which finally sealed the fate of South Vietnam by the erosion of Executive authority, strangulation of South Vietnam by wholesale reduction of aid, and legislated prohibitions against enforcing the peace agreement in the face of unprovoked North Vietnamese violations." See also p. 1095.

30. For a more detailed explanation of this point, see John Spanier and Eric M. Uslaner, *American Foreign Policy Making and the Democratic Dilemmas*, 4th ed. (New York: Holt, Rinehart and Winston, 1985), pp. 5-7. See also the discussion of presidential personality, character, and leadership style in national security in Sam C. Sarkesian, "The President and National Security: An Overview," in Sam C. Sarkesian, ed., *Presidential Leadership and National Security: Style, Institutions, and Politics* (Boulder, Colo.: Westview Press, 1984), pp. 3-36.

31. Hans J. Morgenthau, *A New Foreign Policy for the United States* (New York: Praeger, 1969), pp. 150-51.

32. See, for example, "Harsh Words for Congress Once More," *U.S. News and World Report*, May 20, 1985, pp. 60-61.

33. See Roger Fontaine, "Captured Records Reveal Communist Strategy, Tactics," *Washington Times*, April 25, 1985, p. 1 and Paul Seabury and Walter A. McDougall, eds., *The Grenada Papers* (San Francisco: ICS Press, 1985).

34. Revel, p. 10.

35. Huntington, p. 45.

PART III

Conclusions

9

Democracy and Unconventional Conflicts: The Democratic Imperative

At the end of 1970, a noted authority on the Soviet political system concluded that many Americans were demanding that the United States not only adhere strictly to the highest moral and ethical standards in its foreign relations but that it stop using propaganda in support of capitalism and neoimperialism. He concluded,

> Now sober-minded politicians of both parties, not to mention preachers and professors, make the same demands on the United States, seek national penitence for sins and transgressions which even the most uninhibited Soviet or Chinese Communist propaganda has not thought to attribute to the United States. The mania of guilt and political masochism has assumed proportions which, except for their dangerous implications, would be truly comical.[1]

Although aimed specifically at the anti-Vietnam hysteria (or virtual hysteria) that seemed to grip the United States in 1970, this same attitude is held by a number of Americans today, though some hold such positions in a less strident fashion. Many congresspersons reacting to US policy in Central America, for example, constantly link it to Vietnam. A number of special interest groups, including some church groups, arrayed against US policy, aggressively speak out against capitalism and neoimperialism. Many of these groups follow the same line of thought evident in 1970. Another body of opinion sees the Vietnam experience as a worthy cause that should be honored. It follows that the United States should not be afraid to assert its power again, but next time, in contrast to the Vietnam experience, it must do so to win. A variety of positions evolve from one or the other of these views.

Regardless of the positions taken, however, they must be seen in the context of the problems of Third World conflicts. The United States must live with a variety of Third World systems. It is unlikely that such systems can quickly establish Western-type democracies. As long as such systems are nonexpansionist and committed to and practice sovereignty and self-determination, then they should pose little threat to US security interests. Even left-wing socialist systems are not necessarily threats to the United States as long as they do not adopt an expansionist Marxist-Leninist structure and as long as they adhere to the principles of sovereignty and self-determination.

As history has shown, many Third World states are exposed to a variety of external forces, particularly to the power and influence of expansionist Marxist-Leninist systems. Established socialist systems such as those in Western Europe can limit the influence of Marxist-Leninist systems if they desire. But Third World socialist systems, struggling over ideology and faced with all of the problems of modernity, are hardly in the same position.

It is also true that the Soviet system has legitimate interests in the Third World. As long as these interests are pursued through peaceful competition, the United States stands on firm ground. But peaceful competition as seen through the lens of Marxist-Leninist ideology tends to accept conflict as a way of life. This includes the effort to destroy, or at the least reduce the appeal of, open systems.

The confrontation between the United States and the USSR in the Third World and US efforts in trying to deal with the Third World and unconventional conflicts drive many Americans and their policy makers to seek solutions that aim, on the one hand, to avoid conflicts and, on the other hand, to prevent the expansion of Marxist-Leninist systems. The paradox is that such solutions attempt to reconcile the irreconcilable.

AMERICA'S IRRECONCILABLE WORLDS

In a situation of peaceful competition, the United States would seem to have the advantage, and given its values, economic resources, and political resilience, it should do well in any such competition. It is only when the United States loses sight of how peaceful competition is interpreted by Marxist-Leninist systems that it is likely to be placed at a disadvantage. It must accept the reality that unconventional conflicts are part of this peaceful competition.

Reality and Democracy

The reality is that a great many Americans, including many elected officials, seem to demand the best of two irreconcilable worlds. They do not want to see the establishment of more Marxist-Leninist states, which seek to destabilize particular Third World regions. They do not want another Castro's Cuba, for example. At the same time, they do not want another Vietnam. To achieve these goals, the tendency is to seek the most simplistic solutions based on a world seen through a conventional lens free from conflicts. More often than not, however, the pursuit of such goals cannot avoid involvement in unconventional conflicts. Yet unless Americans are willing to support a policy and strategy based on the possibility, and indeed probability, of becoming involved in unconventional conflicts, there are likely to be more Cubas and more Vietnams. The dilemma of trying to reconcile irreconcilables is at the heart of the moral and philosophical issues of open systems in dealing with unconventional conflicts.

Moral and Philosophical Issues

According to one scholar, the major role of constitutional democracy is in "good actions," which mean the perpetuation and growth of civilization: "The measure of civilization is the extent to which man is helped to develop his potentialities which make life worth living." He further states,

> An effective and responsible democratic foreign policy
> . . . is dependent upon strengthening the ethical and cultural ethos that makes constitutional democracy possible. Popular self-rule is the most demanding of all forms of government. To have a realistic chance of survival for the longer term, democracy must be exceptionally attentive to the need for moral and cultural education and self-education among the citizens. Because of the special danger that comes from abuse of democratic freedom and rights, neglect of that old task of civilization uniquely exposes democracy to extinction.[2]

The author seems to be arguing that a constitutional democracy has the right and duty to protect itself and promote the values of civilization. As such, rigid adherence to moral abstractions without regard to their application and relevance to particular situations is a dangerous position. It follows that this isolates a constitutional democracy from the realities of world politics, creating the false impression that rhetorical commitment to moral abstractions even to the point of self-destruction is the epitome of moral goodness.

This moral and philosophical argument challenges parts of just war theory. But as a number of scholars argue, the concepts of just war often find questionable validity in revolution and counterrevolution. One scholar observes, "Another principle in the law of war is reciprocity which can be taken to imply that if one side violates the immunity of the other's noncombatants, the other side may reciprocate until the initial violation ceases."[3]

Since the center of gravity of revolution, counter-revolution, and terrorism is in the political-social milieu of the political system, it is extremely difficult to distinguish clearly between combatants and noncombatants. Indeed, some scholars argue that on the one hand civilians need to be immune from soldiers and, on the other hand, soldiers must be immune from civilians. When this latter immunity is violated, the issue of reciprocity becomes valid.[4]

In the broader sense, one scholar argues that

> when a fundamental human value, like the rights of noncombatants, is threatened, then action may be taken to preserve that value, even if in the short run protecting it may require disregarding it. This is the principle that justifies acts out of supreme emergency, and it is an extremely dangerous one. When invoked, it must be circumscribed by extreme restraint, or else its actions lead directly to what they were meant to correct.[5]

A recent example of such an act designed to preserve that value was the interception of the Egyptian civilian jet aircraft carrying four terrorists responsible for the piracy of the Italian cruise ship *Achille Lauro* in October 1985. The terrorists were apparently on their way to freedom in Tunisia. The successful interception of the Egyptian aircraft by US fighter aircraft and the arrest of the four terrorists after the aircraft was forced down in Sicily was justified by most Americans and many others because it was in response to a barbaric act: the killing of an elderly and handicapped American and the terrorizing of over 500 other people.

Yet the desire by many Americans to uphold moral principles, regardless of their abstractness, makes it difficult for government to design and carry out effective policies and strategies in response to unconventional conflicts. This is the difficulty in developing a national con-

sensus for support of conflict policies—policies that to
many may appear to challenge moral principles and be
contrary to the norms of open systems.

This brief survey of some moral and philosophical issues does not do justice to the rich traditions and complex
issues addressed in just war literature. But the discussion
does suggest the existence of serious and complex issues
leading to a moral and philosophical muddle for open
systems in coming to grips with unconventional conflicts.

THE NEW BATTLEFIELD

In a 1983 assessment of "peacetime" wars, one news
magazine identified over 40 such wars in progress in the
Third World.[6] More than 30 of these were unconventional. Yet this assessment did not include the number of
terrorist incidents or the range of international terrorist
operations in progress. In the second part of the 1980s, not
only are such conflicts continuing, but the scope of international terrorism seems to broaden, particularly against
open systems.

For most Americans, the 1980s is a decade of peace—if
peace is described in conventional terms; that is, the
United States is not engaged in open conventional war.
Nonetheless, the United States has been involved in and
is linked to many unconventional conflicts, either directly
or indirectly; examples are El Salvador, Nicaragua,
Afghanistan, Kampuchea, and the Philippines.

It is therefore not unreasonable to conclude that the
realities of the international security system make conflict
an integral part of world politics. The principal character
of these conflicts now and for the foreseeable future is
likely to be unconventional, with all that this suggests
about the Third World, superpower relations, the Marxist-
Leninist ideological thrust, and closed systems.

These are the cardinal reference points made in this
study describing the new battlefield. The new battlefield is
not one that shows itself by massive cross-border attacks,
or aerial attacks on US warships, such as occurred at Pearl

Harbor in 1941. Nor will such a battlefield necessarily be characterized by massive troop formations and weapons of mass destruction. Rather, it is one that evolves out of the political-social milieu of a particular system in which there is a high degree of instability and groups contending for power. In the main, such conflicts are not those that suddenly burst upon the international scene. They fester and at some point become visible and increasingly challenging, mushrooming into revolution, either from internal indigenous groups or from external groups, or both.

Revolutions

Popular revolutions led by nationalist and democratic forces are part of the American heritage. These are the kinds of revolutions that should receive sympathetic treatment from the United States because they hold some promise to develop into an open system. How quickly such treatment needs to turn into actual aid and assistance is dependent on the importance of the area to US security interests, the threat to the revolution from external forces intent on co-opting it into a Marxist-Leninist (or other closed system) revolution, and the moral quality of the involvement. The key consideration for US policy is that once it is determined that such revolutions should be supported, this must be done early. Otherwise, left-wing fascist groups are likely to co-opt the revolution or the right-wing dictatorial elite may react so heavy-handedly as to destroy the bases of moderate groups. This is why it is so difficult to conceive of moderate revolutions.

Up to this point, the United States has rarely followed such a strategy. Over the past several decades, it has usually been Marxist-Leninist ideologies and groups that have co-opted such revolutions or have eliminated the truly democratic and nationalistic elements, distorting popular revolutions.

Revolutions that are later shaped by Marxist-Leninist forces usually develop left-wing fascist systems that are likely to be worse than the systems they replace. Equally important, such systems are not usually content with their own states but attempt to spread conflict throughout the region. For example, the Marxist-Leninists in Nicaragua have made no secret of their ultimate aim of spreading the revolution beyond their own borders.[7]

Revolutions that are truly internal and isolated from external forces are in the best position to be democratic and nationalist. But no revolution that has occurred over the past three decades has been isolated from external forces.

What makes the problem more perplexing and dangerous is that revolutionary terror has broadened its dimension, spreading into a vast, if loose, international network. The PLO skyjacking of an El Al aircraft in 1968 was an early incident signaling this new dimension. The massacre of Israeli athletes at the Munich Olympics in 1972 by the Black September group gave a particularly lethal aspect to international terrorism. These early incidents paved the way for the numerous terrorist acts over the past decade and their increasingly lethality.

Peaceful Competition

Democratic systems such as the United States develop best in a peaceful state of affairs, where economic systems and political style determine the outcome of competition. It is the probability of success of open systems that seriously challenges Marxist-Leninist (closed) systems, causing many of them to accept conflict, change, and competition as synonymous.

The perpetuation of democratic values is best pursued in an environment of peaceful competition (peaceful as defined in the traditional sense meaning no conflict) and with systems (regardless of their characteristics) that are committed to sovereignty and self-determination and are nonexpansionist. There are states, however, whose ideological orientation and characteristics are antithetical to open systems and that are intent on initiating and perpetuating unconventional conflict for the purpose of defeating open systems. Much of this is a result of deliberate policy choice, distorting the meaning of peaceful competition and the concept of legitimate state behavior. Further, many revolutionary and counterrevolutionary struggles between contending elites attract the involvement of outside states, internationalizing the conflict. This combination of the character of unconventional conflicts, their propensity, and their internationalization shapes the internal and external dimensions of the new battlefield.

Response to this new battlefield by the United States requires more than recognition of the nature and challenge of unconventional conflict. It requires a reshaping of the US military system toward an effective posture for conflicts across the spectrum. In brief, effective policy and strategy rest on a new US political-psychological posture and revamped military system.

US POLITICAL-PSYCHOLOGICAL POSTURE

The political and psychological efforts to respond effectively are as varied and complex as the character of the new battlefield itself. The primary need is to develop a realistic view of the world, not only in the minds of the public but in the policy-making structures of the government. At the same time, a firm, nonapologetic, and balanced image of US posture and policy must be portrayed to the American people and to the external world. These factors are essential in developing relevant and feasible policy and the necessary national will and staying power to pursue policy goals.

In no small way, the perceptions of a state's moral and ethical basis, its national will, and staying power are a function of the state's ability to project its image to other people. Not only the projection of the image but the quality of that image is contingent on the ability of the United States, for example, to gain access to the information sources and touch the hearts and minds of other systems. The issues and forces involved in achieving these goals have been part of the analysis in the previous chapters.

Much needs to be done in developing a more knowledgeable body politic, more sophisticated policy makers, and a more responsive and flexible policy process. All of this must be based on an understanding of the Third World and its propensity for unconventional conflicts. Finally, it must be recognized that unconventional conflicts includes a war of ideas. Psychological warfare and propaganda in the contemporary period have become a sophisticated and far-ranging undertaking by large and small states alike. In the long run, the battle over ideologies may be the most critical in shaping political systems and determining the outcome of unconventional conflicts.

A number of specific policies and programs need to be put into place if the United States is to compete effectively in the Third World.

First, a firm policy must be adopted that is based on support of like-minded systems and systems that have the potential of developing into open systems. Such a policy must probe closed systems in order to identify areas through which they can be influenced toward openness or, at the least, can be moved in the direction of accepting a more traditional concept of peaceful competition. In brief, a policy of reaction must be replaced by one of initiative and outreach of democratic values and norms. This must include strategic options that can adopt the best mix of economic, political, diplomatic, psychological, and military means.

Second, the intelligence system must be greatly improved not only in its information-gathering function but also in its analytical ability and counterintelligence effort. The concept of intelligence must be broadened to allow initiatives that include penetration of groups and states involved in unconventional warfare. This must be accompanied by a more streamlined and flexible oversight process that places this function in the hands of a select group of congressmen, combining House and Senate functions into one.

Third, the political-military instruments must develop and design strategies that incorporate the best use of the military as a political instrument. This means developing a variety of integrative strategies between military and civilian agencies. It means that the highest levels of national leadership must accept and firmly encourage such strategies.

Fourth, a comprehensive psychological warfare strategy must be designed to sell the US ideology. The idea of democracy, capitalism, and open systems must have a firm and aggressive advocacy projected into the international world, particularly into the Third World. This should include a major effort in attracting the young in Third World areas, especially those who can be accommodated in US institutions of higher learning.

Fifth, planning and the education of policy makers, both civilian and military, must be based on serious considerations of long-range goals. There must be a revitalized intellectual and policy thrust to develop policy and strategic thought focusing on long-range issues incorporating unconventional warfare, US national interests, and effective democratic response.

Sixth, a serious effort must be made by elected officials, policy makers, and influential political actors to educate the American people in the nature and character of unconventional conflicts and the threats they may pose to US national interests. This is not intended as political advocacy but as an educational effort to establish serious and informed dialogue regarding policy and strategy in dealing with unconventional conflicts.

Seventh, the US must make every effort to develop policies and strategies that are based on regional and multinational cooperation. This is a difficult task since national interests and state policies differ, even among friends and allies. This should not preclude the US from pursuing its national interests even if there are disagreements within regions or among allies. In most cases, the

US can do this without undue antagonism to allies and friends, provided it is done with diplomatic sophistication and sensitivity.

Although these specific needs do not encompass the variety of policies and strategies associated with the political-psychological posture of the United States, they do establish a basis for the directions that need to be followed.

US MILITARY SYSTEM

The role of the military in unconventional conflicts is at times ambiguous and at other times clear but always complex.   These are the reasons that particular attention must be given to the military system and its internal composition, shape, and capability in dealing with unconventional conflicts.

Over the past several years, the US military has been criticized not only because of its weapons procurement procedures and waste but also because of its seemingly incoherent strategies, interservice rivalries, duplication of weaponry, ineffectiveness in conducting joint service operations, and an increasingly top-heavy and bureaucratically cluttered command structure.   In a recent criticism, one author concludes,

> Vast sums of money and the true dedication of many have gone into the upkeep of American military power, only to yield persistent failure in the conduct of war and an unfavorable balance of strength for safeguarding the peace. . . . The armed forced have failed us.[8]

In October 1985, the staff of the Senate Armed Services Committee released a 645-page report on the restructuring of the military establishment.[9] The report critically analyzes the US military system, identifies its most glaring deficiencies, and includes a number of recommendations such as the abolition of the Joint Chiefs of Staff to be replaced by an advisory council of senior generals. A number of recommendations are made that are designed to reduce mismanagement and interservice rivalry and to create a more responsive and capable military system.

Most of the analysis, criticism, and call for reform is concerned with strategic forces and general purpose forces, or more generally, conventional capability in nuclear and nonnuclear wars. Although some attention is given to special operations forces and Special Forces, such concern appears marginal to the main issue of strategic capability.

One member of Congress states,

> The individual Services hold SOF [Special Operations Forces] to be peripheral to the interests, missions, goals, and traditions that they view as essential. The Services for the last 40 years have concentrated on deterring nuclear conflicts and the "big" war on the plains of Europe. . . . Because SOF are considered peripheral, they have consistently felt the bite of "fiscal and manpower constraints" and "competition for resources" when it comes time for the Services to allocate their support to their constituent components. . . . The key problem is lack of effective advocacy.[10]

It is clear that a number of changes are necessary in the military system in order to develop a more effective and flexible response across the conflict spectrum. The problems in the general structure and management of the military system are compounded by those created by the challenges of unconventional conflicts.

Regardless of the various positions on special operations forces, there has been little serious debate or analysis regarding the place of special operations forces within the US military system. This is not to suggest that there has not been a great deal of attention within the military services to this issue, but the attention has been aimed at maintaining traditional command and staff career lines and mainstream military capability, with the issue being how to fit the special operations forces into this mainstream as an adjunct to conventional forces. Skill in unconventional conflict and military careers devoted to such skills remain outside the career paths of the military and remain tangential to the accepted concept of military professionalism. The organizational strategy and command structure currently associated with special operations forces virtually ensures control by conventional structures with little knowledge of unconventional warfare. Operational techniques reflect this posture.

The analysis and study of the overall military establishment and the political-psychological posture of the United States raise a number of questions regarding US military capability and effectiveness in dealing with unconventional conflict.

First, there is a great deal of ambiguity, ambivalence, bureaucratic complexity, and political interplay associated with major military commands, their specific missions, command and control authority, and interservice relationships. This has led to serious interservice rivalry and fragmented strategy.

Second, major problems in the military's capability to engage in unconventional conflicts are directly linked to the lack of conceptual synthesis of views and interpretations regarding such conflicts. Without some conceptual harmony, organizational strategy and doctrine are likely to remain wedded to the conventional perceptions of conflicts. Further, such perceptions will continue to reflect the positions of the various organizations and agencies whose missions include some aspect of unconventional conflicts.

Third, in addition to conceptual synthesis, there must develop a professional military and civilian understanding of and capacity for unconventional conflict. Next to developing a conceptual synthesis, this is the most difficult to achieve since it requires revised curricula in military service schools and in regular training of conventional units.

Fourth, unconventional conflicts as defined in this study have two components: special operations and low-intensity conflict. The former is primarily conventional-type operations of a highly specialized nature, usually entailing Range/Commando type forces and missions.

The latter consists of long-range missions associated with revolution and counterrevolution and entails the use of Special Forces. Low-intensity conflicts as defined in this study have two elements: the conduct of low-intensity conflict against an adversary within his own country or in areas occupied by the adversary and the conduct of counteroperations against low-intensity operations being conducted by an adversary. Capability in one does not necessarily lead to capability in the other.

Fifth, a command system and effective operational response to unconventional conflict are not solely military or civilian missions. The characteristics of such conflicts in countering and conducting operations require a mix of civilian and military capabilities.

Sixth, based on experience in Vietnam and the prevailing doctrines for the conduct of unconventional conflict, a distinction must be made between missions and capabilities of organizations designed specifically for low-intensity conflict, special operations, and conventional forces. Although there seems to be some attempt at making distinctions now, there still appears to be very little effort toward preparing conventional units for their role in such operations.[11]

Seventh, the role of the US military officers in the national security policy process must be redesigned to ensure a realistic and meaningful input. At the present time, there are few, if any, military officers seriously involved in strategic political-military issues. Most of the military effort and attention is on planning and operating military instruments and administration of the military system. The US military profession and its role in the policy process has evolved into a managerial role dealing with resource allocation and bureaucratic efficiency. Although this is important, it is secondary to strategic political-military matters and the development of a flexible and effective military posture.

To achieve this type of military posture, high-quality personnel are required to staff and lead civilian and military agencies and institutions. Their sense of professionalism must be based on the understanding of and sensitivity to the needs of unconventional conflicts. It follows that the highest levels of political and military leadership must support the reshaping of the military system and the broader dimensions of military professionalism.

The recasting of the US political-psychological posture and the reshaping of the US military system must be done in the light of the demands and imperatives of democracy. These are fundamental to the operation and values (ideology) of the American political system.

DEMOCRATIC IMPERATIVE

Democratic systems rigidly adhering to abstract moral and ethical principles even when their survival is at stake may quickly destroy themselves. Those who proclaim the "better Red than dead" philosophy ignore the fact that throughout history, human beings have fought and died to break out of slavery or tyranny. It can be argued that there is a higher morality than saving one's life—a morality that transcends the mundane drive for survival and seeks a meaningful life in the concept of Judeo-Christian values (or other religious values of a similar nature). Although such a debate may appear more relevant in terms of nuclear conflicts, they may be just as relevant for the new battlefield, particularly in the long term.

To dismiss the kind of challenges posed by unconventional conflicts as nonthreatening is to ignore history, reality, and the nature of closed systems. To argue that engaging in such conflicts is immoral is to argue that morality must be so interpreted as to be carried to the point of self-destruction. As long as moral and ethical principles remain the fundamental basis of democracy and are used as guides and as long as there is a recognition that any deviation must be made hesitantly, cautiously, and prudently, and only then in the cause of a higher moral call, democratic values survive. Indeed, the highest morality is to ensure the survival of the democratic system.

It is also deceptive to argue that democracies should take no action until there is a clear and present danger. The nature of unconventional conflicts makes useless the notion of clear and present danger in the usual sense. To wait until there is a clear danger may be too late. Even when it is not too late, waiting for a clear sign of conflict may place the United States in an extremely disadvantageous position from which it may not be able to recover. It follows that in response to unconventional conflicts, US policy should evolve from the various factors, dimensions, and characteristics of the new battlefield studied and analyzed here.

This means a policy of response as well as initiation (not simply reactive), ranging from economic aid and assistance to commitment of US ground forces. Such a policy must be based on developing a national consensus in order to establish the national will and staying power to follow through with appropriate strategies. Short-term and ad hoc approaches court disaster. This must be done with the realization that the United States is the prime target for Marxist-Leninist systems, radical closed systems, and a variety of terrorist groups and religious fanatics. In brief, the United States is involved in unconventional conflict but has yet to realize that a war against it is in progress and has been for many years.

The traditions of government responsibility and accountability and the fundamental values in the United States can surely develop effective oversight, control, and accountability of political-military instruments even with a greater latitude for effectively engaging in unconventional conflicts. The knowledge and understanding necessary to respond to unconventional conflicts and Third World states can surely be developed in the US political system and its military to know when and how to respond.

It is not suggested that the United States become a Third World policeman or respond to every unconventional conflict. Indeed, internal conflicts may best be resolved by isolating them from any external involvement, with the outcome determined solely by internal adversaries. But what is stressed is the need to know when and how to respond and the development of policies and strategies that are not solely reactive. There is also a need for greater knowledge and better understanding than Americans have shown in the past for the Third World and unconventional conflicts.

A number of problems associated with the evolution of unconventional conflicts may be prevented, or at least blunted, if the conditions are recognized early and if US policy and strategy set directions early enough to assist moderates and true nationalists in capturing the revolution and preventing the establishment of a closed and/or Marxist-Leninist system.

Finally, the American people and their policy makers must understand that unconventional conflicts are usually protracted and engaged in by those who are patient and persistent. Success for the United States therefore depends on patience and understanding, as well as the proper combination of policies and strategies. These are not the usual characteristics associated with the United States and its political system in dealing with unconventional conflicts.

In sum, clear policy and effective strategies, based on prudency and a realistic assessment of world politics, are essential for developing a national consensus and staying power for Third World issues. From this framework, there can develop the national will and political resolve to establish the staying power necessary to achieve policy goals in the Third World. Such policy goals should make it clear when and where the United States might be expected to stand and fight.

Even with effective policy, strategy, doctrine, and civic literacy and political understanding within the US political system, success is not certain. Open systems can go only so far in using the most effective means to engage in unconventional conflicts. To go beyond democratic sensitivities and overstep the American sense of propriety will surely lead to the erosion of American values and democratic legitimacy.

But it must also be understood that rarely is there a perfect solution for open systems in reconciling morality and democratic propriety with effective response to unconventional conflicts. The dilemmas created by these contradictory forces are enduring within open systems. The most that can be said is that constant attention to democratic imperatives is essential, even if at times these must be redefined in order to preclude a greater disaster or to promote a human value.

In the process of developing the proper posture and in trying to fix the line between barbarism and decency, American blood will probably be shed. This new battlefield is beyond that which Americans are accustomed. There is no such thing as a splendid little war; all are deadly, dirty, and bloody. But this new battlefield gives a more insidious and barbaric dimension to conflict. The real targets and combatants are not the organized armed forces and those whose profession is to engage in battle. The targets are those who make up the political-psychological center of a nation-state and who are least able to withstand systematized and organized death and destruction in the name of a moral cause whose only law is success.

For the United States, the challenge of this new battlefield is particularly serious since its adversaries employ the very virtues and instruments of open systems to pursue their own goals to the detriment of open systems. In the process, these adversaries look with fear as well as disdain at open systems: fear because of the threat these systems pose to closed systems, and disdain because of the nature of open systems that often prevents effective response to the challenges of unconventional warfare.

There is no question that the elimination of war in all of its dimensions, including unconventional wars, should be the highest human endeavor. In the light of history, it is unlikely that this will occur soon. In the meantime, it is prudent to be guided by the proposition that to ensure

peace, prepare for war. To neglect the threats and challenges that war poses to democracies on the presumption
that peace can be sought without war is taking a path
leading to self-destruction.

The challenges of unconventional conflicts, war in the
broader context, and the search for peace seem to pose an
insoluble dilemma to nations, particularly to open systems. Even with the vulnerability of open systems, they
have within them the capacity to respond, once the issues
are recognized and understood. De Tocqueville observed,

> Democratic freedom does not carry its undertakings
> through as perfectly as an intelligent despotism would; it
> often abandons them before it has reaped the profit, or
> embarks on perilous ones; but in the long run it pro-
> duces more, each thing is less well done, but more
> things are done. . . . Democracy does not provide a
> people with the most skilful of governments, but it does
> that which the most skilful governments often cannot
> do: it spreads throughout the body social a restless ac-
> tivity, superabundant force, and energy never found
> elsewhere, which, however little favored by circum-
> stance, can do wonders.[12]

NOTES

1. Adam B. Ulam, *The Rivals: America and Russia since
World War II* (New York: Penguin Books, 1976), p. 385.
2. Claes G. Ryn, "The Ethical Problem of Democratic
Statecraft," in James P. O'Leary, Jeffrey Salmon, and Richard
Shultz, eds., *Power, Principles and Interests: A Reader in
World Politics* (Lexington, Mass.: Gin Press, 1985), p. 117.
3. James Turner Johnson, *Can Modern War Be Just?* (New
Haven: Yale University Press, 1984), p. 56. For a detailed dis-
cussion of just war, see William V. O'Brien, *The Conduct of
Just and Limited War* (New York: Praeger, 1981), and Michael
Walzer, *Just and Unjust Wars: A Moral Argument with
Historical Illustrations* (New York: Basic Books, 1977). See
also *The Challenge of Peace: God's Promise and Our*

Response—A Pastoral Letter on War and Peace (Washington, D.C.: National Conference of Catholic Bishops, 1983). This document examines the just war concept as it relates to nuclear warfare. Unfortunately, the document gives short shrift to the just war issues as they relate to unconventional conflicts.

4. Robert L. Phillips, *War and Justice* (Norman: University of Oklahoma Press, 1984), pp. 98-99.

5. Johnson, p. 57.

6. "Even in 'Peacetime,' 40 Wars Are Going On," *U.S. News and World Report*, July 11, 1983, pp. 44-48.

7. For a discussion of the various categories used by the Soviet Union in identifying and classifying Third World states and the relationship to Soviet policy, see Daniel S. Papp, *Soviet Perceptions of the Developing World in the 1980s: The Ideological Basis* (Lexington, Mass.: Lexington Books, 1985), esp. chap. 3. See also Adam Wolfson, "The Good, the Bad, and the Ugly; Who's Who in Nicaragua," *Policy Review*, no. 33 (Summer 1985): 58-65; Mark Falcoff, "Marxist-Leninist Regimes in Central America: Prospects for the Future," in Uri Ra'anan, Francis Fukuyama, Mark Falcoff, Sam C. Sarkesian, and Richard Shultz, Jr., *Third World Marxist-Leninist Regimes: Strengths, Vulnerabilities, and U.S. Policy* (Washington, D.C.: Pergamon-Brassey's, 1985), pp. 45-82; and Department of State and Department of Defense, *The Soviet-Cuban Connection in Central America and the Caribbean* (Washington, D.C.: Government Printing Office, March 1985).

A number of analysts in the Soviet Union argue that capitalism is the normal outgrowth of feudalism, as Marx stated. Therefore they argue that most Third World states will follow the Western model of development. "They conclude that the Soviet Union should concentrate its foreign policy on the important, industrializing capitalist Third World countries." See Jerry F. Hough, *The Struggle for the Third World: Soviet Debates and American Options* (Washington, D.C.: Brookings Institution, October 1985). See also Jeffrey F. Hough, "Gorbachev's Strategy," *Foreign Affairs* 64, no. 1 (Fall 1985): 33-55. Yet it is true that in the previous decades, the Soviet Union has projected its power into various regions, including Central America and black Africa. If history is any guide, it seems unlikely that the Soviet Union will drastically change this dimension of its foreign policy.

8. Edward N. Luttwak, *The Pentagon and the Art of War: The Question of Military Reform* (New York: Simon & Schuster, 1984), p. 17.

9. See Senate Armed Services Committee, *Defense Organization: The Need for Change* (Washington, D.C.: Government Printing Office, 1985). See also "Defense Organization: The Need for Change," Special Issue, *Armed Forces International* (October 1985). In 1985 criticism of the US military system was coming from a variety of circles, including from within the Pentagon, scholars, and private individuals, as well as from Congress.

10. Congressman Dan Daniel (D-Va.), "US Special Operations; The Case for a Sixth Service," *Armed Forces Journal International* (August 1985): 72.

11. See Sam C. Sarkesian, "Organizational Strategy and Low-Intensity Conflict," in Frank R. Barnet, B. Hugh Tovar, and Richard H. Shultz, eds., *Special Operations in US Strategy* (Washington, D.C.: National Defense University Press, 1984), pp. 261-89.

12. Alexis de Tocqueville, *Democracy in America*, ed. J. P. Mayer, trans. George Lawrence (Garden City, N.Y.: Anchor Books, 1969), p. 244.

APPENDIX

US and USSR Military Assistance to Selected Third World States

Table A-1
US and USSR Military Assistance Deliveries to Countries in
Central America and Caribbean Basin
(not including Mexico and Venezuela)

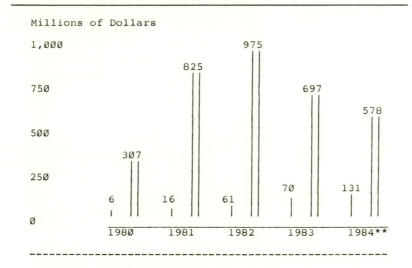

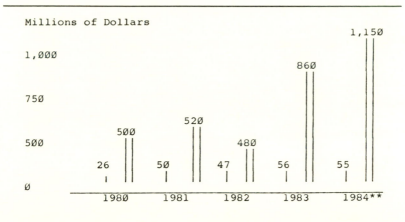

Table A-2
US and USSR Military Assistance Deliveries to Countries in
Central, West, and South Africa

**Includes estimates of Soviet deliveries last half of 1984

Legend: US = | USSR = | |

Table A-3
US and USSR Military Assistance Deliveries to Countries in
the Middle East, North Africa, and Southwest Asia*

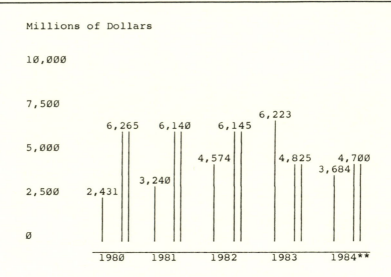

*Includes Israel and Egypt
**Includes estimate of Soviet deliveries last half of 1984

Legend: US = | USSR = | |

Adapted from The Organization of the Joint Chiefs of Staff,
United States Military Posture FY 1986 (Washington, D.C.,
1985), pp. 89-90.

Table A-4
Chief Concentrations of Soviet-Bloc Military Technicians and Advisers, June 1982

Country	Number	Chief Supplying Country
Afghanistan	2,000	U.S.S.R.
Algeria	2,000	U.S.S.R.
Angola	1,000	Cuba
Ethiopia	14,000	Cuba
Libya	2,000	U.S.S.R.
Nicaragua	2,000	Cuba
Syria	3,300	U.S.S.R.
Yeman (Aden)	1,500	U.S.S.R.

Table A-5
Soviet-Bloc Combat Troops outside Home Areas

Soviet-bloc	Country	Troop Strength	Present Since:
U.S.S.R.	Afghanistan	110,000	1979
Cuba	Angola	15-20,000	1975
	Ethiopia	7-9,000	1977
Vietnam	Kampuchea	180,000	1978

Table A-6
Soviet-Bloc Military Presence in the Caribbean Basin*

	Country	Number
Soviet combat troops	Cuba	2,600
Cuban military and security technicians	Nicaragua Grenada**	2,000 30
Soviet and East European technicians	Cuba Nicaragua	2,000 ***

*Excludes 6,000-8,000 Soviet civilian advisers in Cuba.

**Prior to American invasion of Grenada.

***70 officers in addition to other ranks.

Adapted from United States Department of State, *Atlas of United States Foreign Relations* (Washington, D.C.: U.S. Government Printing Office, June 1983), pp. 88 and 93.

Bibliographical Essay

One of the major themes emerging from this study is that there is a great deal of published literature on various aspects of unconventional conflicts. But studies of unconventional conflicts, conceived in broad terms and conceptually coherent, are rare. In the late 1970s and early 1980s, the incidence of terrorism and the terrorist focus on Americans stimulated a parallel surge in studies on international terrorism. Yet there is little in the literature that offers a systematic and conceptual analysis of unconventional conflicts incorporating revolution and terror.

This study has identified much of the literature with extensive notes following each chapter. The purpose of this essay is not to repeat what is at the end of each chapter. It is intended to provide a framework for categorizing the published literature and to give serious readers a method for managing a detailed study of unconventional conflicts based on many sources that have been useful in writing this book.

As a general guide to the subject, the literature is divided into two major groups: bibliographical and nonbibliographical studies. The latter group includes important books that can serve as references and those that are some of the best examples of the published literature. The literature on terrorism is included only inasmuch as it is closely linked to revolution and counterrevolution.

BIBLIOGRAPHICAL GUIDES

One of the earliest attempts at sorting out the available material on revolution and guerrilla warfare is A. Thomas Ferguson, Jr., "Sources for the Study of Revolutionary Guerrilla Warfare." The author describes the available inventories on revolutionary guerrilla warfare, including a number of sources that are generally unknown to the public, such as the Special Operations Research Office (SORO), which was sponsored by the American University of Washington, D.C., but funded by the US Army. Some of the most extensive bibliographies emanated from this office. The author identifies a number of other important sources, including Henry Bienen, *Violence and Social Change*, which includes a review essay of the works in English, and Ronald H. Chilcote, *Revolution and Structural Change in Latin America: A Bibliography on Ideology, Development, and the Radical Left, 1930-1965*.

More recent is the article by Sam C. Sarkesian, "American Policy on Revolution and Counterrevolution: A Review of the Themes in the Literature." This work includes much of the published material on Vietnam and the post-Vietnam period. It is limited to material published in the United States, with only a few exceptions. The author divides the material into six categories: concepts of revolution; causes of revolution; revolutionary systems; counterrevolutionary systems; external forces and geopolitical considerations; and revolutionary and counterrevolutionary outcomes and consequences (progress). Each category is further divided into general themes. Many of the works and much of the assessment from this article are included in chapters 2, 3, and 5 of this book.

A recent and important work is Benjamin R. Beede, *Intervention and Counterinsurgency: An Annotated Bibliography of the Small Wars of the United States, 1898-1984*, an essential reference for those studying unconventional conflicts. The book focuses only on works in English. While the preface provides an explanation of the organizational scheme for the volume, the introduction offers brief, but valuable, insights into concepts and perspectives on small wars.

NONBIBLIOGRAPHIC SOURCES

A number of nonbibliographic sources can serve as guides to the type of published literature in unconventional conflicts. An example is Walter Laqueur's *Guerrilla: A History and Critical Study*. Beginning with biblical times and extending through the early 1970s, this book provides a broad sweep of guerrilla warfare across the international landscape. The volume has extensive footnotes and a brief but useful bibliography.

Other historical and comparative studies include Theda Skocpol, *States and Social Revolutions: A Comparative Analysis of France, Russia, and China;* Jack A. Goldstone, *Revolutions: Theoretical, Comparative, and Historical Studies;* and John Dunn, *Modern Revolutions: An Introduction to the Analysis of a Political Phenomenon*. The Skocpol book has extensive footnotes and bibliography. The Goldstone book includes a brief but useful bibliography. Dunn's book contains extensive notes and an even more extensive bibliography.

Other books of an analytical focus and of importance are J. Bowyer Bell, *On Revolt: Strategies of National Liberation;* Jacques Ellul, *Autopsy of a Revolution;* Crane Brinton, *Anatomy of a Revolution;* and Mark Hagopian, *The Phenomenon of Revolution*. The value of these books is in their scholarly analytical and comparative approach.

A volume particularly useful for the study of modern insurgencies and operational in its approach is Bard O'Neill, William R. Heaton, and Donald J. Alberts, *Insurgency in the Modern World*. In a similar vein is Thomas Greene, *Comparative Revolutionary Movements*.

An earlier book aimed at an academic audience is Hannah Arendt, *On Revolution*. This is an incisive philosophical analysis of the political and social dimensions of revolution. The extensive footnotes and bibliography include a variety of non-English sources and are particularly valuable to researchers.

Biographies and studies of revolutionary leaders and personalities provide original source material and a personal dimension to the study of unconventional conflicts. These include the *Selected Works of Mao Tse-tung,* edited by Bruno Shaw; Mao Tse-tung, *Selected Works;* General Vo Nguyen Giap, *People's War, People's Army;* Che Guevara, *Guerrilla Warfare; "Che" Guevara on Revolution* by Jay Mallin; and Samuel B. Griffith, *Sun Tzu, The Art of War.*

US Policy and Strategy: Vietnam

The literature on Vietnam from an American perspective is extensive and continues to grow. A necessary starting point for the study of US involvement is the *Senator Gravel Edition* of the Pentagon Papers. A shorter work is *The Pentagon Papers as Published by the New York Times,* although this latter volume is less authoritative and tends to be overly journalistic. Important historical and analytical works are Stanley Karnow, *Vietnam: A History,* and Michael Maclear, *The Ten Thousand Day War, Vietnam: 1945-1975.* Of special note are the two volumes by Joseph Buttinger, *Vietnam: A Dragon Embattled.* They provide a detailed study of Vietnam history through the 1960s and are probably the best work on the subject. Ronald H. Spector's *United States Army in Vietnam: Advice and Support: The Early Years* is useful for an analysis of US military involvement.

An excellent analysis of US strategy is Summer, *On Strategy: Vietnam in Context.* Applying Clausewitzian principles, the author provides a serious critique of US strategy. The Summer volume has become essential reading in many senior US military schools.

Other volumes of importance in analyzing US policy include William C. Westmoreland, *A Soldier Reports;* U.S. Grant Sharp, *Strategy for Defeat: Vietnam in Retrospect;* and Bruce Palmer, Jr., *The 25-Year War: America's Military Role in Vietnam.*

Sam C. Sarkesian's *America's Forgotten Wars* is useful in its historical and comparative analysis and its application of this framework to Vietnam. The volume edited by Richard Hunt and Richard Shultz, *Lessons from an Unconventional War,* follows a similar pattern but focuses specifically on the lessons of Vietnam, projecting into the future.

Aside from the studies on policy and strategy, many books examine various aspects of US involvement in ground, sea, and air operations. To grasp the essentials of the US experience, serious attention must surely be given to such literature. Examples of the ground operational environment include Al Santoli, *Everything We Had;* Michael Herr, *Dispatches;* and S. L. A. Marshall, *Vietnam, Three Battles.* A good analysis of the use of air power is James Clay Thompson, *Rolling Thunder: Understanding Policy and Program Failure.*

International Dimensions

A serious study of unconventional conflicts must go beyond US involvement in Vietnam. In this respect there are important studies of the French involvement, as well as studies of the Vietcong. Bernard Fall, *Street without Joy: Insurgency in Indochina,* is an example of the former and Douglas Pike, *Viet Cong,* of the latter. Both are instructive in their insights into the problems that faced the United States. The conflict in Malaya is well covered by Richard Clutterbuck, *The Long, Long War;* and Sir Robert Thompson, *Defeating Communist Insurgency: The Lessons of Malaya and Vietnam.* Benedict J. Kerkvleit's *The Huk Rebellion* is instructive of how the revolution in the Philippines was defeated by the leadership of Magsaysay. It is conceivable that Americans who made policy and strategy decisions for the Vietnam War might have avoided some mistakes had they learned from the lessons of Malaya, the Philippines, and the French in Indochina.

Useful volumes for the study of revolutions in Central and Latin America include Richard Gott, *Guerrilla Movements in Latin America,* and an edited volume by Georges Fauriol, *Latin American Insurgencies.* An important book on earlier US involvement in Nicaragua, particularly from the operational perspective, is Neill Macaulay, *The Sandino Affair.*

An excellent historical overview is *War in Peace: Conventional and Guerrilla Warfare Since 1945.* Sir Robert Thompson served as consulting editor for the volume. Of equal value is the edited volume by Beckett and Pimlott, *Armed Forces and Modern Counter-Insurgency.* This is one of the few comparative studies, and although there are some shortcomings, it is an important contribution to the literature.

BIBLIOGRAPHICAL GUIDES: TERRORISM

One of the first attempts in the recent period to assess the literature on terrorism is Martha Crenshaw, "Terrorism against the State." The author states, "As is often true of a new field of study, most work on terrorism is recent, uneven in quality, and noncumulative" (p. 473). The literature is categorized into general studies, case studies, autobiographies, terrorism and democracy, policy responses, international relations and foreign policy, nuclear terrorism, chronologies, bibliographies, and journals. In each category, the author identifies and comments briefly on some of the major works.

An important volume of bibliographical studies on terrorism is Edward F. Mickolus, *The Literature of Terrorism: A Selectively Annotated Bibliography*. The book contains over 3,800 entries.

Several other bibliographical volumes are also useful, including Myron J. Smith, *The Secret Wars: A Guide to Sources in English, Vol. 3: International Terrorism;* and Yonah Alexander, *International Terrorism: National, Regional, and Global Perspectives*. Guides to works of a historical nature include Walter Laqueur, *The Terrorism Reader: A Historical Anthology,* and Jennifer Shaw et al., *Ten Years of Terrorism: Collected Views*.

PRINCIPLES OF WAR: JUST WAR THEORIES

It is important to place unconventional conflicts in the general scheme of the conflict spectrum. One of the first studies to do this is a volume edited by Sam C. Sarkesian and William L. Scully, *U.S. Policy and Low-Intensity Conflict: Potentials for Struggles in the 1980s*. This book includes studies on the British and French experience and uses these as a comparative basis for studying the capability and effectiveness of US political-military instruments for low-intensity conflicts. In addition to detailed endnotes, the book includes a brief bibliography.

An important dimension to the study of unconventional conflict is its relationship to the principles of war. *Clausewitz, On War,* edited by Anatol Rapoport, is extremely helpful in this respect. More recent is Raymond Aron, *Clausewitz: Philosopher of War,* an important contribution since it includes a critical analysis and commentary on Clausewitz by the author, a well-known French political scientist. Complementing these volumes is the study *The American Way of War* by Russell Weigley. This book is essential to the understanding of the difficulties faced by the US military in responding to unconventional conflicts.

Involvement in unconventional conflicts invariably raises the issues of just war and moral and ethical behavior. Some of the best books on these matters include the National Conference of Catholic Bishops, *The Challenge of Peace: God's Promise and Our Response;* James V. Schall, S. J., *Out of Justice, Peace: Winning the Peace;* Michael Walzer, *Just and Unjust Wars: A Moral Argument with Historical Illustrations;* William V. O'Brien, *The Conduct of Just and Limited Wars;* and Robert Tucker, *The Just War: Exposition of the American Concept.* These books focus on most major issues associated with just war and show how difficult it is to apply such theories to unconventional conflicts.

An added dimension to the literature are studies, both bibliographic and nonbibliographic, published by US military sources such as the US Army War College, the Air University, the Naval War College, and the National Defense University. One example is the three-volume work, *The Role of Air Power in Low Intensity Conflict,* published by the Air University. These volumes are a collection of symposium papers prepared for the Air Power Symposium in 1985 and include some of the best work from a military perspective.

Further, the literature on the US intelligence system and methods is an integral part of unconventional conflicts. Important volumes include publications by the US Defense Intelligence School such as *Bibliography of Intelligence Literature* and the series edited by Roy Godson, for example, *Intelligence Requirements for the 1980's: Elements of Intelligence,* revised edition.

CONCLUSIONS

The study of unconventional conflicts in all of their dimen-sions demands more than a study of guerrilla war, revolution, counterrevolution, or terror. The nature of such conflicts strikes at the heart of open systems, challenges the notions of traditional concepts of war, and reflects violence aimed at po-litical systems as well as the international order. An assess-ment of the published literature dictates attention to all of these issues.

REFERENCES

Books

Air University. *The Role of Air Power in Low Intensity Conflict.* Symposium Papers. 3 vol. Maxwell Air Force Base, Ala.: Air University, May 1985.

Alexander, Yonah, ed. *International Terrorism: National, Regional, and Global Perspectives.* New York: Praeger, 1976.

Arendt, Hannah. *On Revolution.* New York: Viking Press, 1965.

Aron, Raymond, *Clausewitz: Philosopher of War.* Translated by Christine Booker and Norman Stone. Englewood Cliffs, N.J.: Prentice-Hall, 1985.

Beckett, Ian F. W. and Pimlott, John, eds. *Armed Forces and Modern Counter-Insurgency.* New York: St. Martin's Press, 1985.

Beede, Benjamin R. *Intervention and Counterinsurgency: An Annotated Bibliography of the Small Wars of the United States, 1898-1984.* New York: Garland Publishing, 1985.

Bell, J. Bowyer. *Revolt: Strategies of National Liberation.* Cambridge: Harvard University Press, 1976.

Bibliography of Intelligence Literature. 7th ed. (rev.). Washington, D.C.: Defense Intelligence School, August 1981.

Brinton, Crane. *Anatomy of a Conflict.* Rev. and expanded ed. New York: Vintage Books, 1965.

Burns, Richard Dean and Leitenberg, Milton. *The Wars in Vietnam, Cambodia and Laos 1945-1982: A Bibliographic Guide.* New York: ABC-CLIO, 1983.

Buttinger, Joseph. *Vietnam, A Dragon Embattled.* 2 vols. New York: Praeger, 1967.

Clutterbuck, Richard. *The Long, Long War: Counterinsurgency in Malaya and Vietnam.* New York: Praeger, 1966.

Department of the Army. *Field Manual 100-20, Low Intensity Conflict.* Baltimore, Md.: US Army Adjutant General Publications Center, January 1981.

Dunn, John. *Modern Revolutions: An Introduction to the Analysis of a Political Phenomenon.* London: Cambridge University Press, 1972.

Ellul, Jacques. *Autopsy of a Revolution.* New York: Alfred A. Knopf, 1971.

Fall, Bernard. *Street without Joy: Insurgency in Indochina, 1946-63.* 3d. rev. ed. Harrisburg, Penn.: Stackpole Co., 1963.

Fauriol, Georges, ed. *Latin American Insurgencies.* Washington, D.C.: National Defense University Press, 1985.

Giap, General Vo Nguyen. *People's War, People's Army.* Washington, D.C.: Government Printing Office, 1962.

Godson, Roy, ed. *Intelligence Requirements for the 1980's: Analysis and Estimates.* Washington, D.C.: National Strategy Information Center, 1980.

————, ed. *Intelligence Requirements for the 1980's: Elements of Intelligence.* Rev. ed. Washington, D.C.: National Strategy Information Center, 1983.

Goldstone, Jack A., ed. *Revolutions: Theoretical, Comparative, and Historical Studies.* New York: Harcourt Brace Jovanovich, 1986.

Gott, Richard. *Guerrilla Movements in Latin America.* Garden City, N.Y.: Anchor Books, 1974.

Greene, Thomas. *Comparative Revolutionary Movements.* Englewood Cliffs, N.J.: Prentice-Hall, 1974.

Guevara, Che. *Guerrilla Warfare,* translated by J. P. Morray. New York: Vintage Books, 1969.

Hagopian, Mark N. *The Phenomenon of Revolution.* New York: Dodd, Mead, 1974.

Herr, Michael. *Dispatches.* New York: Avon Books, 1978.

Hunt, Richard A. and Shultz, Richard H. *Lessons from an Unconventional War; Reassessing U.S. Strategies for Future Conflicts.* New York: Pergamon Press, 1982.

Karnow, Stanley. *Vietnam: A History.* New York: Viking Press, 1983.

Kerkvleit, Benedict J. *The Huk Rebellion: A Study of Peasant Revolt in the Philippines.* Berkeley: University of California Press, 1977.

Laqueur, Walter. *Guerrilla; A Historical and Critical Study.* Boston: Little, Brown, 1976.

————. *Terrorism.* Boston: Little, Brown, 1977.

Livingstone, Neil C. and Arnold, Terrence E. *Fighting Back: Winning the War Against Terrorism.* Lexington, Mass.: Lexington Books, 1985.

Maclear, Michael. *The Ten Thousand Day War—Vietnam: 1945-1975.* New York: Avon Books, 1981.

Macaulay, Neill. *The Sandino Affair.* Chicago: Quadrangle Books, 1967.

Mallin, Jay, ed. *"Che" Guevara on Revolution.* New York: Delta Publishing Co., 1969.

Mao Tse-tung. *Selected Works of Mao Tse-tung.* Vol. 2. Peking: Foreign Language Press, 1965.

Marshall, S. L. A. *Vietnam, Three Battles.* New York: Da Capo Press, 1971.

Meraria, Ariel, ed. *On Terrorism and Combatting Terrorism.* Frederick, Md.: University Publications of America, 1985.

Mickolus, Edward F. *The Literature of Terrorism: A Selectively Annotated Bibliography.* Westport, Conn.: Greenwood Press, 1980.

National Conference of Catholic Bishops. *The Challenge of Peace: God's Promise and Our Response.* Washington, D.C.: United States Catholic Conference, 1983.

O'Brien, William V. *The Conduct of Just and Limited War.* New York: Praeger, 1981.

O'Neill, Bard E.; Heaton, William R.; and Alberts, Donald J., eds. *Insurgency in the Modern World.* Boulder, Colo.: Westview Press, 1980.

Palmer, General Bruce, Jr. *The 25-Year War: America's Military Role in Vietnam.* Lexington: University of Kentucky Press, 1984.

Pike, Douglas. *Viet Cong: The Organization and Techniques of the National Liberation Front of South Vietnam.* Cambridge: MIT Press, 1967.

Ra'ana, Uri; Pfaltzgraff, Robert L., Jr.; Shultz, Richard H.; Halperin, Ernst; and Lukes, Igor, eds. *Hydra of Carnage, International Linkages of Terrorism: The Witnesses Speak.* Lexington, Mass.: Lexington Books, 1985.

Rapoport, Anatol, ed. *Clausewitz, On War.* Baltimore: Penguin Books, 1968.

Revel, Jean François. *How Democracies Perish.* Garden City, NY: Doubleday, Inc., 1983.

Rocca, Raymond G. and Dziak, John J. *Bibliography on Soviet Intelligence and Security Services.* Boulder, Colo.: Westview Press, 1985.

Santoli, Al. *Everything We Had.* New York: Ballantine Books, 1981.

Sarkesian, Sam C. *America's Forgotten Wars: The Counterrevolutionary Past and Lessons for the Future.* Westport, Conn.: Greenwood Press, 1984.

————, ed. *Revolutionary Guerrilla Warfare.* Chicago: Precedent Publishing, 1975.

Sarkesian, Sam C., and Scully, William L., eds. *U.S. Policy and Low-Intensity Conflict: Potentials for Military Struggles in the 1980s.* New Brunswick, N.J.: Transaction Books, 1981.

Schall, James V., S. J., ed. *Out of Justice, Peace: Winning the Peace.* San Francisco: Ignatius Press, 1984.

Schmid, Alex P. *Political Terrorism: A Research Guide to Concepts, Theories, Data Bases and Literature.* New Brunswick, N.J.: Transaction Books, 1984.

Senator Gravel Edition: The Defense Department History of United States Decisionmaking on Vietnam. 4 vols. Boston: Beacon Press, 1971.

Sharp, Admiral U.S. Grant. *Strategy for Defeat: Vietnam in Retrospect.* San Rafael, Calif.: Presidio Press, 1978.

Shaw, Bruno, ed. *Selected Works of Mao Tse-tung.* New York: Harper Colophon Books, 1970.

Shaw, Jennifer, et al. *Ten Years of Terrorism: Collected Views.* New York: Crane, Russak, 1979.

Sheehan, Neil; Smith, Hedrick; Kenworthy, E. W.; and Butterfield, Fox. *The Pentagon Papers as Published by The New York Times.* New York: Bantam Books, 1971.

Skocpol, Theda. *States and Social Revolutions: A Comparative Analysis of France, Russia, and China.* Cambridge: Cambridge University Press, 1979.

Smith, Myron J. *The Secret Wars: A Guide to Sources in English.* Vol. 3: *International Terrorism, 1968-1980.* New York: ABC-CLIO, 1980.

Spector, Ronald H. *U.S. Army in Vietnam; Advice and Support: The Early Years, 1941-1960.* Washington, D.C.: Government Printing Office, 1983.

Summers, Harry G., Jr. *On Strategy: The Vietnam War in Context.* Carlisle Barracks, Penn.: US Army War College, 1981.

Sun Tzu, *The Art of War,* trans. and with an introduction by Samuel B. Griffith. New York: Oxford University Press, 1971.

Thompson, James Clay. *Rolling Thunder: Understanding Policy and Program Failure.* Chapel Hill: University of North Carolina Press, 1980.

Thompson, Sir Robert. *Defeating Communist Insurgency: The Lessons of Malaya and Vietnam.* New York: Praeger, 1966.

Thompson, Sir Robert, consulting editor. *War in Peace: Conventional and Guerrilla Warfare Since 1945.* New York: Crown, 1985.

Tucker, Robert. *The Just War: Exposition of the American Concept.* Baltimore, Md.: Johns Hopkins University Press, 1960.

Walzer, Michael. *Just and Unjust Wars: A Moral Argument with Historical Illustrations.* New York: Basic Books, 1977.

Weigley, Russell. *The American Way of War: A History of United States Military Strategy and Policy.* Bloomington: Indiana University Press, 1977.

Westmoreland, General William C. *A Soldier Reports.* Garden City, N.Y.: Doubleday, 1976.

Articles and Chapters

Crenshaw, Martha. "Terrorism against the State." *Choice* (December 1981): 473-80.

Ferguson, A. Thomas, Jr. "Sources for the Study of Revolutionary Guerrilla Warfare." In Sam C. Sarkesian, ed., *Revolutionary Guerrilla Warfare.* Chicago: Precedent Publishing, 1975.

Sarkesian, Sam C. "American Policy on Revolution and Counterrevolution: A Review of the Themes in the Literature." *Conflict* 5, no. 2 (1984): 137-84.

Journals

Air University Review.
Conflict.
Military Review.
Naval War College Review.
Parameters.
Terrorism.

Index

Achille Lauro, 121, 291

Adversaries: access to American media, 255–56; fear of open systems, 205; sympathetic groups, 255; the United States and, 255, 280; use of disinformation, 255

Afghanistan: invasion of, 26; Carter Administration, 26; Central America and, 210

Africa: divisiveness in, 21; government in, 19; ideology in, 21; politics and economics in, 19; regionalism in, 21. *See also* Colonialism

Aid and assistance to the Third World, 229

AirLand Battle, 124 n.2

Algeria, 17

America: and aftermath of World War II, 180; attitudes towards Third World, 251; and battlefield behavior, 178; constraints on military, 113–14; disillusion in, 148; fear of Soviets, 205; focus on Soviet Union, 9; historical suspicion of Old World, 272; "Never Again" syndrome in, 24; Pearl Harbor concept, 186; perceptions of war, 130, 132; self-criticism, 178; self-righteous views in, 178; Third World culture and, 279; Vietnam and, 24; views on war and peace, 186. *See also* New realism

American heritage, revolution and, 293

Americanization of conflicts, 233, 236

American mind-sets: characteristics, 186; Soviet Union and, 184

American realism, unconventional conflicts and, 279

Americans: Central America and, 204; difficulty of in understanding revolutions and counterrevolutions, 74, 280; distorted views and confusion of Third World, 75,

United States Special Forces;
Vietnam War
United States military missions,
301
*United States Military Posture for
FY 1986*, 164 n.42
US military professionalism:
civil control, 179; conventional
wisdom, 134, 300; need for
change, 301–2; special operations
and, 160; unconventional
conflicts, 300
US military thought. *See*
Clausewitz, Carl von; Sun Tzu;
Western military thought
United States national security,
258–59. *See also* National
interest
US Navy SEALS, 156. *See also*
First Operations Command, US
United States policy: Americanism, 272; beyond Europe, 258,
261; Central America, 199–200,
205; characteristics, 173; conceptual and doctrinal confusion, 132;
consensus and, 275, 303; conventional lenses, 165; dangers, 229,
230; dilemmas, 165, 224; domestic
forces, 205–6; foreign policy and
national security, 256–57; history
of unconventional conflicts, 135;
inconsistencies and inadequacies,
225; intervention and non-Americanization, 113; Latin America,
216, 229–30, 272; low intensity
conflict, 113, 122, 132; needs, 293,
303, 304; new dimensions, 191;
Nicaragua, 241, 273–74; no assurance of success, 281; notions of
good and evil, 270; purposes and
goals, 227–30; reactive posture,
191; realism and, 206; Soviet
Union and Europe, 172–73; Third

World, 202, 206, 217, 224, 225–26;
three components of, 272–73;
values and the political system,
208; Vietnam, 147, 154. *See also*
National interests; Vietnam
literature; Vietnam War
United States policy makers,
91–92
United States policy and strategy,
114, 119
United States policy requirements,
296–98
United States political system,
160, 189, 276–77. *See also*
Democracy; Open systems;
United States; United States
policy
United States posture, 193, 243.
See also United States policy
United States reawakening, 155
United States Special Forces, 160,
161 n.2; adjunct to conventional
operations, 132; lineage, 132; low
intensity conflict, 132; proper
missions, 133; Vietnam and, 155.
See also First Special Operations
Command, US; Special Forces;
United States military; US
military professionalism,
Vietnam War
United States special operations:
critics of, 158; economy of operations, 159; problems in 1985, 159.
See also low intensity conflicts;
United States military
United States strategy: Central
America, 192; changed needed,
186; Clausewitz and Sun Tzu, 173;
contrast, conventional and unconventional, 114; criteria for success, 232, 233; dilemmas, 173,
185–86; doctrine and, 235; domestic support, 236; evolution of,

About the Author

SAM C. SARKESIAN is Professor of Political Science and Chairman of the Inter-University Seminar on Armed Forces and Society at Loyola University of Chicago. He is the author of *America's Forgotten Wars* (Greenwood Press, 1984) and other books, as well as numerous journal articles, book chapters, and papers, and co-author of a recently published study entitled *Third World Marxist-Leninist*